AF560672

CULTURE AND CIVILIZATION SERIES

THE
CLASSICAL AGE

Edited by
Dr. R.K. Pruthi

First Published-2004

ISBN 81-7141-876-7

Published by

DISCOVERY PUBLISHING HOUSE
4831/24, Ansari Road, Prahlad Street,
Darya Ganj, New Delhi-110002 (India)
Phone: 23279245 • Fax: 91-11-23253475
E-mail:dphtemp@indiatimes.com

Printed at :
ARORA OFFSET PRESS
Laxmi Nagar, Delhi-92.

PREFACE

The period of Indian civilization from AD 320 when the Gupta empire was founded to about AD 740 when Yashovarman of Kanauj died, is called the classical age of India.

Our purpose in this volume is to trace the development of the Indian civilization during the above period. We have attempted to provide a cross section of the account of the period from political, social, diplomatic details and through classical literature. Appended to it are chronological and bibliographical sources for information and further studies.

We are indebted to the authorities whose works we have included in attempting to prepare this work.

Professors R.S. Sharma, G.C. Pande, Lalanji Gopal, Romila Thaper, K.V. Raman, B.N. Puri, S. Gupta, and B.B. Lal have always been kind and helpful.

Librarians and staff members of USI, ICHR, ICSSR, IIC and Supreme Court have been helpful.

My publisher and his staff at production and printing level have work hard. I thank them all.

R.K. Pruthi

Contents

Introduction

Throughout the history of India, the process of integration comprises two simultaneous movements: one owes its origin to Aryan culture and operates by virtue of the momentum which the values of that culture possess; the other works itself upward from the way of life of the early Dravidian and other non-Aryan cultures in the country into the framework of the Aryan culture modifying its form and content, though not the fundamentals, weaving a harmonious pattern continuously. The first movement provides vitality and synthesis; the second contributes vigour and variety. But it is the harmonious adjustment of both that gives India, age after age, her strength, tenacity and sense of mission.

The evolution of India, during the period of the Magadhan supremacy, began with the dawn of history in India, in the seventh century before Christ. But long before this, Indians, who had adopted the Aryan way of life, had developed a common way of life; and their sense of unity, preserved by tradition and activated by racememory, recaptured in each generation, was expressed through common action. By vitalising the fundamental values of their culture, they had created vigorous adjustments necessitated by the conditions of each age. During this process, the best elements in the society had, from the earliest times, developed a ruling purpose—the fulfilment of *Rita* or *Dharma*—which gave them the capacity to will themselves into a well-defined and vigorous social organism.

The Magadhan Period closed with the invasion of the Yueh-chis. Disintegration followed in the northern and western India and was accentuated by the break up of the Kushana Empire which they had founded. The process of integration was also hindered by Buddhism which was not organically rooted in race memory and race tradition, and stood, in many respects, in antagonism to them. But it was an expansive movement and naturally attracted foreigners; in India, it stimulated the national mind and culture by impact rather than by inspiration. The Shungas and the Satavahana conquerors however drew strength from its roots.

The third century after Christ is still shrouded in obscurity. But, according to the *Bhagavata-Purana,* northern India was undergoing a period of disintegration. Nagas ruled in Champavati and Mathura; Abhiras ruled in Saurashtra and Avanti; in the region of Abu and Malava the rulers were devoid of culture "like unto the *Mlechchha*". In Sindh, on the banks of the Chandrabhaga, in the Kunti in Kashmir, the Shudras, Vratyas and the *Mlechchhas* ruled. These rulers, the author says, lacked the power of the Spirit, disregarded *Dharma* and Truth, and were "contemptible and irascible". His only hope lay in the new rulers, Vishvasphani in Magadha and Vindhyashakti, a Brahmana, ruling on the banks of the Narmada.

But there is little doubt, that by the beginning of the fourth century, the forces of disintegration had lost their momentum. In southern India the old forces were being given new forms and directions.

In the beginning of the fourth century, the powerful Pallava king Shivaskandavarman in southern India celebrated the *Ashvamedha.* About A.D. 320, Chandragupta I, the founder of the Gupta Empire, revived the *chakravarti* ideal in northern India. His marriage with Kumaradevi, the Lichchhavi princess, probably resulted in the union of her principality with Magadha and launched him on a career of wide conquests. Fortunately for him, there was no other rival for imperial supremacy in northern India at the time and no foreign invader threatened the country from the north-west.

Placed between A.D. 355-380, Samudragupta, the next Emperor, laid the foundation of an irresistible military machine which probably included a Navy. With his large standing army, he wiped out the feeble kings and effete republics of the Gangetic basin. The territory from Hardwar to the borders of Assam was consolidated into a compact homeland which he directly administered under a system which, with suitable modifications, was soon adopted in many parts of the country and persisted in some form even up to the British period. Samudragupta's sacred horse, followed by his army, extracted tribute from the kings ruling in most parts of the country and served to bring about friendly relations with the Shahanushahi kings of the north-west. He reached the zenith of his power when he performed the *Ashvamedha* sacrifice and gave munificent donations.

Politically, this was the age of integration in India. After more than three hundred years of fragmentation and foreign domination, northern India was again united under the vigorous rule of a powerful monarch of versatile talents. A brilliant general, a farsighted statesman, he became the symbol and architect of a mighty creative urge among the people which, while drawing vitality from tradition and race-memory, took on a new shape and power.

Samudragupta was succeeded by his no less brilliant son, Chandragupta II, known as Vikramaditya, acclaimed as the greatest of the Gupta Emperors. In his reign, which is placed between A.D. 376 and 414, the last vestige of foreign rule disappeared from the land the direct sway of Pataliputra extended from the Bay of Bengal to the Arabian Sea. The country to the south of the Narmada was dominated by two friendly powers—the Vakatakas and the Pallavas—who shared the Gupta Emperors' enthusiasm for strengthening *Dharma*. The dominions of the descendants of Vindhyashakti extended from Bundelkhand to Hyderabad. A daughter of Chandragupta II was married to one of them, and she ruled as regent for thirteen years; and till the dynasty disappeared, the Vakatakas continued in friendly alliance with the Guptas. The Pallavas, who help unquestioned sway in the south, also maintained friendly relations with the Guptas, even when they were not subject to their hegemony.

Under the leadership of Chandragupta II, the Gupta eagles flew over parts of Balkh across the Hindu Kush. Peace, plenty and power, associated with an all-pervading moral sense, were, in his reign, integrated with an intellectual and cultural efflorescence, and to the mind of the succeeding generation, it symbolised the fulfilment of the highest national aspirations.

Chandragupta was succeeded by his son, Kumaragupta (A.D. 415-455) and, later, by his grandson, Skandagupta (A.D. 455-467) who inflicted a defeat on the invading Hunas. Both of them stabilised what their predecessors had acquired and consolidated. These one hundred and fifty years of Gupta rule can rightly be called the Golden Prime of India.

The Gupta Emperors upheld *Dharma* in all its aspects and, in consequence, its content was enriched and its scope enlarged. An overarching law of life, though it existed from Vedic times, it received under them the form which in the main it still retains. They drew their inspiration from it, and in so doing carried the people with them. Historical continuity and conscious unity were preserved by a faith in the Vedas as the source of all knowledge and inspiration. Within the framework of this faith, myths, traditions and rituals, language and literature, and canons of conduct, ideals and modes of life, became integrating agencies. Through the Puranas, which sang of sacred legends of rivers, mountains, cities, of royal houses, and of semi-divine heroes and sages, the past remained a glorious heritage to inspire the future with fresh vigour.

In this age, the most powerful integrating force were the Dharmashastras. They provided the basis of Aryan society and the mode of social adjustment; prescribed laws of inheritance and of civil and criminal justice; and laid down rules to govern all major situations from birth to death. Of them all, *Manu-smriti* was held in the highest sanctity throughout the country, not only in the north but in the south as well. The Tamil kings upheld its authority; one of the oldest classics of Tamil literature bears the clear impress of its great influence.

Theoretically, according to the Dharmashastras, the social structure envisaged a four-fold order of social groups, Chaturvarnya; in fact, it was hierarchy of such groups ranged according to the standard of culture attained by each with intervening groups to accommodate products of racial fusion. The Brahmanas stood at its head as devoted to learning, culture and self-discipline. The hierarchy was cultural, not a racial one. Outsiders were allowed to enter and benefit by it, but not so fast as to destroy the social equilibrium. Opportunity was thus given to those who were aliens to Indian culture to rise in the scale of life, but never so rapidly as to endanger the stability of the existing social order.

Castes mixed in marriage with comparative freedom; *anuloma* marriages were very common; the *pratiloma* marriages were by no means rare.

The Dharmashastras were not enforced at the point of the sword. Even the backward and the immigrant classes dropped their group-customs and usages, and cheerfully adopted the social system prescribed by them. Thus, Aryanisation of India was not achieved by the fiats of rulers or mass coercion by superior classes, but by the willing acceptance by all those who realised that the dynamics of the Dharmashastra provided, for the age, the best conditions for social, spiritual and cultural uplift.

Sankrit, a living language, elastic in structure and rich in expression, possessing a rich, varied and beautiful literary achievement, was the living embodiment of the *Dharma* and a powerful integrating force. Inscriptions began to be written in Sankrit, even in the far South. A new thought or a new literary masterpiece in the language attracted the attention of all the intellectual centers. For instance the works of Kalidasa, a contemporary of Chandragupta II Vikramaditya, became the models of literary beauty throughout the country within a few years of his death.

Under the Gupta Emperors, the *Mahabharata* acquired a unique position as an integrating psychological force. It immortalised the proud and joyous manhood of Bharatavarsha, and provided a common source of inspiration in courts, schools and in society as a whole.

The cultural uprising was based upon the central idea underlying *Dharma* from early time. It predicated an unalterable faith in human endeavour, self-restraint and self-discipline. Emphasis was laid on individual experience and becoming rather than on belief and the scriptural word; it was reached only when a man could shed his limitations and become divine in this life. Running through a diversity of religious beliefs and social outlook, it also laid an emphasis on the observance of the great vows of truth, non-stealing, continence and non-possession as essential steps in progress. All conduct, in order to be worthy of respect, had to be harmonised and regulated by ethical and spiritual values calculated to help the fulfilment of this ideal.

The four Gupta Emperors,—omitting, of course, the ignoble Ramagupta,—in maintaining the ideals of a *chakravarti,* made the state at one and the same time, powerful, stable, dynamic and happy. The age saw the speculative thought among others of Vasubandhu and the Nayanmars; the perfect lyric and drama of Kalidasa; the astronomical discoveries of Varahamihira; the beginnings of the structural temples;

the beauty of the early Ajanta frescoes; the rise of Vaishnavism and Shaivism; the completion of the *Mahabharata* and the composition of *Vayu*—and the *Matsya-Puranas*. The empire was not merely based on conquests or administrative efficiency; its greatness lay in its integral outlook. Its strength was based as much on military strength as on internal order and economic plenty; the sap of its vitality was drawn from the roots of ancient tradition and race memory which they maintained, re-interpreted and replenished. The upsurge of the Kshatriya hierarchs of Madhyadesha and Magadha, loyally pledged to stability, constituted the steel-frame of the imperial structure. Nor was the splendour of the empire an isolated phenomenon surrounding the individuality of the rulers. The people, having discovered in their traditional way of life something noble and splendid, only saw it reflected in the greatness of their rulers. The Vakatakas and the Pallavas of the far south, the two other dominant powers in the country closely allied with the Guptas, joined in availing themselves of the agency of the Brahmanas, the missionaries and instruments of *Dharma,* by lavish generosity.

The Gupta Emperors became the symbols of a tremendous national upsurge. Life was never happier, our culture never more creative than during the Golden Prime of India.

About A.D. 455 the Hunas began to enter India. Emperor Skandagupta drove them back by a supreme effort. Twelve years later he died. A war of succession appears to have followed the death of Skandagupta weakening the empire in the hour of its danger. Five Gupta Emperors including Narasimhagupta Baladitya held precarious sway over parts of the empire between c. A.D. 500-570. Many parts of the empire became independent.

By A.D. 512, the Hunas under Toramana overran north India upto Eran in Madhya Pradesh. Toramana's son Mihirakula, a veritable terror, spread fire and carnage from the Punjab to Gwalior and by A.D. 525 became the master of a vast territory.

The Huna domination fortunately did not last long. There is no doubt that the power of Toramana was completely crushed and it may be true that having lost his kingdom he had to take refuge in Kashmir. The detalis of this struggle for liberation is unfortunately lost. We only know the name of three liberators: Emperor Narasimhagupta Baladitya, Yashodharman and Ishanavarman, the Maukhari king.

Yashodharman passed like a meteor without leaving any trace behind him, but Ishanavarman laid the foundation of the greatness of his dynasty—the Maukharis—and his capital, Kanauj.

The Golden Prime of India became a thing of the past; the military superiority of Magadha disappeared. Out of the welter emerged a new set of dynasties: the Maukharis of Kanauj, the Pushpabhutis of Thaneshvar, the Maitrakas of Valabhi and the Chalukyas of Badami. The Pallavas of Kanchi continued to flourish. In the west the Pratihara, head of a well-knit hierarchy, began to emerge from obscurity near Mt. Abu.

Soon the Maukharis also disappeared and Harshavardhana emerged as the most powerful king of north India.

Due to the exaggerated eulogies of his biographer, Bana, and the enthusiastic Hiuen Tsang, Sri Harsha has been given more than his share of importance. No doubt he preserved the unity of Madhyadesha, but he suffered a serious defeat at the hands of Pulakeshin II of Badami and had to make terms with the Maitrakas of Valabhi. The territories he conquered were neither as extensive as the empire of Guptas who preceded him, nor that of the Pratiharas who followed him; nor did he leave behind an empire.

Sri Harsha, unlike the Guptas, was not able to release a new integrating impulse. The Emperor, with a large army had conquered far and wide, staged spectacular festivals, made generous gifts; his character stood high. But he left no hierarchs and no successors; on his death the fabric he had erected, fell to pieces. The causes which led to this sudden collapse of Kanauj may be found not only in the circumstances that brought him to supremacy, but also in his personal character.

The empire he had won simply disappeared. After Sri Harsha, his daughter's son, Dharasena IV, the ruler of the comparatively small kingdom of Valabhi, assumed the pretentious title of an Emperor. Within fifty years of Sri Harsha's death Yashovarman, a powerful ruler and the patron of Bhavabhuti, restored Kanauj to its glory—but for a while.

But the strength and vigour of India, between A.D. 550 and 750, was found in the south. While the Maukharis were founding an empire which had its seat at Kanauj, Pulakeshin II, of the Chalukya family

(c. A.D. 550), had already founded a kingdom in the Bijapur district of Bombay with its capital at Vatapi, modern Badami. About the end of the sixth century, his son, Kiritivarman, embarked on wars against the kings who ruled to the north of Godavari.

Pulakeshin II, who had already subdued the Pallavas of Kanchi, repelled the invasion of Sri Harsha in c. A.D. 620. He annexed Vengi, modern Godavari district, and appointed his brother Vishnuvardhana as its governor on the east coast. Vishnuvardhana later became virtually independent and founded the dynasty of the Eastern Chalukyas. After a rule of about two centuries, during which the Chalukyas provided the greatness stabilising influence in the south, they were replaced by the Rashtrakutas.

The great Pallava king, Narasimhavarman I (c. A.D. 630-668) defeated even Pulakeshin II and captured his capital. Though the Chalukyas avenged this defeat soon after, the Pallavas remained the most powerful kings in the far south.

Throughout the period of over four hundred years from A.D. 320 to 750, India was administered by well-organised governments. The political interest during this time is primarily confined to the history of northern India. This was due mostly to the power and extent of the Gupta Empire. But the contribution of the Chalukyas and the Pallava kings in stabilising the country and fostering the integrating forces should not be under-estimated.

The foundation of life, shaped during the Gupta period, remained unshaken in a large part of the country, though its pattern was changed.

The Puranas, some of which were redacted or newly written in the Gupta age, became the popular gospels of the new impulse. The Puranas were not merely texts, they revived the glory of the distant past, sanctified new places in the country weaving the unity of Bharatavarsha, and gave the old values a new vigour by re-interpreting them in the light of new conditions.

Shaivism an old cult became a vigorous integrating movement. The Gupta Emperors were Vaishnavas, but Shaivism was more popular, and Buddhism also had a large number of supporters. After A.D. 500 the Bhakti cult introduced into the religious movements the emotional element which dominated Indian life for centuries.

Sanskrit continued to be the vehicle for expression of thought, for the Sanskrit speaking world was one, all-Indian. Another factor in uniting the nation was the sacred literature, *Ramayana, Mahabharata* and the Puranas. The Pauranikas were the missionaries of the new age. The *Katha* became the most powerful educative and integrating force.

The Empires of Ancient India

The seventh century B.C. was notable not only for the appearance of new religions but also for the consolidation of political units into a number of independent kingdoms. There were at this time at least sixteen kingdoms in India north of the Vindhya range, but by the sixth century four Gangetic states had become the major actors in Indian politics: Kosala (the realm of the legendary figure Rama), Vatsa, Avanti, and, destined for greatness, Magadha. Magadha controlled strategic sectors of the major trade routes of northern India—via both land and water. And Magadha had access to the important iron deposits. These were the primary economic foundations of an expansion that culminated in the vast imperial system of the Mauryas. "In its own way," Kosambi has remarked, "it corresponds to the Roman Empire in Europe." In this process of consolidation, popular institutions were gradually replaced by forms of government more amenable to the political integration of large areas.

Max Weber and, more recently, several other scholars have remarked on a fact often overlooked in studies of ancient Indian history. Contemporary with the rise of powerful territorial states, and more than simple coincidence, was the appearance of capitalist enterprise. The Ganges provided a natural trade route, and wealthy nobles, beginning to move to urban centers to spend their rent, provided a market. The city, which had begun its development in the eighth and seventh centguries B.C., ceased to be primarily a fortress as opportunities for the accumulation of wealth through trade expanded. The king became increasingly dependent on the guilds, and the financial power of these craft and merchant associations qualifies them for comparison with those of medieval Europe. But the Indian guilds never developed an organisation capable of resisting the state's efforts to meet expenses by means other than capitalistic tax farming. The new mercantile class, with its need for security of property and an orderly setting for business operations, could be expected to lend willing support to the autocracies of the Gangetic plain. And in return for financing the imperial ambitions of the prince, these merchants often gained important rights and privileges. Wealth made possible greater social mobility, and it was not uncommon for members of the lower orders of society to attain positions of prestige. We know that the Mauryan dynasty employed a considerable number of shudra officials.

The *purāṇas* (compendia of ancient legends and lore covering a wide variety of topics) do not provide a reliable account of the rise of Magadha, and the Sinhalese *Mahāvaṁsa,* a Buddhist text, is now usually taken as the basis for reconstructing the early history of the kingdom. In the time of the Buddha and the Persian emperor Cyrus, Magadha was ruled by the efficient and resolute Bimbisāra, a man distinguished for military prowess and administrative acumen, who knew what to do with territory after he had conquered it. Bimbisara reigned for fifty-two years before his death at the hand of his own son (eight years before the Buddha's own demise). Ajātaśatru, his son, succeeded in establishing hegemony over neighbouring kingdoms and republics incorporating, among other states, the once-powerful Kosala. By the fourth century B.C. Magadh—its capital now at Pāṭaliputra (modern Patna)—controlled the basin of the Ganges and the area as far north and west as Rajasthan and the Punjab. The foundations of imperial Magadha had been well laid by the Nanda rulers when the remarkable Chandragupta Maurya entered the scene.

Plutarch has written that "Androkottos himself, who was then but a youth, saw Alexander himself." The discovery by the early Sanskritist Sir William Jones that "Androkottos" (sometimes "Sandrocottos") referred to Chandragupta is one of the great chronological anchors of Indian history. Alexander left the Punjab in 324 B.C., having dramatised the military weakness of the small states ‹ northwestern India. It is difficult to reconstruct the ensuing campaign of Chandragupta against the Greek forces. Justin says simply that one Sandrocottos was responsible for liberating India after the death of Alexander. The Greek position had deteriorated, morale was low, and the conquered peoples proved difficult to govern. Chandragupta, already having proclaimed himself king, engaged his army in a series of battles with Greek forces that must have preoccupied him until Eudemus and his troops retired from the Punjab in 317, ending the threat of the Greek garrisons and leaving Chandragupta supreme in the northwest.

But he had managed during this time to march on Magadha, turning an almost certain disaster resulting from poor strategy into victory. Pataliputra was besieged, the Nanda ruler killed, and Chandragupta was anointed by his adroit brahman minister, Cāṇakya (or Kautalya), c. 321. The *Mudrārākṣasa,* a political play of the Gupta era, suggests that a palace revolution may have placed the Mauryas on the Nanda throne, and it is of course possible that some such intrigue may have been involved. The Mauryan ruler's position was finally secured by his triumph in 305 over the Greek king Seleucus, Alexander's successor in the eastern reaches of the empire, who sought to reclaim the area that had been lost. The Greek sources enlighten us little on this conflict, but they do state that Seleucus ceded extensive territories to the Indian leader in return for 500 war elephants—an exchange which indicates that Chandragupta had the upper hand. At the time Seleucus surrendered Afghanistan and Baluchistan, the Indian army is reported to have numbered 650,000 men, 30,000 cavalry, 9,000 elephants, and 8,000 chariots. Arrian maintains that these soldiers were paid so well that they supported themselves and their dependents with comparative ease. Even allowing for the usual exaggeration in these figures, the burden on the Mauryan treasury must certainly have been enormous.

Although the sources present us with a number of problems, we probably know more of Mauryan polity than of any other period before the rise of the Mogul dynasty. The administrative organisation and regulations of Kautalya[1] are generally taken to be a description of the Mauryan system. However, the *Kautaliya* never purports to give an account of a specific policy. It is a theoretical work, and any attempt to deduce more than the broad outlines of the Mauryan administrative system from it must bear this in mind. Despite its formal structure it is a *shastram,* a philosophical study. Those who insist on a late date for the Kautalya *Arthashạstra* are usually willing to concede that the work refers to conditions which, by the Mauryan epoch, had come to characterise Indian polity. The *Arthashastra* is supplemented by the observations of the Greek ambassador to the Mauryan court,

Megasthenes, who exists for us only through citations in the subsequent writings of Diodorus, Strabo, the elder Pliny, Plutarch, Justin, and Arrian. In a recent article, R.C. Majumdar argues that the classical writers had little confidence in Megasthenes' veracity; his *India* was not highly regarded. Arrian considered his descriptions generally unreliable: Megasthenes did not take pains to verify what he heard and frequently recorded quite fantastic things. It would appear that classical writers were not as influenced by the accounts of Megasthenes as Indologists have assumed. It must be remembered also that Megasthenes was presumably describing Magadhan institutions in terms that would be meaningful to his countrymen. His extravagant description of Magadha under Chandragupta may have been partially inspired by a desire to make of India an example for his fellow Greeks. India, a land of villages and country states, does not translate well into the vocabulary of the city-state, although some similarities are no doubt present. If this allowance is made, the differences between his account and Kautalya's are not significant. For the later Mauryan period the most reliable information comes from the imperial edicts—pillar and rock inscriptions—of the Emperor Ashoka (*Aśoka*). Perhaps the greater number of these inscriptions had no binding authority. They were essentially the idealistic pronouncements of a spiritual leader.

There is some question about the class origin of Chandragupta. The Punjabi king, Porus, is reported by Curtius to have tole Alexander that the Nanda king ruling at this was of low birth—a barber who had become the queen's lover and accomplice in the assassination of the former king. Mahāpadma, the founder of the dynasty (c. 364 B.C.), is described in the Puranas as another Paraśurāma (the exterminator of the warrior class). If we are to believe the Buddhist sources, the youngest of the nine Nanda brothers, and the last to rule, was begotten by a man of unknown origin, probably a shudra. Plutarch reports that Chandragupta referred to the base origin of his predecessor, which suggests his own higher status. Kautalya accepts him as a kshatriya, but it is likely that the role of king conferred kshatriyaship by this time. Foreign sources reveal nothing about Chandragupta's alleged humble origin, and there is little evidence to indicate that the himself was of the Nanda dynasty, as some have held. The theory that Chandragupta came from the lower orders runs counter to the puranas and the Buddhist literature. However, the Gupta suffix was most common among members of the vaishya class. Professor Mookerji believes that the clan name Moriya provides a more convincing explanation of the dynasty name Maurya than other theories (such as those which would derive the name form "Mura," suggesting humble birth). This argument is based on Buddhist tradition, which holds that the emperor was the son of the chief of this clan.

By the time Chandragupta's son Bindusāra ascended the throne in the early years of the third century B.C., the empire of the Mauryas had reached vast proportions. It was divided and subdivided into provinces,[2] divisions, districts, and villages. Most large empires followed this administrative pattern. Members of the royal family often served as provincial governors: Ashoka, Chandragupta's grandson, served his apprenticeship in this capacity. In the absence of princes, military officers respected for their valor were appointed to these governorships. The talent for military leadership was a necessary qualification, since the governors were responsible for preserving order and protecting the marches of the empire. The provincial governors maintained their own courts and ministerial councils, and, owing to the difficulty of communication with the central government, autonomy tended to vary proportionately with distance from the imperial capital.

Megasthenes mentions three groups of officials: the *agronomoi,* district officials; *astynomoi,* town officials; and the War Office. The district officials superintended irrigation and surveying, hunting, agriculture, metallurgical and forest industries, mining, and road maintenance. The town officials were attached to six boards of five members each, which were charged with the care of foreigners, supervision of factories, registration of vital statistics, inspection of goods, collection of taxes and regulation of certain marketing operations. The committee of the War Office dealt with affairs of the admiralty, transport and supply, the cavalry, the elephants, the chariots, and the infantry. A headman (*grāmaṇī* in the village, *gopa* in the town), guided by the panchayat of elders, supervised the affairs of the smallest administrative units. He was registrar, tax administrator, and general arbiter. Villages were classified according to the contribution they made to the central government: those supplying troops, those giving free labour, those providing produce instead of taxes, those paying in either grain or coin as they wished, those exempted. Mauryan administration seems to have involved two coordinate divisions of government: city and country. This division was continued into succeeding centuries. At this time the cities of the realm, like other corporate entities, enjoyed a high degree of independence. The central government rarely interfered with the administration of local affairs, and Megasthenes hints that at least some of the cities had arrived at a democratic form of government.

Pataliputra, the capital city, was located at the point where the river Son joins the Ganges. It is described as a handsome city, more than nine miles in length, about one and a quarter miles broad, and surrounded by a moat sixty feet deep and two hundred yards wide. A timber palisade with sixty-four gates and 570 towers ran along the moat. It is possible that the audience hall at Pataliputra was modeled after a design used at Persepolis. The social and economic activities of the city were, for the most part, administered by the thirty-member council.

The king relied mainly on his Chief Minister (*mantri*) and on his purohita. Three or four councilors composed his immediate advisory cabinet, and there was a larger council, or mantri-parishad, charged with the execution of royal orders. The central government had eighteen departments headed by *tirthas.*[3] A committee of five superintended the operations of each department, and a number of inspecting officers served to coordinate the activities of all departments. There were also military and economic officials. As administration increased in complexity, the power of the ministers grew. By the later Mauryan era evidence of ministers' refusing to execute the orders of the king can be found.

Reconciling bureaucratic responsibility with autocratic control must have posed a major problem for the Mauryan ruler. The position of the minister may have been similar in some respects to that of the present-day Soviet bureaucrat confronted with the demand for efficient administration by a government reluctant to delegate the control over resources necessary for such efficiency because it fears the development of independent centers of power in the bureaucracy. As a consequence of such a dilemma the central government is burdened with the details of administration. Megasthenes reported that the Mauryan king was kept so busy that his daily rubdown with wooden rollers had to take place while he continued to hear cases in court. The ministers were appointed by the king, whose actions they advised in the interests of the people (at least in theory); they were usually chosen for their disposition to judge impartially and for those qualities of character that Hindu doctrine identified with the governing classes. There was no actual check on the executive power, although sacred law supposedly guided the policy of the king and he was expected to have the advice and approval of his ministers before acting. Chandragupta and his successors took on considerable legislative power, and the *Arthashastra* mirrors this new emphasis on the sovereign authority of the king's law.

The state decribed by Megasthenes and outlined in the *Arthashastra* is a bureaucratic polity—perhaps a resurrection of the ancient Harappa administrative pattern. This power structure, centered in a great citadel within the walled city of Pataliputra, might be described as a mixed system of rational and bureaucratic relationships on the state level, with guild, tribal, and caste associations absorbing residual administrative functions. These associations were destined to increase in importance—until by Gupta times the situation had reversed and the state was all but reduced to military and diplomatic functions.

In referring to the Mauryan bureaucratic structure, we imply a distinctively political area of activity with its own characteristic roles and purposes, which can be differentiated from the institutions, organisations, and goals of economic, religious, and other sectors of society. Chandragupta had established himself as a relatively independent force in politics, possessing a new freedom from tribal, clan, and caste restrictions and able to develop and pursue his own ends through agencies which were not affiliated with and legitimated by other social groups, but which were committed rather to the king and the governing elite. The function of these organisations was to implement policy by mobilising material resources and popular support.[4]

In addition to the struggle for power in the bureaucracy itself (particularly the attempt to prevent the growth of clusters of power within the hierarchy), there is of course the larger struggle between the political decision-making group and other foci of power within the community. Mauryan consolidation was aided by the failure of traditional institutions to integrate and stabilise society effectively and to cope with changes capable of disrupting equilibrium. The territorial expansion of the earlier Magadhan rulers and the Mauryas made available new sources of wealth and power, which also served to upset the established position of different groups in society. We have earlier indicated that members of the lower classes began to gain at least some measure of prosperity as economic advances created new demands for their services. By encouraging the organisation of a money economy and the increase in the volume of international trade and contacts with the Hellenistic world, the Mauryan rulers hastened the deadline of the isolation upon which the traditional society depends for the preservation of the customary and the sacred.[5] The shrewd Kautalya may have seen the consequences of territorial expansion and concentration of political power, and may have sought to utilise these developments to strengthen the brahman position by encouraging the expansion of Aryan culture, curtailing the growing influence of heterodox religion (especially an alliance with the state), and providing an effective check on the kshatriya nobility. But the motives of the brahman minister we may only surmise.[6]

Raising money to finance the extensive undertakings of the state with out inducing widespread popular discontent must have called for considerable ingenuity. The war with Seleucus made further demands on the resources of the state, and if the *Arthashastra* does in fact date from this period, we can easily understand its preoccupation with the financial needs of the state. Chandragupta, as we have noted, maintained a vast army numbering hundreds of thousands of troops. The Greek ambassador remarked that the soldiers constituted a "class" second only to the agriculturists in size. They were salaried and equipped by the state, and when not fighting, which was their only duty, they "abandon themselves to enjoyment."[7]

Mauryan economic policy eventually had the effect of pushing production into the villages. As a part of the programme to augment the wealth of the state, Chandragupta established many village communities, which appear to have been subject to extensive controls by the bureaucracy, although they often became virtually self-sufficient economic units.[8] The Mauryan king had the right of eminent domain over all the land in the kingdom. Evidently this right was so broadly interpreted in the Mauryan state that it suggested to Greek observers a parallel with Egypt, where the king owned the land. Export and import duties, excise and *octroi* taxes were often burdensome, but despite this and the fact that the Mauryan king did not encourage small private enterprise as such, commerce expanded and Megasthenes was able to comment enthusiastically on the prosperity of Magadha. With land taxes sometimes reaching a third of the yield, the coffers filled. The state operated the mines, supervised the forests, managed its own dairy, cotton, sugar, and oil industries, and controlled the manufacture and sale of liquor.

The government provided many public services, which included rural development programmes and experimental farms for the improvement of crops and animals. The dharmic code dictated a charitable programme, and the state provided for the less fortunate members of the community. Food was allotted to the hungry, and care given to orphans, the sick (animal as well as human), and the aged. Travellers and foreigners in distress were similarly provided for. Places of worship and entertainment were sponsored and subsidised by the government. The forests were made to yield scholarship as well as timber; the government set up learning "reservations," and was as assiduous in furthering education as in backing religion. The state also sought to protect the consumer from fraud and from unauthorised commodity prices. A series of judicial bodies, ranking from the village court, presided over by the headman, to the imperial court, administered the law. With the possible exception of the village court, these bodies differentiated between criminal and civil cases.

The Mauryan emperor, or his representatives, conducted periodic tours of outlying regions to renew contacts with the people as well as to inspect provincial administration. Megasthenes reports that the king relied on spies. There were apparently so many of these special agents that the Greek concluded that they constituted a separate class in the Mauryan state. It was their duty to relate to the king or the magistrates everything that transpired in the cities and army and countryside. Prostitutes were often employed in this way. The attention Kautalya devotes to the intelligence system may reflect the importance attached to spying activities the Mauryan empire. The spies and the army may be said to have been the pillars of the Mauryan power, making possible the reasonably effective administration of a great territory in a time when transportation and communication systems were still primitive.[9]

Although slavery was recognised in Hindu theory, slaves were treated with more human consideration than was the case in most ancient states. Megasthenes claimed that the institution did not exist, which may indicate that by the time of the Mauryas many slaves were receiving their freedom and the worst evils of the system were being abolished.

THE REGIME OF ASHOKA MAURYA

Occasional shafts of light pierce the dense tangle of the Indian past and reveal the teaching of a religious virtuoso, the career of a monarch, the exploits of a hero. The reign of the emperor Ashoka in the third century B.C. left its monument in the form of inscriptions that remain to us today. These records make it possible for us to reconstruct the heyday of Mauryan power with some confidence. The empire of Ashoka, the last great Mauryan king, embraced all of India with the exception of the Tamil country at the southern extremity, stretching north to the Hindu Kush and Kashmir and Nepal.[10]

The chronicles of Ceylon, the *Dīpavaṃsa* and *Mahāvaṃsa,* probably dating from the fourth and fifth centuries A.D., tell us something of period of Ashoka's reign, although these Buddhist sources can hardly be considered disinterested commentaries. The chronicles state that Chandragupta ruled for twenty-four years, Bindusara for twenty-eight years followed by a four-year interregnum, and Ashoka for thirty-seven years. Ashoka was apparently not crown prince, and the sources touching on his early reign indicate a struggle for power among the Mauryan princes—which would account for the four-year interval after the death of his father. He acceded to the throne of Magadha in 269 or the following year.

Buddhist texts imply that Ashoka was extremely wicked before his conversion to the faith, but we may assume that this characterisation is intended to dramatise the change wrought by the emperor's acceptance of the teaching. Accounts of conversions to Christianity are not free of such exaggerations, and some Augustine scholars believe that the saint deliberately overstated his own youthful sins and indiscretions in order to emphasise the power of his new-found faith. The distress and destruction caused by the war with Kalinga, in which, we are told, "150,000 persons were deported, 100,000 were slain, and many times that number died," are reputed to have had a profound effect on the great emperor, causing him to renounce future armed conquest and to dedicate himself to imbuing the world with the Buddhist ethic and sacred duty. But we can be reasonably sure that Ashoka's desire to control the routes to southern India must have been an important motive for the war. And with the defeat of Kalinga, Ashoka overcame the last significant obstacle to the control of India. (The edicts point to generally amicable relations with the kingdoms of the south, and there appears to have been no need for their subjection.) For all his remorse, it is interesting to note that Ashoka did not confess these feelings in Kalinga itself. To do so would surely have been unwise. We may, however, speculate that in embracing Buddhism,

Ashoka had determined on a faith capable of cementing the empire he and his grandfather had built. It may well be that Ashoka was not the first of his line to show partiality to a nonorthodox sect. His father is said to have been influenced by the Ājivikas,[11] and Chandragupta himself very possibly became a Jaina in his later years.

The Buddhist chronicles are surprisingly quiet regarding the Kalinga war. The Ceylon texts do not refer to it, although it is commonly assumed to have been the event that stimulated the famous conversion. A recent study of Ashoka concludes that the emperor's acceptance of Buddhism actually preceded the Kalinga campaign. In the Brahmagiri Minor Rock Edict (c. 256), Ashoka remarks that he has been a lay Buddhist for more than two and a half years, but he says, "for a year I did not make much progress." His conversion thus seems not to have been the dramatic transformation that we have come to expect in such situations. After a year of exposure to the heterodox teaching, Ashoka was able to announce that at last he had drawn close to the Order. The Bhabra edict (which was most probably intended for the monks of the sangha rather than for the general population) further attests to his acceptance of the major elements of Buddhism. But the dhamma, the expression of this ethic, is more a concept of social responsibility than a purely religious ideal. Ashoka evidently did not seek to identify dhamma as a Buddhist principle, but rather tried to emphasise the universalistic content of the idea and its freedom from any specific doctrinal roots. Dhamma represents a civic ethic, something that would not, of course, be stressed in orthodox Buddhism.

The Mauryan ruler made it clear the he considered the welfare and happiness of the people his mission; to bring them contentment in this world and heaven in the next is the purpose expressed in the Rock Edicts.[12] We know that Ashoka provided for groves of shade trees along the major highways of the realm to accommodate merchants and other travellers.[13] In the sixth Rock Edict he says that no matter where he is "in the enclosed [female] apartments, in the inner chamber, in the royal ranch, on horseback or in pleasure orchards, the Reporters may report people's business to me. People's business I do at all places."

But it was not comfort of this world that most concerned the great king. Ashoka took it upon himself to establish a code of ethics that amounted to a rejection of the sacrificial cult and the brutalities and inequities it justified. The military programme of his grandfather was replaced with a policy of "righteousness": only through dharma could lasting conquests be made. "The sound of drum has become the sound of Dhamma." This was the basis of the practice of nonviolence (*ahiṃsā)* advocated by the Mauryan emperor. A more skeptical assessment might suggest that expansion was no longer profitable. The costs of maintaining the empire were more than the income from the less fertile Deccan could bear."[14] And yet, despite its cost and despite Ashoka's rejection of aggressive war, there is no mention in the edicts of his reducing the size of the imperial army. Ashoka, for all his dedication to humanitarian ideals, gives no evidence of having relaxed the methods of punishment prescribed by earlier Mauryan kings. Nor did the principle of nonviolence lead him to abolish capital punishment.

In the ninth year of his reign he embraced Buddhism, which, of all religions, he saw as the most perfect embodiment of ahimsa. Under the patronage of the great emperor the Buddhist ethic spread beyond the confines of the peninsula; within several centuries most of southern Asia was exposed to the religion, and during the first five centuries of the Christian era central Asia and the Far East came under Buddhist influence.[15] But tolerance was the keystone of official policy under Ashoka. "The king, beloved of the Gods,[16] honours every form of religious faith, but considers no gift or honour so much as the increase of the substance of religion; whereof this is the root, to reverence one's own faith and never to revile that of others. Whoever acts differently injures his own religion while he wrongs another's." All men should respect the doctrines professed by others, and, in the administration of the realm, the customary law of different peoples must be allowed to prevail. The ideal had a secularising effect on society for it must have meant the end of many special concessions and immunities to the priests. It should be noted that Rock Edicts III and IV recommend respectful and generous behavior toward brahmans as well as toward heterodox ascetics. More often than not the brahmans are mentioned in the edicts before the Buddhist holy men. These inscriptions indicate that Ashoka was always careful to avoid antagonising the priests directly. But Ashoka certainly did not share the deference to the sacrificial order that marked Kautalya's acceptance of varna.[17]

It is relevant to ask at this point what dhamma (dharma) may have meant for Ashoka. Surely there had been a decisive modification in the concept as it developed from the Vedic rita. Under brahman influence, dharma had become intimately linked with caste. And though caste continued to be recognised by the Buddhists as an institution fundamental to social order, it had lost its former significance for personal salvation.

Despite the declared intentions of Ashoka, it can be argued that the tradition of royal patronage of religion had its real beginning in his regime. Although he counseled tolerance and demanded that men be restrained in their speech regarding religious matters and that all sects be allowed to flourish, Ashoka was intent on encouraging certain types of conduct and he must have infringed on religious freedom when he condemned practices such as the killing of animals for sacrifice. His very sympathy toward heterodox groups, his active proselytising and establishing of missions, held a danger to the traditional balance of power. The royal authority had become the protector of sacred law in a way that was new to India. Government had always been an instrument of religion, but less actively so. Now the king must concern himself directly with the common good, an idea anticipated in the *Arthashastra* (if it is not, indeed, Ashokan experience that inspired the ideal commonwealth of Kautalya).

Ashoka's conversion to Buddhism ended the ability of the brahman ministers to check the royal power. When the state combined Brahma and Kshatra in its own authority it approached a self-legitimating caesaropapism. And now there existed the opportunity for religion to become the instrument of government—in a more insidious fashion than that devised by the author of the *Arthashastra*. The individual could accept official policy or oppose it, but there were no effective agencies of protest and social change. Before the advent of Buddhism, the inchoate caste system had at least served as an intermediary institution between the individual and the state. Freedom was still only the freedom to prepare oneself for salvation. And here the state justified its intervention, since its function was conceived in moral terms. The state recognised no sphere of life beyond the pale of state regulation, and Ashoka himself decided what constituted the good of the people.[18]

We may wonder what law Ashoka employed in dealing with those, such as Jainas and Buddhists, for whom the traditional caste-based codes would have been inappropriate or inadequate. What replaced Brahmanical law? We should, of course, assume that the emperor relied on the usage and custom of non-Brahmanical peoples.

But this would still require a technique for adjusting disputes arising among persons of different religious commitments. The development of positive law must have been at least in part the consequence of the need for equitable administration of a people professing a variety of faiths. To a considerable extent the tradition of pluralism which allowed different groups to regulate their activities in accord with their own laws and customs, could be extended to these peoples. But there were always problems of conflicting local laws, and the secular authority would have to arbitrate such problems. This pattern of development may have been similar in some respects to the evolution of the Roman *ius gentium*. There were ample opportunities for Ashoka to promulgate law, and the emperor did in fact issue orders that cannot be called in any sense the application of customary or sacred law. He had appropriated the legislative function, although in theory the rules he handed down were in accordance with sacred law.

The Buddhist king governed directly, announcing his policy in imperial edicts which, whether of a civil or ecclesiastical nature (no careful delineation was made), were communicated to the citizens by his viceroys and governors. Thirty-three of these inscriptions remain.[19] These edicts, which mirror the ethical ideas of the early Buddhist canonists,[20] are concerned with dhamma and methods of disseminating these ethical principles. The edicts are similar in expression to those of Darius. With several exceptions in the northwest, the inscriptions are in Prakrit (popular dialects) and are written in the Brāhmī script, which is usually read from left to right. The use of Prakrit indicates that the edicts were meant to be accessible to all literate men. Most of the Minor Rock Edicts are concerned exclusively with Buddhism and Ashoka's relation to the Order,[21] and the Minor Pillar Edicts are devoted to Ashoka's religious activities.[22] The pillar edicts date from the twenty-seventh and twenty-eighth years of his reign. They are his last testament. The seventh edict, which summarises his achievements, is followed by ten years of silence. If the emperor left further records, they have yet to be discovered.

The central government undertook to propagate dhamma; in the fourteenth year of his rule Ashoka established a corps of dhamma-mahāmattas (dharma-mahāmātras) to serve as religious supervisors as well as welfare agents.[23] The mahamatta seems to have had access to the homes of all members of society. In the first pillar edict (twenty-seventh regnal year) we learn that it was sometimes necessary for these officials to persuade men who wandered from the true path. But we are not enlightened as to the form this persuasion takes. The dhamma appears to be more narrowly defined by this time and to have taken on the nature of a comprehensive civil code.

The higher officials were ordered to tour at regular intervals in order to learn the wishes of the people as well as to instruct them in the moral life. It could be argued that the emissaries of dharma were less expensive representatives of the law than the usual officials and soldiers (and the spies necessary to watch their activities). Ashoka himself was frequently on the move. This entrusting of government officials with moral as well as political functions has been cited as the most important single innovation in the political organisation of Ashoka's regime. Every few years a council of administrative officials met to consider methods of promoting justice and advancing the ethical concepts which, in the Buddhist Law of Piety, were conceived as the foundation of religion.

In addition to illuminating Ashoka's religious faith and his missionary activity, the edicts tell us something of his administrative system. Two of the Rock Edicts (III and VI) refer to the Ashokan council. The ministers had the right to debate the orders of the king and his departmental advisors.[24] This was meant to imply not that the authority of the king was limited, but rather that the advice of the council should be sought before the people were informed by local officials of administrative decisions.[25] Members of the parishad appear to have been free to express opinions contrary to the king's, and, in the later years of Ashoka's regime, to have successfully deterred or modified actions contemplated by the king. Parts of the empire (especially frontier areas) were governed by local rajas, but the governors and district officers (*rājūkas* and *prādeśikas*) were the important administrative figures. One of the edicts grants these officials sovereign jurisdiction in governing the provinces. They need not fear contradiction from the central authority. Here is the first suggestion of the diminishing power of the central government.

The Buddhist legends imply that Ashoka's control began to loosen toward the end of his regime, but there is little of a specific nature to suggest how or where this weakening came about. In its attempts to regulate life—first in the material sphere, under Chandragupta and his able minister, and later in the spiritual, under

Ashoka—the state at length over-extended itself. Difficulties of communication and finance and pressures from discontented or ambitious elements of the community were to prove too much for the Mauryan state. If Magadha had been able to produce leadership of comparable talent, these obstacles might have been overcome. But such ability is rare: Chandragupta and Ashoka were, respectively, India's greatest organiser and India's greatest king.[26]

Although the economic, military, and religious policies of the Mauryan rulers and their innovations in political organisation did not appreciably transform the daily life of the humbler member of society, the effects of their administrations must surely have altered the traditional social structure. By traditional (or communal) society we mean one in which norms and goals are established by custom, and there is little capacity for change and invention. Ascribed status determines the political elite, and social groups are relatively free of domination by the central authority or by other groups, and are able to control many aspects of their members' lives. When the state itself asserts control over these groups, the structure begins to take on a totalitarian character. Without the technological devices available to modren totalitarian states, the state could not hope to alter the behaviour of the individual to the degree possible today. But indirectly, by controlling the economy, introducing new classes into political life and excluding others, actively promoting particular religious ideals, administering sanctions efficiently in various areas of conduct, mobilising for expansion, and the like, the Mauryan state was threatening the time-honored institutions and modifying customary social relationships.

We should not be surprised to learn of a reaction on the part of those groups whose position in society was dependent on the older patterns of conduct. Although there is little evidence of actual maltreatment of the brahmans, the priests lost much of their former influence on political policy and religious life. Some historians postulate a brahman uprising, and attribute the collapse of the empire to Ashoka's patronage of Buddhism and commitment to pacifism. The theory of a brahman uprising was possibly inspired by the fact that Puṣyamitra, who led the palace revolution (c. 184 B.C.) against the Mauryan king Brihadratha, ending a dynastic rule that had lasted for 137 years,[27] was evidently a brahman.[28] A less dramatic, but more realistic theory of the downfall of the Mauryas would have to emphasise the practical problems of administering a territory that included most of India—as well as the need to rely on officials who were often ambitious and of divided loyalty. An empire of these proportions depends on effective control at the center. This direction appears to have been lacking in the later years of the empire. The movement for local autonomy was encouraged by foreign invaders such as the Bactrian Greeks. In the court itself there were undoubtedly factional disputes and ministers eager to arrogate more power to themselves.

Pushyamitra, who organised the *coup d'état* that overthrew Brihadratha, held a high office under the king as commander-in-chief of the army. He established his own family, the Shungas (*Śuṅga*), on the throne of Magadha; they ruled, if tradition is correct, until Sīmuka, the first Sātavāhana king, vanquished the Shunga empire sometime around 72 B.C. By this time Ujjayinī, the capital of the old kingdom of Avanti, had regained its prominence, and, with Magadha cut off from the ports of the west, it replaced Pataliputra as an economic and cultural center. In northern and western India foreign conquerors consolidated their positions. The Kushans (*Kuṣaṇa*) controlled almost all of this area in the first century A.D., shifting the political focus to Peshawar. The domain of the powerful Kushan king Kaniṣka, a patron of Buddhism, extended as far east as modern Bihar. But the Kushan power was already so decentralised as to justify the use of the term feudatory in describing the political structure. The successors of Kanishka ruled until the third century, when, with the victory of Shapur I, the northwest was brought under Persian influence. In the northwestern Deccan, the kingdom of the Satavahanas (*Āndhras*) was paramount for the first three centuries of the Christian era. In this unstable period between the empire of the Mauryas and that of the Guptas, the term matsyanyaya gained increasing currency. Lawlessness characterised large parts of India; it was indeed a "time of troubles" marked by pillaging invaders and almost constant struggle among the Indian states.

Small kingdoms as well as a number of republics had begun to reappear as early as the concluding years of Mauryan rule. It was not uncommon for the leadership of these republics to become hereditary, and for the rulers to take the title of maharaja. Of these republics, the Yaudheyas, in the southern Punjab, the Mālavas in what is now Rajasthan, and several others survived into the Gupta period—but not beyond the fourth century A.D. More often than not, kings followed the traditional advice to refrain from annexing conquered territory. The vanquished king, or a close relative, would be restored to the throne—the state becoming a feudatory. Or, when annexation did take place (as it did occasionally in the Gupta epoch), the former king might serve as a provincial officer.

These tributary states were independent in domestic and foreign policy, save for their duties of homage on ceremonial occasions and their obligations to assist their lords in time of war. The elaborate gradation of rank (ranging from king to "supreme king of kings"[29]) reflected the relative position of these states in the political structure of the time. These grandiose titles appear to have been largely the contribution of invading tribes that descended on India during these centuries and all but exhausted kshatriya power.

Yet in this time of barbarian encounter and religious competition that followed the decline of Mauryan rule, the institution of kingship was strengthened. If the invaders were to be repulsed, the king must have full responsibility and the state must be effectively organised to take maximum advantage of its resources. And it was in the interest of religion to buttress the authority of the king. In the acute religious conflict that followed the break-up of the Ashokan empire, the states usually took a strong partisan position (most of them disposed to renascent Brahmanism) and the king was rewarded with a sanctification that had never been equaled in earlier Indian history. It is at this time that the divinity of kings really emerges: the innovations of Ashoka, the new interpretations of the royal function, and the introduction of Near Eastern and Greek concepts encouraged this development.

IMPERIAL ADMINISTRATION OF THE GUPTAS

The second century A.D. saw a reassertion of guild power, which Weber believed coincided with the new influx of money from the Roman Empire; the availability of precious metals may have encouraged Indian kings to mint coins of their own. But between the second century and the early Gupta period the great urban centers had begun to decline. Archaeologists tell us that by this time coins had become coarser and cruder and the fine pottery of an earlier age had disappeared. The Gupta rulers, Kumāra Gupta excepted, issued almost no copper coins. Trade was diminishing in importance and the money economy was declining. Officials were, with increasing frequency, paid in kind or by grants of revenues. The village had become the basic unit of the economy. Commodity production and purchasing power were reduced to a level that discouraged capitalistic development. When the costs of centralised administrative control became prohibitive the village assumed increasing political importance as well. And the village, practically self-contained politically and economically, would remain the fundamental social entity until modern times. With the replacing of the city by the village in the Gupta epoch, commodity production was no longer equal to the rich cultural development that had earlier flowered under the Satavahana dynasty.

Records of a number of land grants to brahmans have survived. These gifts of land were intended by their donors as a kind of spiritual investment. By the fifth century A.D. the grants comprised control over revenue sources, including even the mines (which had long been considered the king's personal domain), as well as administrative control over the villages included in the land grants.[30] The practice of granting land and administrative rights to the brahmans in the Gupta era was one of the factors leading to feudalising of Indian society.[31] During this period land appears to have been sold for religious purposes only, though we cannot be certain of this. There is evidence (if the *Arthashastra* can be considered evidence) that in Mauryan times there were land transactions for other reasons. The descriptions of Gupta society provided by Chinese pilgrims in the fifth and seventh centuries A.D. indicate that the state did not keep registries of households, which suggests, in turn, that the state was not directly involved in collecting taxes, but assigned this function to intermediaries. We have the statement of Fa-hsien that Gupta officials were granted land revenues. The power of the guilds had long been challenged by princes jealous of their wealth and influence, and though there had been revivals of these mercantile associations, in the Gupta period they remained subordinate to the feudal barons, who controlled the village surplus and constituted the market for luxury goods.

This was the economic setting of the second of the great Indian empires. Again it was Magadha that succeeded in realising the ancient ideal of the chakravartin. The Guptas and their allies, the Vākāṭakas, ruled most of central and northern India in the fourth and fifth centuries A.D. The second Gupta ruḷer (though the fourth of his house mentioned in the inscriptions), Samudra Gupta, who ruled for forty years in the fourth century, established a dominion that stretched from the Punjab to modern Assam in northeastern India and was centered in the old Mauryan capital. His son, Chandra Gupta II, who reigned until A.D. 415, extended Gupta sovereignty over almost all of northern India and the adjacent Deccan. It was he who consolidated the alliance with the powerful Vakatakas, who were paramount in west central India. Fa-hsien records that the government of the Guptas interfered little in the affairs of the people, and then always with a gentleness he found impressive. The Chinese pilgrim was able to report that travellers could journey from one end of India to the other without fear of violence. (How different was his experience from that of his countryman several centuries later whose movements were always in jeopardy!). By this time Hinduism was entrenched as the dominant form of religious expression, and the subsidence of warfare enabled the country to profit from the enlightened heterodox ethical systems that infused Hindu religion. Poets and dramatists who flourished in these regimes portrayed the refinement and splendor of Indian courtly life. Samudra Gupta himself was an intellect and musician of the first order. Toward the end of the rule of Kumāra Gupta I, son of Chandra Gupta II, India was again beset by invaders who, like the Greeks and Central Asians, poured over the mountains of the northwest into the fertile plains. Now an Iranian people (hūṇas) appeared to herald the collapse of Gupta power.

Before we turn to the main features of Gupta polity, mention should be made of the sources of information available to us. In addition to fairly extensive numismatic evidence, we have the puranas, which tell us much about the history of the early Guptas. The *Nārada Dharmaśāstra* (in many ways reminiscent o the *Arthashastra* of Kautalya) and the *Bṛhaspati Dharmaśāstra* may both date from the fourth century. A number of inscriptions of the period are evidence that these codes (or smritis) greatly influenced the Gupta kings.[32] One of the most valuable of the sources available to us is the record left by the Chinese Buddhist pilgrim whose observations we have already noted. He spent fifteen years in India during the reign of Chandra Gupta II (three of them in the capital at Pataliputra).

The *Kāmandakīya* belongs to the fourth or fifth century A.D., and it is reasonable to ascribe it to the late fourth century when the empire of the Guptas had been consolidated. There is some speculation that the author may have been Śikhara, the minister of Chandra Gupta II; however, it is generally believed that its author was an academic theoretician removed from active participation in politics. In our brief examination of Gupta polity we shall depend in part on this treatise.[33]

The *Pañcatantra,* a book of fables belonging to the late fifth or early sixth century and intended for the instruction of statesmen, is also in the arthashastra tradition and quotes frequently from the treatise of Kamandaka. The *Harṣacarita* of Bāṇa and the literature of India's laureate poet, Kālidāsa, belong to this era—the former (a biography of the emperor Harsha) to the seventh century, the twilight of the grand empire. Kalidasa has been located everywhere from the first century B.C. to the middle of the fifth century A.D. The problem of dating his works is complicated by the number of "Kalidasas" and "Vikramadityas" (with whom the poet was associated) that appear throughout historical references, but most historians now place this foremost of Sanskrit writers in the time of the Gupta monarchs Chandra Gupta II and Kumara Gupta I (375-455). The political passages in his *Raghuvaṁśam* would suggest this brilliant period of Gupta power.

Then there is the undistinguished *Kaumudīmahotsava,* a five-act drama of unknown authorship, which illumines the opening years of the dynasty. The *Devīcandraguptam,* which exists only in fragments, and the *Mudrārākṣasa* (both dramatic works) contribute to our picture of the Gupta court. The *Mudrarakshasa* is of particular interest in that ostensibly it refers to the establishment of the Mauryan empire through the efforts of Chandragupta Maurya and Kautalya, and emphasises the importance of diplomacy and expediency. Although the setting is Mauryan, the events probably mirror conditions contemporaneous with its author, Viśākhadatta. The play is essentially a rationale of Kautalyan stagecraft, which is put forth as a model for political negotiation. It illustrates the dictum that political ends justify the means of their accomplishment: Kautalyan opportunism definitely pays. (Portions of the play have been included in the Appendix.) Parallels in Mauryan and Gupta politics and the inspiration that Kautalya provided the later dynasty have often been remarked upon.

Evidence other than these literary sources must, however, be given more weight. The stone pillar of Samudra Gupta at Allahabad is the most important of the inscriptions that remain. It attests to the vastness of Gupta dominions. Even the king of Ceylon admitted the supremacy of the Gupta kings. The pillar, though it makes clear that primogeniture is the traditional basis of succession, indicates that the final decision lies with people and the ministers.[34] Other inscriptions suggest that the eldest son was not always selected, qualification being a more important consideration. Popular opinion and law appear to have been honoured to a degree almost unparalleled in Indian history. Authority was (in theory at least) confined to a prescribed area. The office rather than the king himself was revered; the Guptas appear not to have claimed supernatural authority. Again law and tradition, if the one could be separated from the other, were considered the supreme powers. The king could not modify or even interpret the law; at best he could stress one aspect of the code rather than another through the methods he chose to execute the law. The Gupta inscriptions are not edicts as were the notices of Ashoka. And though the inscriptions of Ashoka are certainly not injunctions, they had more legal significance than those of the Guptas.

Discipline of mind and body is stressed as strongly by Kamandaka as by Kautalya. Drink and sex could be enjoyed in moderation—but the other two corrupters, hunting and gambling, should be avoided altogether. Fashion implies that men may have been aided in living up to these standards by the prohibition of both drink and the killing of animals. He saw no shops where meat[35] or intoxicating drink was sold. Dikshitar remarks that this must have deprived the government of the considerable income the earlier Mauryas obtained from the tax on these commodities. As for the conduct of the king himself, we learn from Gupta sources that he must be impartial, not given to anger. He must be righteous in behavior, vigorous but controlled in his actions, cultivated in mind. His education should include practice in the use of weapons as well as the study of dandaniti and vartta (economics) and the Vedas. Because danger was always present, the king must take every precaution to safeguard his person.

The king submitted his plans to a council (parishad, or *mantri maṇḍalam*), which deliberated the proposals put to it. Discussion must take place in strictest privacy. At the head of the council was the *mantri mukhya,* the first minister, who acted in the king's behalf when the king was not present. The number of ministers was greater than that recommended by Kautalya, but probably did not exceed eight or nine. They were carefully selected; character, wisdom, and dedication to the service of the state were the main criteria. But records indicate that at least in many instances, office was hereditary. And we know that the ministers were almost invariably brahmans. There is little reason to believe that the king dared act without consultation, or that he could controvert the decision of a cabinet constituting the best minds in his kingdom. He might ask for further debate, but he was expected to approve the opinion of the council without further question. The council, on the other hand, must anticipate all contingencies. The king emerges as an approving and administering agent.

Moral guidance was provided by the purohita, who was charged with what a later age might call judicial review—interpreting the decisions of the parishad in the light of the sacred texts. Kamandaka also speaks of a war council, which possessed great power. The nature of the assembly must remain for the present in relative darkness. The sabha was a representative organisation intended to give some kind of political significance to the wishes of the people. It evidently played a role in approving the choice of a king. We are told that the sabha forced the nomination of Rama Gupta, but it was essentially a rubber stamp, initiating little or no policy.

The central duty of the king is still to hold other men to the performance of their own prescribed duties. Protection receives the same emphasis in the *Kamandakiya* as it did in the *Shantiparva* and the *Kautaliya*. The rod of danda must be wielded in accord with the offense and without prejudice. Protection involves more than the punishment of disorderly men. The king must preserve his people from disease, flood, fire, and economic privation. He is charged with installing and maintaining irrigation and with taking those measures necessary to protect the health and economic prosperity of his subjects. Encouraging commerce and agricultural improvement and providing sanitation and medication are among his duties. The construction of shrines and temples came within this sphere of activity.

To meet expenses—the costs of military campaigns, the salaries of government employees, the upkeep of the palace, gifts to deserving institutions and individuals, and so forth—the Gupta kings depended primarily on the land tax, the customary sixth of the produce. The state had a monopoly on salt production, and first claim to other minerals. Fa-hsien refers specifically to the royal lands, and it is probable that these holdings were an important source of income throughout the Gupta era, although the Mauryan designation for the demesnes (*sita*) had been abandoned. (Some 250 years later, another Chinese pilgrim, Hiuen Tsiang, listed four uses of income from crown lands: expenses incurred by the affairs of state and sacrificial gifts, subsidies for the officers of government, honorariums for men of merit and distinction, and charity.) The village rendered certain services and payments to the state directly, or to the army when it was nearby. Military conscription seems to have existed, although whether it extended beyond the kshatriya caste is a moot point.[36] Associations of artisans, merchants, and bankers were taxed. And in emergency situations the king resorted to inflating the currency.

Final appeal in the execution of justice was to the king, but it is likely that he did little more than restate the position of the chief judge. It was the king's duty to appoint those who would administer the law. The law itself was a combination of sacred code, custom,[37] and the opinion of the sages. The principle of equity supplemented ordinance and convention. And arbitration was allowed to determine certain cases involving no actual crime. Three great codifiers of the law lived during this time: Nārada, Brihaspati, and Kātyāyana. Their task was to relate earlier smritis (especially *Manu*) and arthashastra principles to the changing needs of the time. Distinction between civil and criminal law was more sharply drawn than it had earlier been. Judges seeking appointment had to meet rigorous requirements, but once in judicial office they were relatively free of state coercion. A series of appellate courts further protected the citizen. According to Narada, a case tried in the village assembly went to the city council, and one tried in the city court might be appealed to the king.

Gupta administration was decentralised and, as patrimonial bureaucracy reached its logical conclusion in hereditary land grants, it reflected the quasi-feudal character of the economy. It comprised a network of self -governing tribes and tributary kingdoms, their chiefs often serving as representatives of the imperial power. The central authority was remarkably tolerant of local variation and evidently extended patronage equitably to Hindus, Buddhists, and Jainas. The empire was essentially rural in character, and official policy generally encouraged village settlement. District officers were usually appointed by the provincial governor. The emperor had *jure* power to dismiss his officials, but there is little doubt that the tenure of these district officers rested in fact on their local strength.Such offices tended to become hereditary as did the ministries, and records attest to four or five generations' having held a commission.[38] The district officer consulted a council composed of prominent citizens (probably caste or guild leaders) before making important decisions. A Gupta inscription honoring the official who instigated the rebuilding of the

Girnar dam in A.D. 455 provides a most attractive picture of one of these Gupta administrators.

> He caused distress to no man in the city, but he chastened the wicked. Even in this mean age he did not fail the trust of the people. He cherished the citizens as his own children and he put down crime. He delighted the inhabitants with gifts and honours and smiling conversation, and he increased their love with informal visits and friendly receptions.

The towns were governed by an official (*purapala*) who may have been aided by a council. But the fundamental unit of administration was the village, and the Guptas allowed the village executive bodies the usual autonomy. The village headman was known as *grāmeyaka*. He, too, had a council with which he generally worked closely. The district and village councils exercised the bulk of governmental functions, protective and developmental.[39]

The later history of the Guptas is obscure, but historians are reasonably certain that the empire maintained a unity despite barbarian incursions and feudalisation from within until the time of Budha Gupta, whose reign ended in 495. Gupta power survived in northern Bengal through the first half of the sixth century. There are a number of later "Gupta" princes who may or may not have been connected with the great line of Chandra and Samudra Gupta. The early sixth century saw the Hunas clearly in ascendance, but by mid-century the Chālukyas in the Deccan and the Maukharis of the Ganges basin had become the dominant powers in India. When Grahavarman, king of the latter people, died in A.D. 606 without an heir, the nobles, it is said, offered the throne to Harṣa (or Harshavardhana as he is sometimes called). The forty years of his reign were to revive the imperial glory of the Guptas and see Harsha, suzerain of an empire increasingly feudal in structure, recognised as supreme in northern India.

The reign of this king, who was reputed to be a vaishya, is relatively well documented. The court poet Bāṇa has left a narrative in the *Harṣacarita* (which tells of the indefatigable energy of the king and his devotion to duty and justice), and the account of the Chinese pilgrim Hiuen Tsiang has survived. Harsha, we are told, was a great patron of learning, religion, and the arts. We have mentioned Hiuen Tsiang's description of how the king parceled out the revenue from royal lands with a portion for state-sponsored worship, another for gifts to the different sects, and a third to reward cultural achievement. The beliefs of the royal family are an indication of the religious eclecticism of the time. Prabhākara, father of Harsha, was a sun-worshiper; Harsha's brother was a devoted Buddhist of the Hīnayāna mode; Harsha is mentioned by Bana as a Shaivite, but later (under the influence of his Chinese guest) became sympathetic to Mahāyāna Buddhism.[40]

Harsha died leaving no heirs, and Indian political history sank once again into the chaos of warring dynasties. No one power was sufficiently strong to bring the princes of India under its control, nor were the princes to prove able to cooperate for their own defense against the rising Muslim menace. During the reign of Harsha, Kashmir was a major power in the north—its pre-eminence challenged only by Harsha's own authority. Śaśāṅka, fervent anti-buddhist and murderer of Harsha's older brother Rājyavardhana, ruled ancient Bengal and Assam and extended his authority as far west as Benares.[41]

The topography of the Deccan early encouraged political fragmentation. As Mahalingam has remarked,

> The history of South India from the earliest times is largely the history of small kingdoms and principalities. There was no lordly imperialism or great empire with considerable concentration of power in the hands of one authority, except probably for short periods under distinguished rulers of some dynasty or other, as for instance under the imperial Colas or under some of the kings of Vijayanagar. In such periods, the acceptance of the overlordship of the suzerain authority was only personal. Further, the extension of the imperial control did not necessarily and always mean the complete removal of the older kingdoms and rulerships and the establishment of colonies or military governorships by the conqueror.

It is sufficient for our purposes to note that southernmost Dravidian India was divided among the Pāṇḍyas, who governed the southern tip of the peninsula, the Cholas (*Cōlas*) on the southeastern, or Coromandel coast, and the Cheras (*Cēras*) on the southwestern, or Malabar coast. Although imperial consolidation was not the typical political experience of the south, these monarchies have been described as almost Byzantine in their splendor and elaborate court ceremonial during the post-Gupta period.

This magnificent courtly life must have entailed a substantial revenue. The Tamil kingdom spent an enormous amount of its wealth on irrigation. We know also that the encouragement of culture and religion constituted an important item of expenditure. The sources of revenue were approximately the same in the south as in northern India, the tax on the produce of the land being also a sixth of the yield. The theory of the tax as payment for protection seems to have been as characteristic of the south as of the Aryan kingdoms. The king is warned in similar terms of the dangers of onerous taxation. The Cholas had a more centralized and exacting administration than the other kingdoms of the Tamil country. The land was carefully classified for tax purposes and the bureaucracy was distinguished by fine gradations of rank. It appears that the Cholas were the only Indian state to develop a regular navy and make it an effective instrument of military policy.

REFERENCES

1. The *Arthashastra* of Kautalya will be discussed in some detail.
2. Avantiraṣtra, Dakṣinapatha, Kalīnga, Prāchya, and Uttarāpatha are known to us today.
3. It is not clear from evidence we have whether department heads were generally distinguished from ministers.
4. We assume here that hierarchical patterns employed in the administration of large territories may take the form of (1) rational bureaucracy, characterised by the allocation to each post of rights and duties that are arranged in a definite chain of command with relationships assuming an impersonal and formal nature, or (2) charismatic bureaucracy, which is characterised less by loyalty to office than by loyalty to the person of the leader. Charismatic bureaucracy may be a totalitarian bureaucracy, which allocates functions and responsibilities frequently without requisite control of necessary facilities, or it may be patrimonial bureaucracy, which amounts to an extension of the ruler's household and introduces a paternal element into the relation of the leader to his subordinates. (Though the latter may acquire hereditary land grants, they remain more like bureaucratic officials than vassals.) Decentralised types of control (i.e., control over areas of limited size) include the households, dominated by the patriarch; the feudal relationship, based on a contract that stipulates rights and duties instead of the paternal relationship; *polis* democracy; and the tribal, caste, or village council of elders or influential members of the community.
5. As early as the sixth century B.C. trade united Magadha with Persia. Silver coins attest to this development.
6. In terms of basic forms of social organisation it would appear that the tribal group represented a greater challenge than the bureaucratic state to the caste order. We might go so far as to say that though it brought with it a certain leveling of society, the Mauryan state in its struggle with the older tribal elements found that the alternative to the former

horizontal divisions involved social controls that only the system of sanctified stratification could provide.

7. Megasthenes records also that they had hired attendants to wait on them, so that evidently they were well paid. This may indicate that their loyalty was uncertain and that the king was forced to purchase their allegiance. Chandragupta's title to the throne rested on conquest, and suspicions about his origin may have threatened his legitimation.

8. "The idiocy of village life was carefully fostered as a state economic measure; for the increased wealth which was hardly any use to the villager found its way into the hands of the state, which supplied him with cattle, tools, utensils, on its own terms and charged heavily for irrigation and any special service." (Kosambi [218], p. 219.)

9. We are not certain whether regular embassy posts were established. Ambassadors were often primarily envoys of good will, or were intent on specific missions, such as negotiating commercial or diplomatic treaties, or espionage.

10. Kāmarūpa (modern Assam) seems to have remained outside the empire.

11. An ascetic group somewhat like the Jainas in the discipline that guided their conduct (*vide* Basham [23]).

12. Rock Edict VI: "For the welfare of the whole world is an esteemed duty with me....There is no higher duty than the welfare of the whole world. And what little effort I make is in order that I may render some happy here and that they may gain heaven in the next world." Probably the *Singālovāda Suttanta* or similar Pali texts are the source of the moral rules laid down in Rock Edict. VI.

13. "On the roads have I planted the banyan trees. They will offer shade to man and beast. I have grown mango-orchards. I have caused wells to be dug at every eight koses; and I have had rest-houses [built]. I have made many watering sheds at different places for the enjoyment of man and beast. This [provision of] enjoyment, however, is, indeed, a trifle, because mankind has been blessed with many such blessings by the previous kings as by me." (Pillar Edict VII. *Vide* also Rock Edict II.)

14. Professor Kosambi makes the point that between the regimes of Chandragupta and Ashoka the silver content of coins was diminished from three-quarters to less than a third—and this debasement continued.

15. Migration, political upheaval, the development of sects, the brahmanic revival, and the Muslim conquests all contributed to the destruction of Buddhism as the basis of a common Asian civilisation, and drove the religion from India—where it survives only in monuments and shrines. But elements of the Buddhist faith were assimilated by Hinduism, and in this highly altered form it survives.

16. *Devāṇampiya,* "beloved of the gods," is the title Ashoka took for himself.
17. But *vide* Mookerji [272], Appendix III, for parallels between the Rock Edicts and the *Arthashastra.* A number of the reforms undertaken by the king would appear to be the realisation of changes proposed by Kautalya, if we are correct in assuming the earlier date of the *Arthashastra.*
18. Emile Durkheim discusses the relationship between the state and the group life of society in these words: "In holding its constituent societies in check, [the state] prevents them from exerting the repressive influences over the individual that they would otherwise exert. So there is nothing inherently tyrannical about state intervention in the different fields of collective life; on the contrary, it has the object and the effect of alleviating tyrannies that do exist......[But] if that collective force, the state, is to be the liberator of the individual, it has itself need of some counterbalance; it must be restrained by other collective forces..." (*Professional Ethics and Civic Morals* [Glencoe, Ill., 1958], pp. 62f.) *Vide,* e.g., Hegel, *Philosophy of Right,* pars. 302f.
19. Fourteen Rock Edicts, the minor Rock Edicts, seven Pillar Edicts, and the minor Pillar inscriptions. Not all of the pillars are in the places in which they were originally inscribed. Many of the inscriptions begin with the phrase "Devanam-priyo Piyadasi Raja Evam aha," "Thus saith King Priyadarshin, beloved of the gods." Ashoka refers to himself as Priyadarshi.
20. It is not often observed that the emphasis of the Ashokan inscriptions has shifted to a value more "positive" than Nirvana; we learn of a heavenly reward (*svarga*) for pious and dutiful behaviour in this life. (Cf. Rock Edicts IV, IX, XIII; Zimmer [441], pp. 499f.)
21. These include the Bhabra and Rummindei edicts.
22. Evidently Ashoka did not consider himself head of the sangha. Had he, he would surely have played a more instrumental role in convening the Third Council at Pataliputra.
23. In Rock Edict V he relates that "Dhamma-mahamattas were created by me when I had been consecrated thirteen years. They are employed among all sects; and [are concerned with] the establishment of Dhamma, promotion of Dhamma, and the welfare and happiness of those devoted to Dhamma." In Pillar Edict IV he says: "They will make themselves acquainted with what gives happiness or pain, and exhort the people of the provinces so that they will find happiness in this life and the next... Certainly, just as [a person] feels confident after turning over his children to a competent nurse, [saying to himself] the nurse desires the welfare of my offspring, so have I appointed the rajukas for the welfare and happiness of the country people. In order that they may perform their

duties without fear, confidently and willingly, I give them independent authority in judgment [reward] and punishment. But uniformity in administration and punishment is desirable." Although the *missidominici* of the Frankish kings (with whom the mahamattas are compared) were charged with the promotion of religion, their duties were far more secular than those of the mahamattas.

24. The third Rock Edict indicates that Ashoka's council did little more than approve the policies of the king. But in the sixth Rock Edict the authority of the ministers is somewhat greater, though the council is rarely more than an advisory body.

25. The size of Ashoka's privy council is not known, but his father's is said to have numbered five hundred members.

26. Thapar ([407], pp. 194f.), relying on passages in the *Kunālasūtra,* a Kashmere account, has suggested that on the death of Ashoka the empire was partitioned between Kunāla and Ashoka's grandson, Dasaratha. Kunala, who governed in the west, was very possibly Ashoka's son. If this theory is correct, Kunala could be expected to have had administrative difficulties that the eastern empire, governed from Pataliputra and based on the organisation inherited from Ashoka, would not have experienced. But evidence for all this is far from conclusive.

27. According to the puranas the Mauryas ruled for this period of time, the regimes of Chandragupta, Bindusara, and Ashoka accounting for eighty-five years. After Ashoka the dynastic chronicle becomes confused.

28. Most scholars consider Pushyamitra to have been a brahman, but though the family name suggests brahman lineage, we know that by this time members of the twice-born castes were taking the names of their priests—rather than the priests taking the name of the tribal chieftains, as had been the custom in Vedic times.

29. By Gupta times the title maharaja could no longer compete with such lofty descriptions of the monarch as "son of the gods." "Maharaja" had become the title for the rulers of modest feudatories—a hollow memory of the grandeur and potency the term once connoted.

30. In the days of tribal organisation, land was jointly held. By Gupta times the concept of private property was fully developed. Land in the new settlements sponsored by the state seems to have been frequently assigned for the life of the tenant cultivator on the condition that he perform his economic duties.

31. Administrative rights appear to have been first surrendered in grants made by a Satavahana ruler in the second century A.D. *Vide* Sharma [390], p. 297.

32. J.F. Fleet's monumental *Corpus Inscriptionum Indicarum,* III, 1888, is a catalog of inscriptions of the imperial and later Gupta periods.

33. The work is considered at greater length.
34. Chandra Gupta, his father's choice, was passed over in favour of the eldest son, Rama Gupta, who was later removed by Chandra Gupta.
35. Though there were butchers in the society depicted in the *Mudrarakshasa.*
36. Such characteristics of European feudalism as the granting of land in return for military service were not present in India—a reason for circumspection in describing social developments in post-Mauryan India as "feudal."
37. Local deviation from general convention was respected.
38. Public servants were subject to a system of regulations that shares much with the civil service code of today. Included were a number of benefits such as vacations, pensions, sick leave, and incentive payments, which are described in terms often strikingly modern.
39. Ghoshal has criticised Majumdar's suggestion that the Indian political system be viewed during the millennium that began with the rise of Magadha as a checking and balancing of the popular, bureaucratic, and royal power. Majumdar (*Ancient India* [Banaras, 1952]) argued that by the fourth century A.D. the popular element in this tripartite division of power had all but disappeared as a viable political factor—the result of renascent Brahmanism which supported the social hierarchy and the monarchy. Ghoshal observes ("The Genius of Ancient Indian Polity," in [143]) that Gupta incriptions point to the representation of various community interests on district governing boards, that a brahman-court coalition had existed before this time, and that there is a lack of any convincing evidence that the Guptas encouraged the interests of one group over those of another. The balanced constitution, if it ever existed, belonged to a much earlier period of history.
40. Hiuen Tsiang undoubtedly exaggerates Harsha's partiality for Buddhism. By this time Buddhism had lost its original purity; it was being absorbed into Hinduism, and Harsha's faith is probably best described as a mixture of the two faiths. *Vide* Bagchi [12], pp. 405ff.
41. Among the evils for which he is remembered is the burning of the sacred bodhi tree at Bodh Gaya, the scene of the Buddha's enlightenment.

The Vākāṭakas

Like Delhi of the present day, Magadha was the then seat of the central government; whosoever occupied it was regarded as the sovereign power. Accordingly, the Guptas gained their importance; but due to the efforts of Vindhyaśakti, the founder of the Vākāṭaka dynasty, and his son Pravarasena I, who had performed all the seven soma sacrifices, at least three Vājapeyas[1] and four Aśvamedhas[2] and had assumed the title of Samrāṭ,[3] the dynasty rose to such a great prominence that Guptas thought it indispensable to win over them by matrimonial alliance. The Poona[4] copper-plate grant and Riddhapur[5] plates bear testimony to the fact that Prabhāvatī Gupta, daughter of Candragupta II, was married to the Vākāṭaka prince Rudrasena II. According to Dr. Altekar[6] this alliance had some political purpose. It made the Guptas secure from the rising power of the Vākāṭakas. This might have resulted in Guptas concentrating on the uprooting of the Hūṇas from India.

The history of the Vākāṭakas is shrouded in such a mystery that one still hesitates to say anything definitely about their home, caste, chronology and capital. Their obscure origin is referred to in the Purāṇas[7]:

विन्ध्यशक्तिसुतश्चापि प्रवीरो नाम वीर्यवान्
भोक्ष्यते च समाः षष्टिं पुरीं का काञ्चनकां च वै।

"The valiant ruler by name Pravīra son of Vindhyaśakti will enjoy for sixty years the city of Kāncanakā. Jayaswal in his "Imperial History of India"[8] relies also on the text of *Manjuśrīmūlakalpa,* in which there is a list of successive dynasties. But a very reliable source of information is the Ajantā cave inscriptions and copperplate grants of the Vākāṭakas. Jayaswal[9] deciphered Vākāṭaka coins and furnished us with some more information. He says[10], "From coins we get the names of the two Vākāṭaka emperors—Pravarasena I and Rudrasena I." He[11] writes that later coins of the Vākāṭakas are not available as they afterwards adopted the Gupta coinage. But according to Prof. Mirashi[12], Jayaswal's readings are all doubtful and have not been accepted by other scholars. He firmly maintains that the Vākāṭakas never issued any coins but used the currency of the Guptas throughout their kingdom.

The Vākāṭakas as such are not known to literature except that some inference can be drawn from Pravarasena II's *Setubandha K*āvya. In the *Meghadūta*[13] of Kālidāsa there is mention of Rāmagiri mountain which is according to Prof. Mirashi[14] the same as Rāmṭek near Nagpur which lay about a mile and a half from the then Vākāṭaka capital Nandīvardhana. This fact is well attested by other records[15] which also mention that Kālidāsa stayed at the court of the Vākāṭakas.

Coming to the home of the Vākāṭakas we are faced with a great controversy whether they hailed from the north or from the south. Of course, it is certain that they came neither from the extreme north nor from the extreme south. The Purāṇic description[16] of the Vindhyaka or the Vindhyan dynasty limits the problem to the Vindhyan region. But again the question arises whether they hailed from the north or the south of the Vindhyas.

One view is that they originally hailed from Bijnaur-Bagāt, a village in Bundelkhand[17]. It is quite possible that a family from the village of Bagāt or Vakāt may have been known as Vākāṭaka, but the connection of early Vākāṭaka with this territory is not yet definitely proved.[18] Dr. Altekar[19] suggests that the village Vakāṭa to which Vākāṭakas belonged was rather to the south than to the north of the Vindhyas. In support of this argument he[20] refers to a third century inscription from Amarāvatī in Āndhra country which shows that a Vākāṭaka pilgrim had paid a visit to the local stūpa. He might have come from the Vakāṭa village.

Prof. Mirashi[21] seems to be almost certain that they hailed from the south of the Vindhyas. He relies on Sanskrit and Prākrit inscriptions of the Vākāṭakas which bear a remarkable similarity with the Pallava grants. The early Vākāṭakas called themselves Hāritīputras the descendants of Hāritī while Śātakarṇis, Kadambas and Cālukyas also called themselves Hāritīputra.[22] Porf. Mirashi is definite that Vākāṭakas also originally belonged to the south. The Purāṇas[23] mention two Vākāṭaka capitals—Purikā and Canakā, and from the description in the *Harivaṁśa* the former seems to have been situated somewhere at the foot of Ṛkṣavat or Satpura mountain[24]. Ṛkṣavat is mentioned in the Viṣṇu Purāṇa[25] as the source of Tāpī, Payosnī etc. तापी पयोष्णी निर्विन्ध्या प्रमुखा ऋक्षसंभवाः ।

If we put reliance on Bhau Daji[26], a well-known antiquarian, who remarked while editing the inscription in cave XVI at Ajantā that the Vākāṭakas were a dynasty of the Yavanas or Greeks who took lead in the performance of Vedic sacrifices, the theory of their belonging to the south would not stand, but while interpreting Purāṇic records Dr. Altekar[27] tried to show that Vindhyaśakti came after Kilakila kings and not from Kailakila (Yavana) countries. On this interpretation we are again inclined to hold the view that this home was in the south. However, Dr. Altekar has kept this question still open to further research.

Buhler[28] while concluding his article on Illichpur grant warns against the identification of Vindhyaśakti Vākāṭaka with the Kailakila Yavana Vindhyaśakti; but Aiyangar[29] does not support Bühler's objection. Dandekar[30] is also of the opinion that Bühler's objections against the generally accepted identification of Vindhyaśakti and Pravīra of the Purāṇas with Vindhyaśakti and Pravarasena of the Vākāṭaka dynasty are without any valid evidence.

Regarding the caste of the Vākāṭakas there are arguments in favour of their being Brāhmaṇas and this, Prof. Mirashi[31] holds, is the prevailing view. Jayaswal[32] and Altekar[33] also hold the same view. But the arguments on which this view is based are subject to refutation. It cannot be definitely said that they were Brāhmaṇas, because the word "dvija" does not necessarily mean Brāhmaṇa; it may refer to Kṣatriyas and Vaiśyas as well.[34] Again, the view that because they belonged to Bharadvāja gotra they were Brāhmaṇas is not quite tenable. It was the practice of the royal families to be affiliated to the Vedic gotra of their preceptor.

Jayaswal's[35] theory of Cedi Era is also not reliable. However, fortunately Vākāṭaka-Gupta matrimonial alliance is a fixed point to settle this question. Almost all the writers on this subject, viz. Aiyangar,

Altekar, Mirashi and others have equally asserted that it is convenient to take this alliance as starting point for determining Vākāṭaka chronology.

Dr. R. C. Majumdar[36] has discussed the chronology every successfully but Prof. Mirashi[37] has at some places differed from him; both the distinguished historians, however, are unanimous in assigning 250 A.D. and 270 A.D. to Vindhyaśakti and Pravarasena I respectively. Majumdar[38] regards the dynasty to have come to an end on the succession of the last king Harisena in 475 A.D., while Mirashi[39] takes it to be 500 A.D. a son of Harisena whose name, he says, is not known. According to the XIV Ajantā cave inscriptions[40] and also one of the most complete copper-plate grants[41] of the Vākāṭakas it is found that there had been eight Vākāṭaka rulers. From all this it may safely be concluded that they ruled at least for three centuries.

Regarding the extent of their kingdom, the copper-plate grants of Pravarasena II[42] and Ajantā cave inscriptions[43] furnish us with a very vivid account. According to the latter the emperor Harisena Vākāṭaka had conquered Kuntala, Avantī, Kaliṅga, Kośala, Trikūṭaka, Lāṭa, Āndhra etc. (i.e. 490-520 A.D.).

The Bālāghāṭ plates[44] further mention that the Vākāṭakas had their own feudatories. The Seoni[45] and Illichpur[46] copper-plates roughly indicate the boundary of Vākāṭaka empire during Pravarasena II's time. Relying on this Bühler[47] suggested that the proposal of Gen. Cunningham[48] to fix the boundaries of the Vākāṭaka kingdom between Mahādeo Hills in the north, the Godāvarī in the south, the Ajantā hills on the west and the sources of the Mahānadī on the east might be accepted.

So great was the prominence of the Vākāṭaka that Prof. Dubreuil,[49] one of the foremost writers of ancient Indian History, is inclined to say "of all the dynasties of the Deccan that have reigned from the 3rd to the 6th century the most glorious, the most important, the one that must be given the place of honour, the one that has had the greatest influence on the civilisation of the whole of the Deccan is unquestionably the illustrious dynasty of the Vākāṭakas".

What a great influence the Vākāṭaka might have exercised on the minds of the then rulers of India can be very well imagined from their matrimonial relations. As already shown the famous inscription of Riddhapur[50] copper-plates and Poona[51] plates of Prabhāvatīgupta bear a clear testimony that a Gupta princess by name Prabhāvatīgupta, the daughter of the famous king Candragupta II, was married with the Vākāṭaka Prince Rudrasena II. The daughter of Bhava-nāga, one of the Nāga rulers of Padmāvatī, was married to Vākāṭaka crown prince Gautamīputra, the son Pravarasena I. The Vākāṭaka records never fail to mention that Bhavanāga was the maternal grandfather of Rudrasena I[52]. It is to be noted that during Pravarasena I's reign his son Gautamīputra might have died, for the fact that he received no title of any kind and that he is only incidentally mentioned shows that he did not actually rule. This is also confirmed from the Ajantā cave XIV[53] inscription where genealogy of the ruling kings of the Vākāṭakas is given and the name Gautamīputra is omitted. That the Kadambas gave their daughter to Vākāṭakas is inferred from Talaguṇḍa Pillar[54] inscription which is a posthumous record of Kākusthavarman put up by his son Śāntivarman.

Dr. (Miss) Virji[55] in her thesis *"Maitrakas of Valabbī"*, has tried to show that a marriage had taken place between the Vākāṭakas (ruling over Avantī) and Maitrakas (ruling over Valabhī) and that an alliance had been concluded for the specific purpose of ending the Hūṇa menace. This reminds us of a similar alliance between the Guptas and the Vākāṭakas, so we are led to the inference that the then native rulers of India might be very shrewd and at the same time keen to drive away the foreigners out of India by uniting internally for a common cause. The Princess chosen for the marriage seems to have been Candralekhā, who is described in the *Darśanasārā* of Devasena as the daughter of the king of Ujjayinī and the queen of Dhruvasena I of Valabhīpura[56]. Dr. Miss Virji[57] in support of her argument maintains that Ujjain had by that time definitely come under the sway of the Vākāṭakas. This she relies on the Ajantā inscription of Harisena[58]. But there is no data available for Vākāṭaka-Valabhī matrimonial alliance from any of the inscriptions nor is there any such reference in Valabhī inscriptions.

By the combined labours of Vindhyaśakti and Pravarasena, the Vākāṭakas must have reached a stage of glory. King Pravarasena I assumed imperial titles like *Samrāṭ* and performed Aśvamedha sacrifices. He was succeeded by his grandson Rudrasena I who gave up the title of *Samrāṭ,* and the Purāṇas state that the dynasty of Vindhyakas (Vākāṭakas) came to an end after Pravīra[59]. The cause of their sudden change might be due to the glorious conquest of Samudragupta. What is clear so far is that the high position achieved by Pravarasena I suffered an eclipse either at the very end of his reign or as the direct result of his death, and when the Vākāṭaka state emerged under his grandson, it did so with diminished lustre[60].

Rudrasena I was succeeded by his son (A.D. 345) Pṛthvīsena who rehabilitated his dynastic fortunes. The Ajantā inscriptions seem to give him credit for the conquest of Kuntala (Western Deccan and Northern Mysore). An inscription at Nacaneka-Talai[61] in Bundelkhand refers to "Vyāghradeva who meditated on the feet of the Mahārāja of the Vākāṭakas, the illustrious Pṛthvīsena". This record conveys a good idea of his extensive dominion. Thus once again we see the revival of the Vākāṭaka power.

Pṛthvīsena I was succeeded by his son Rudrasena II, the son-in-law of the illustrious Gupta king Candragupta II, but he died soon after his accession; and thereafter began the period of regency of Prabhā vatī Gupta during which the Guptas virtually assumed the reigns of the Vākāṭaka kingdom by sending several officials including the poet laureate Kālidāsa to the Vākāṭaka court. It was during this period that the Gupta culture was spread among the Vākāṭakas.

Pravarasena II was the successor of Rudrasena II but came to the throne after the end of regency of Prabhāvatī Gupta. His original name was Dāmodarasena, but on accession he assumed the coronation name[62] of Pravarasena II. His reign was very successful. There are some nine copper-plate grants issued in his time. His close contact with the poet Kālidāsa is inferred from *Setubandba Kāvya* of Pravarasena II. It marks a great literary advance in his time. His later successor. Pṛthvīsena and Devasena were not so powerful.

At last the great Vākāṭaka Harisena of Vatsagulma branch annexed the kingdom and is said to have made extensive conquests in all directions.

The Vākāṭaka empire which was at the zenith of its glory at about 510 A.D. during Harisena's reign disappeared within less than forty years[63]. The dominion of the Vākāṭakas soon passed into the hands of the Cālukyas. It has been argued that the immediate cause of the disappearance of the Vākāṭaka power was the rise of the Rāṣṭrakūṭa empire which ruled over the whole of Deccan during the sixth century A.D.[64]. But Dr. Altekar does not agree with this view. He says that its real causes are still unknown, but after all it is certain that by c. 540 the Kadambas of Kārṇāṭaka, the Kalacuris of Northern Mahārāṣṭra and the Nalas of Bastar State managed to absorb most of the territories during the weak rule of the successor of Harisena[65].

Thus by the middle of the sixth century this powerful dynasty vanished into thin air.*

B. S. Purohit

REFERENCES

1. Chammak Plates: *Indian Antiquary,* vol. 12, p. 246.
2. *Ibid.,*
3. *Ibid.,* p. 243. (विष्णु वृध्यसगोत्रस्य साम्राजो वाकाटकानां महाराज श्रीप्रवरसेनस्य)
4. *Epigraphia Indica,* vol. XV, pp. 42-43.
5. *Indian Antiquary.* vol LIII, p. 48.
6. Altekar and Majumdar, *Vākāṭaka-Gupta Age,* p. 169.
7. Pargiter, *Dynasties of Kali Age,* p. 50.
8. p. 2.
9. *History of India,* p. 71-73.
10. *Ibid.,* kp. 71, 61.
11. *Ibid.,* p. 71.
12. *Annual Bulletin of Nagpur University Historical Society,* No. 1, p. 9.
13. Stanza i. Line 4.
14. "Location of Ramgiri" *Nagpur University Journal,* vol. IX. p. 8f.
15. (a) K. H. Dhruva. Padya racnā-nī-aitihāsika ālocanā, p. 235.

    (b) Kṣemendra: *Kāvyamālā-Aucitya-vicār-carcā,* p. 139.
16. Pargiter, *Dynasties of Kali Age,* p. 50.
17. Jayaswal, *History of India,* pp. 66-68.
18. Altekar and Majumdar, *op. cit.,* p. 96.
19. *Ibid.*
20. *Ibid.*
21. *Annual Bulletin of Nagpur University Historical Society,* No. I, p. 10.
22. As quoted by Mirashi *Ibid.,* p. 9.

---

*Paper read at the 15th All-India Oriental Conference held in Bombay in 1949.

23. Pargiter, *op. cit.*, p. 50.

24. Cf. *Harivaṁśa, Visṇupurāṇa*, 38, 22, ऋक्षवन्तं समभितस्तीरे तत्रैव च निरामये, निर्मिता सा पुरी राज्ञा पुरिका नाम नामतः। Relied on Mirashi, *op. cit.*, p. 10.

25 Bk. II, Chapter III, sl. II.

26. *JBBRAS.*, vol. VII, p. 69f.

27. *Op. cit.*, footnote 3.

28. *Indian Antiquary,* vol. XII, p. 242.

29. *Ancient India,* vol. I, p. 134.

30. *A History of the Guptas,* p. 38.

31. *Op. cit.*, p. 9.

32. *Op. cit.*, p. 66.

33. *Op. cit.*, p. 96.

34. Bühler, *Archaeological Survey of Western India,* vol. VI, p. 138.

35. *Op. cit.*, p. 108.

36. *IRASB.*, vol. XII, pp. 1 f.

37. *Indian Historical Quarterly,* vol. XXIV, No. 2. p. 155.

38. *Op. cit.*

39. *Op. cit.*

40. Bühler, *op. cit.*, vol. IV, pp. 124ff.

41. *Indian Antiquary,* vol. XII, pp. 239ff.

42. *Ibid.*

43. Bühler, *op. cit.*

44. *Epigraphia Indica,*vol. IX, pp. 270ff.

45. *JASB.*, vol. V, pp. 726ff.

46. *Indian Antiquary,* vol. XII, p. 240.

47. *Ibid.*

48. *Archaeological Reports,* vol. IX, p. 123.

49. *Ancient History of the Deccan,* p. 71.

50. *Op. cit.*

51. *Op. cit.*

52. Jayaswal, *History of India*, p. 62.

53. Bühler, *op. cit.*

54. *Epigraphia Carnatika,* vol. IV.

55. *Manuscript Copy,* p. 43.

56. Shah, *Jainism in Northern India,* p. 68.

57. *Op. cit.*, p. 43.

58. Bühler, *op. cit.* IV, pp. 129ff.

59 As quoted by Aiyangar, *Ancient India,* p. 137.

60. *Ibid.*, p. 141.

61. *Indian Antiquary,* vol. LV, p. 225 (Dec. 1926).

62. अभिषेक नाम, *Indian Antiquary,* vol. XII, p. 240.

63. Altekar & Majumdar, *op. cit.*, p. 123.

64. *Ibid.*, p. 124.

65. *ABORI.*, XXIV, p. 149.

Post-Mauryan India

The Mauryan empire lost its unity and strength soon after the death of Aśoka, but its decadence dragged on for half a century till the last Maurya; Bṛihadratha was murdered by the first Śunga about 185 B.C. The history of India after this up to the rise of the Guptas is almost a welter of confusion. Our sources of information are mainly *Purāṇic* and numismatic. The *Purāṇic* chronicles preserve the continuity of Indian history up to the last quarter of the first century B.C. Then the narrative loses itself in the darkness of uncertainty which is occasionally dispelled by the light thrown by coins and inscriptions. For the period immediately following the overthrow of the Mauryas, the *Gārgī Samhitā,* the *Mahābhāshya* of Patanjali, the *Divyāvadāṇa.* the *Mālavikāgnimitra* of Kālidāsa and the *Harshacharita* of Bāṇa supply interesting and important details. For the third century A.D. coins constitute our main source of information but they are often insufficient, inconclusive and difficult to interpret.

Soon after Aśoka's death Panchāla under the dynasty of mitra kings different from the Śungas, and Mathurā under another dynasty seem to have become independent States. According to the *Purāṇas,* the Śungas, Kāṇvas and Andhras were the successors of the Mauryas to the imperial position. The Andhra rulers of the *Purāṇas* were those who called themselves Sātavāhanas and ruled in the Deccan till the first half of the third century A.D. The kingdom of Kalinga declared its independence but its history is dependent mainly on a single inscription which is by no means well preserved and full of gaps and difficulties. In the farther south, the Tamil kingdoms and fiefs were flourishing in a relatively high state of civilisation. These kingdoms were having their full share of the prosperous maritime commerce with the West and probably also in the movement of colonisation across the Bay of Bengal in Malaysia. The most important aspect of this age lies in the contacts of India with the Western world and their far-reaching consequences. The maritime commerce of South India included a growing trade with the Roman empire. The north-west of India may have had a growing trade with the Roman empire. The north-west of India may be said to have remained completely under Hellenistic influence. In this period it entered fully into the State system of Central and Western Asia with consequences of no mean import for the rest of the country. During the life-time of Aśoka, Parthia and Bactria separated themselves from the Seleucid kingdom of Syria. Commanding important land routes to India, they sought for outlets towards the Indus and the Ganges. By the beginning of the second century B.C. the Greek power reached the Jumna. A hundred years later the Scythians of Seistan (Śakasthāna) occupied the delta of the Indus (Śakadvipa). The land routes to the West were thus practically closed to the rulers of Magadha. Therefore they had to resort much more than before to the sea routes connecting the Narmadā valley with Mesopotamia and Egypt. This resulted in the southern regions of the Mauryan empire getting economic advantage. It was at this time that Ujjayini in Avanti became a centre of international commerce. From Broach to Patāliputra arose prosperous towns at regular intervals marking the routes of caravans and also of Buddhist pilgrimage. Little by little Magadha ceased to be the seat of imperial supermacy.

The history of North-West India during the first centuries before and after Christ is of great interest for many reasons. The contact of India with the north and west became close and constant. Greeks, Partho-Scythians, and Yue-chi or Kushāns entered India. They founded colonies and established States some of which were long-lived e.g. the empire of the Satraps of Ujjain lasted till the fourth century A.D. The most important feature of the period, is the assimilation of the invaders by the indigenous population. They, who came as barbarians, became civilised Hindus. At one time the Greek condottere advanced as far as the Ganges and possibly up to Patna. The ethnic character of the western marches of India was considerably changed by the new admixture. Out of the mingling of the Greeks and Hindus was born the Graeco-Buddhist art of Gandhāra whose influence radiated on all sides reaching Amarāvati and even Central Asia and Indonesia and

Indo-China beyond the seas. Buddhism underwent a profound modification and the Mahāyāna doctrine, born perhaps at Amaravati is said to bear the stamp of Iran. Thus enriched, Buddhism crossed the Pamir and reached China by way of Turkestan. There was a great deal of exchange of merchandise, symbols and ideas between the remotest regions of the west and the east. Some kings of India issued coins of Mediterranean origin and are said to have assumed the Chinese title of 'Son of Heaven'. This period is in every way a fascinating one through bristling with difficult problems of interpretation and chronology but in this book we can give no more than the barest outline of it.

Political Geography. The political geography of India of this period may be broadly stated thus: south of the Ganges were four States namely Magadha. Kāsī. Kausāmbī and Mathurā. To the east were Videha (North Bihar), Kosala (Oudh) and Panchāla. These States occupied most of the Gangetic plain. The Central Indian kingdoms of Barhut. Vidisā and Ujjain formed the bulk of the territories outside the Gangetic plain which were still held by the later Mauryas and their immediate successor, Pushyamitra. During the reign of the first of the Śunga dynasty, the Andhras of Southern India began to play an important role in the politics of the north. The situation in India at the beginning of the first century B.C. saw the Śungas holding the centre of the country and probably the western side of the Gangetic plain, the Andhras occupying the north of the Peninsula and Mālwa, and Kalinga strongly established on the east coast. South of the Andhras, the Peninsula was divided mainly between the Tamil kingdoms—the Cholas in the east, the Keralas in the south-west, and the Pāṇḍyas in the south-east. To the north-west remained the Indus plain.

Śungas and Kāṇvas

We owe to Bāṇa's *Harshacharita* some details of the story of the overthrow of the Maurya power by Pushyamitra. According to this, the occasion of the military coup was provided by a review of the forces. This incident shows that Pushyamitra had already prepared his ground by seducing his army from its loyalty to the Maurya king. The *Purāṇas* also affirm that Pushyamitra slew his master and reigned in his place.

According to Pāṇini the Śungas were brāhmins of the Bharadvāja gotra. Kālidāsa, however, in his drama *Mālavikāgnimitra* describes

Agnimitra, son of Pushyamitra, as a scion of the Baimbika family of Kaśyapa lineage. But the Śunga origin of Pushyamitra is generally accepted. The *Purāṇas* assume the rule of the Śungas and Kāṇvas from Magadha, but there is no evidence, epigraphic or numismatic, connecting them with that country or Pāṭaliputra. The inscription of Khāravela gives the only known epigraphic evidence on Magadha in this period and this excluded the possibility of an imperial power established at Pāṭaliputra. The Śungas are mentioned by name in a brief inscription at Bhārhut. In this they are specially associated with the kingdom of Vidisā; perhaps they inherited from the last Maurya only a part of the old Mauryan empire. The Sungas are said to have ruled for 112 years (184-72 B.C.) and there were ten kings in all. The first of them was Pushyamitra who ruled for thirty-six years and the last Devabhūti who had a ten years' rule. In between them except the ninth ruler, Bhāga who ruled for thirty-two years, others had short reigns of three to ten years. Although there is uncertainty regarding the length of individual regions, the total duration of the dynasty may well be correct.

Pushyamitra. *Divyāvadāna* and *Tōranātha* depict Pushyamitra as a veritable enemy of the Buddhist doctrine. The story goes that he wished to destroy the *Kukkutarāma* of Aśoka at Pāṭaliputra, but his attempt was foiled by the mysterious roar of a mighty lion. After burning other monasteries he went to Sākala (Sialkot in East Punjab) and offered a reward of 100 *dināras* for the head of every monk. It is said that Pushyamitra's end was due to superhuman interposition. The net purport of this story seems to be that Pushyamitra favoured brāḥmaṇism more than Buddhism. But in fact the Śunga period was marked by the rise of important Buddhist monuments at Sānchi, Bhārhut and other places. There were numerous donations to the *sanghas* from merchants and corporations. A short Sanskrit inscription from Ayodhya mentions two *aśvamedhas* performed by *Senāpati* Pushyamitra and a relative of his who was perhaps ruling there as viceroy of the Śungas.

The *Mālavikāgnimitra* of Kālidāsa (A.D. 400) dramatised the love of Agnimitra, the viceroy at Vidisa, for Mālavikā, a princess of Berar, who was living at the king's court in disguise. The play refers to the war between Vidisa and Vidarbha ending in the victory of Vidisa and the recognition of the Wardha as the boundary between the two States. The kingdom was ruled by a Sātavāhana king. The play also refers to

Vasumitṛa, the son of Agnimitra, defeating a band of Yavanas on the right bank of the river Sindhu when they tried to capture the sacrificial horse of Pushyamitra. Patanjali attests to both the horse sacrifice and the Yavana invasion of Central India. There is a difference of opinion over the location of the Sindhu; probably it is Kāli Sindhu, a tributary of the Charmaṇavati (Chambal) flowing within a hundred miles of Madhyamikā which was besieged by the Yavanas, or another Sindhu, a tributary of the Jumna. We would discuss the Yavana invasions later.

Agnimitra must have succeeded his father and ruled for eight years. Among the coins found near Ahicchatra are some bearing the name of the king, but it is doubtful if they belong to the Śunga king or a feudatory line of kings who ruled in that city and bore names ending in *mitra*. According to Bāṇa's *Harshacharita*, Sumitra, the son of Agnimitra, was overfond of the drama, was attacked by Mitradeva in the midst of actors, and killed. The fifth ruler of the line was Odraka, a name which has many variant forms. An inscription at Pabhosa records the excavation of a cave in his tenth regional year. It seems therefore that the *purāṇic* version that he ruled for seven years is mistaken. The ninth ruler Bhāga or Bhāgavata according to the *Purāṇas* was undoubtedly the Kāsiputra Bhāgabhadra, king of Vidisa in whose 14th regional year the Garuḍa column of Besnagar was erected by Heliodorus (son of Dion), the Yavana ambassador representing Antialcidas, king of Takshasilā, at the court of Vidisa. This inscription of about 90 B.C. furnishes a valuable link between Śunga history and that of the Yavanas in India. The last king Debabhuti ruled for ten years. According to Baṇa he was killed at the instance of his minister Vāsudeva by a daughter of his slave woman disguised as his queen. This minister was a Kāṇva brāhmin. According to the *Purāṇas* Vāsudeva became the founder of a line of four kings who ruled altogether for forty-five years after the Śungas (72-27 B.C.).

One thing is certain about the Śungas—that they played an important part in history. Pushyamitra stemmed the tide of foreign invasion and maintained his authority over a large part of the empire. The Bactrian kings maintained friendly relations with the Śungas. Though the Śungas lost Magadha, they did not altogether disappear from the stage but continued to rule in Viḍisā until that region passed into the hands of the Andhras. Many kings of Central and Northern India, such as those of Kausāmbī (Kosam on the Jumna), Mathurā and Ahicchatra, who are represented by coins and inscriptions became their feudatories. In those days Vidisā was the meeting place of many important trade rotues. Its neighbourhood is studded with monuments of the Mauryas, Śungas and Andhras. This region affords the earliest example of an inscribed coin bearing the inscription *Rano Dhamapālasa* (of king Dharmapāla) in Brāhmi characters written from right to left and most probably of an earlier age than the Aśokan inscriptions.

Kāṇvas. The first ruler of the Kāṇva line was Vāsudeva, as we have seen, who was succeeded by his son, Bhūmimitra. Vāsudeva's kingdom apparently consisted only of a part of the Śunga territory, perhaps confined to Magadha alone. The Punjab had already been occupied by the Greeks. The greater part of the Gangetic plain to the west of Magadha had been parcelled out amognst the various 'mitra' king and Vidisa was still in the hands of the Śungas. The *Purāṇas* speak of thee Kānvas as 'enjoying the allegiance of the feudatories'. But it is impossible to say who these feudatories were. Perhaps the naming of Kāṇvas as an imperial power is only a conventional compliment to a dynasty ruling over Magadha. It is best to state that nothing definite is known about the Kāṇva rulers and there is an unsettled dispute over the interpretation of coins bearing the legend Bhūmimitra. That Suśarman, the last ruler of the Kāṇvas was overthrown by the Andhras is certain. But the identity of the Andhra king who conquered Magadha from the Kāṇvas cannot be ascertained now.

Republics. In the Southern Punjab and Northern Rajputānā there were several Kshatriya clans, the ancestors of the Rājputs of later days and this fact is attested by coins. These clans had a republican or monarchical form of Government. When the Śunga power fell, the tribes living between the Rāvī and the Jumna asserted their independence. These were the people described as professional warriors by Pāṇini.

The Yaudheyas living in the country between the Sutlej and the Jumna were notable warriors. Coins furnish period of the independence of this tribe during the period. To the south-west of Mathurā lay the tribal republic of to Ārjunāyanas who are known to us from their coins bearing legends in Brāhmi characters of the second and first century B.C. Later Indian tradition regards them as the descendants of the epic hero Arjuna. They seem to have been subdued by the Śakas about 75 B.C. The Udumbaras of the Gurdaspur district claimed descent from

Visvāmitra who is figured on the coins of their king Dharaghosha (latter half of the first century B.C.). The Kulūtas of the Kulu valley (Kangra district) are know from coins of a later date—first or second century A.D. The earliest issues of Kuṇindas on the Sutlej in the Simla hills States belong to the same age as the coins of Udumbaras.

The Sātavāhanas (Andhras)

There has been much controversy over the original home of the Sātavāhanas and the meaning of their dynastic name and the title Śātakarṇi. The kings called Śātavāhanas and Śātakarṇis in inscriptions and on coins are styled by the *Purāṇas* as Andhras, Andhrajātīyāh and Andhra-bhṛityāh.

Andhra is both a tribal and territorial name. Andhras as a people are mentioned as early as the fifty century B.C. The *Aitareya Brāhmana* speaks of them as exiled and degenerate sons of Visvāmitra. The elder Pliny also mentions the Andhras as a powerful race. The inscriptions of Aśoka mention the Andhras along with the Pārindas as border people. It appears that the Bhojas, the Peṭenikas, the Raṭṭhikas, the Pārindas and others soon after Aśoka's death united under the rule of the dynasty (*kula*) of Śātavāhanas who belonged to the Andhra nation (*jāti*). Pliny's mention of the Andhra territory in Eastern Deccan together with the late traditions about Śrikākulam on the lower course of the Kṛishṇā being the capital of the Andhras led to the assumption that the original seat of their kingdom was in the Godāvarī-Kṛishnā delta region from where it expanded rapidly to the west right across the Deccan. But there are on traces of the early Sātavāhanas on the east coast. The Bhaṭṭiprolu inscriptions in this region (near the mouth of the Kṛishṇā) reveal only the existence about 200 B.C. of a king Kubiraka who is otherwise unknown. All the inscriptions and the coins of the early Andhra king are concentrated in Western Deccan. This points to a western origin, the region around Pratishṭhāna modern Paithan in the Aurangabad district of Mahārāshtra State. Pratishṭhāna is famous in literature as Śālivāhana's capital, therefore the theory of the expansion of the Andhras or the Śātavāhanas from west to east rather than the reverse is more plausible.

The name Śātavāhanas took the forms of Śālivāhana later. The name Śātakarni was borne by many kings of the dyanasty. It is very difficult to explain these names. Śātavāhana is connected by some with Satiyaputas. Others say that it is the equivalent of Sapta-vāhana (the sun's chariot is believed to the drawn by seven horses). This interpretation would give a solar origin to the dynasty. A third view derives the name from the Muṇḍā words, *sadam* meaning horse, and hapan meaning son. According to this view Sātavāhanas means 'son of the performer of Aśvamedha'. Some Sātavāhana coins carry the figure of horse. The name Śātakarṇi (Sankritized into Śatakarṇī, i.e. son of Śatakarṇa, hundred-eared) is derived from the Muṇḍā word *kon,* (*koni*) which means 'son'. Yet another form of the same name appears as Nurruvar-Kannar, the hundred Kannas, described in the Tamil epic Śilappadikāram as the friends of Śeran Śenguṭṭuvan and as the rulers of some territory on the banks of the Ganges. These and other legends are of too puerile a character to be mentioned here.

Whether the Sātavāhanas were brāhmins or not is also a debated point. One of the greatest kings of the line, Gautamiputra Śri Śātakarṇi is called *'ekabamhaṇa'* which means 'unrivalled brāhmaṇa', R.G. Bhandarkar translates *ekabamhhaṇa* as 'the only protector of the brahmins'. Another epithet used is '*khatiya-dapa-māna* damana', meaning 'the restrainer of the might and pride of the Kshatriyas'. Legend treats Śālivāhana as of mixed brāhmaṇa and Nāga origin.

The *Purāṇas* regard all the Andhras as the successors of the Kāṇvas. In them the slayer of Suśarman, the last Kāṇva king is identified with Śimuka, the first of the Andhra line. But this is against the reliable evidence of the inscriptions, which show that independent rule of the Sātavāhanas must have begun soon after the death of Asoka about 230 B.C. The end of the Kāṇvas came about 28 or 27 B.C. Therefore this will fall in the reign of a later king among the Sātavāhanas, No. 11, 12 or 13 of the *Purāṇic* list of thirty kings. The *Matsya Purāṇa* gives a list of thirty kings and states that their rule lasted altogether for about 460 years. This is manifestly correct and should be preferred to the shorter list of the Vāyu Purāṇa which gives the names of only 17, 18 or 19 kings with a total of 300 years' reign.

The *Purāṇic* name Āndhrabhṛtiya is interpreted as servants of the Andhras, but it can also mean Andhras who were servants. Perhaps the Andhras were at first tributary to Aśoka. The Sātavāhanas family which had risen in the service of the Mauryan empire in Western deccan was quick to take advantage of the death of the great emperor, organise an independent kingdom of their own and start it on a career of expansion. Their first conquest was Mahārāshtra north and south.

Then they conquered Mālwa west and east, and the modern Madhya Pradesh. In this task they were ably assisted by the Raṭṭhikas and Bhojas for which these were amply rewarded with high offices, titles and matrimonial alliances.

The first ruler of the Sātavāhana line was Simuka. According to Jaina tradition he became wicked after a time, wash dethorned and killed at the end of a rule of twenty-three years. His brother Kaṇha (Kṛishṇa) succeeded him and extended the kingdom to west up to Nasik, if not beyond. The third king, Śātakarṇi 1, was a powerful ruler. He was Śimuka's son. He conquered Western Mālwa, come into conflict with the Śungas and performed many sacrifices including *Asvamedha* and *Rājasūya.* During these sacrifices he gave away large sums as *dakshiṇā* (fees) to the priests. This incident is recorded in the inscription of his widow, queen Nāganikā, daughter of a Mahārathi. He had the titles Lord of Dakshiṇāpatha and the ruler of the unchecked wheel (*apratihataratha*), i.e. free to march wherever he liked, the sixth king of the line was Śātakarṇi II who had the longest rule of the line (56 years). Towards the end of his reign he conquered Eastern Mālwa (Vidisā) from the Śungas. Most probably this is the Śātakarni mentioned in the inscription of Khāravela who will be found described later. The eighth king of this line was Āpilaka who brought Madhya Pradesh under Sātavāḥana rule. The seventeenth king Hala (A.D. 20-24) is famous in literature as the compiler of *Sattasai* which is a collection of 700 erotic *gāthās* in the Āryā metre in Mahārāshṭrī Prākṛit.

Kshatrapa Invasion—Set back C. A.D. 40-80: The steady growth of the Satavahana empire for more than two centuries and the rapidly mounting prosperity which reached its culmination in literary and maritime activities received a serious set-back in the second quarter of the first century A.D. There followed half a century of great crisis in Sātavāhana history. This was also a period of Kushāna advanced in Northern India.

The inroads of Śaka *satraps* of the Kshaharāta family were probably the result of the advance of Kushāṇa poet in Northern India. The four immediate successors of Hāla had short reigns making up altogether less than a dozen years. This itself is a sufficient evidence of the troubled time. In this period the 'Western Satraps' came into prominence. The earliest known member of the Kshaharāta dynasty was Bhūmaka known to us from coins only. The greatest conqueror of the line was Nahapāna who succeeded Bhūmaka immediately or after an interval. Nahapāna is known from numerous coins and a few inscriptions. On coins he bears the title *rājan,* and in inscriptions for a great extension of the Kshaharāta empire at the expense of the Sātavāhana. The *Periplus* states that the kingdom of Mambanus (Nahapāna) began with Arake (Aryaka of Varāhamihira) and that the Greek ships coming into the Sātavāhana port of Kalyan were diverted to Barygaza (Broach). Nahapana ruled over Gujarat, Kathiawar, nothern Mahārāshṭra and even parts of southern Mahārāshṭra for a time. Nahapāna's capital was Minnagara (*min* means Scythian), perhaps Dohad, half-way between Ujjain and Broach. This spread of Śaka-Pahlava power at the expense of Sātavāhanas is best placed in the period A.D. 40-80 about the time of the *Periplus.*

Sātavāhana Recovery. After half a century of great tribulation the Sātavāhana power made a sharp and total recovery in the reign of Gautamiputra Śātakraiṇi (No. 23 in the list, C.A.D. 80-104), the greatest of the Sātavāhanas. The first sixteen years of his reign would seem to have been spent in great preparations for an all-out attack on the well-entrenched Kshaharāta power. He is described as the destroyer of the Śakas, Pahlavas and Yavanas. He overthrew Nahapāna restruck large numbers of his silver coins.

Political Order and Ideas

Historical Development

Traditionally political authority has been held in high esteem in India. The state was expected to provide security against internal disorder and external invasions, maintain the external condition of virtue, promote the happiness and welfare of the people and patronise learning and culture. To protect the people, the state was required to wield force in accordance with Law. By regulating social behaviour, it was to hinder the hindrances to the pursuit of virtue. It was to promote public prosperity through a wise policy of taxation, public works, charitable works, assistance to economic activities and organising economic enterprise. It was to promote culture by maintaining and rewarding learned men and scholars, poets, authors and artists. The fabric of culture, thus, depended on the state at three levels—at the level of security, at the level of general prosperity, and at the level of direct patronage. Till the end of the Mauryan period, the state was generally successful in its tasks but in the post-Mauryan period, it failed to meet the challenge of foreign invasions though it continued to follow an enlightened economic and cultural policy till the Gupta period. In the post-Gupta period, the political order is now increasingly held to have become relatively more oppressive in the socio-economic sphere and it had certainly become more anarchic, though it continued to partronise culture till its overthrow by foreign invaders.

According to the commonly accepted opinion about Vedic polity, the people were then divided into clans or tribes called *Janas.* Five

Janas are commonly mentioned *Puru, Anu, Yadu, Trtsu* and *Druhyu* are examples of *Janas*. Similarly we hear of the *Bharatas* or the *Bharata Jana*. It may be mentioned that the most ancient commentarial tradition regarded the names as simply names of men.[1] Sayana occasionally follows this, at other times following the epic tradition which makes these simply as names of ruling families or Ksattriya dynasties. It is possible that ancient tribes, calling themselves simply as human collectivities, came to survive in later times as simply ruling clans or families. It is, however, not clear as to where exactly the early Vedic period belongs in this process of evolution. The prevalence of agriculture certainly rules out a nomadic tribal polity for the period. By the later Vedic times, we might assume that *Puru* etc., were simply ancient ruling families because the *Janapadas* which were formed at this time do not correspond to these ancient names. Later Vedic Janapadas suggest clans like *Sivi, Kuru* or *Pancala*. The continuity between clan and family may be seen in the history of mediaeval Rajput *gots* like Sisodia etc of Rajasthan.

Again, general opinion holds that the Vedic *Janas* were ruled by kings with the help of *Sabha* and *Samiti*. Several scholars, most prominently Jayaswal, have argued that Vedic kingship was elective.[2] Some other scholars have sought to amend this by arguing that the election might have been simply selection or approval. One recent author has sought to reconstruct the diversity and developmental stages of Vedic polity, arguing that Vedic literature evidences monarchy as well as aristocratic republics.[3] This is not impossible in view of what we know of later times but the republican form was conceivably of later origin than the popular monarchy since the early Vedic pantheon seems to be organised as a monarchy rather than as a republic.

Samiti appears to have been the larger body, a gathering of the clans or of all the people, while *Sabha* might have consisted of the companions of the king or the elders. The resolution of the *Sabha*, expressing the opinion of many, was held inviolable and its connection with the dispensation of justice is clear in the later Vedic age. The two are called the 'twin daughters of Prajapati'. It is clear that although the Vedic king was the leader in war, the final judge and the representative of the people and thus invested with authority which made him an earthly parallel to India and Varuna, the divine rulers, he was no autocrat. He was the leader of a free people and responsible to their assemblies and councils. The responsible character of the king did not mean that he was to pander to the whims of the common people or was continuously required to obtain a favourable vote in the assembly. The *Samiti* could not meet occasionally to elect a king or decide on war, while the *Sabha* was more a body of councillors and assessors. The leadership and authority of the king were undisputed. His responsibility was primarily to Law, not to mere men and opinions. Law (*vrata, dharman*) was not the mere fiat of one man or many men. Law was revealed and traditional and echoed in the sense of equity in the community. The king was expected to conform to high ideals and tradition. The body of priests was the custodian of the revealed law but the people in their assemblies voiced the traditional mores.Governance was a matter of high moment and the role of the people in it was neither that of passivity nor of detailed interference. The priests and the people were interpreters of an order of which the king was the chief custodian and executive. The early Vedic king was a hero, the companion and patron of seers whose immortal hymns commemorate the names of some of their patrons. The priest declared the revealed law but did not rule. The king accepted the law and strove to enforce it. The priest and the king worked in coordinate independence and constituted a unique hierarchy.

In the later Vedic age, we find divergent tendencies. While the principle of heredity replaced that of election in the monarchical states, some states appear to have developed as republics. At the same time, within the monarchies the notion of approval by the people did not die out. The *Ratnins* remained as the representatives of the people. They included persons from the household of the king, his administrative officials, representatives of the villages of the estates. The king sought to become superior to others and to attain an imperial status not merely by war but by ritual. The kinsmen of the king formed an aristocracy which, as the epics depict, was engaged in fighting, hunting, drinking and gambling. The lure of power brought the aristocracy into not merely internecine conflicts such as reflected in *Mbh.*, but also in conflict with the Brahmanas, which is illustrated by the legends of the *Haihayas* and the *Yadavas*. The notion of the exploitation of the Vaisyas and the Sudras probably arose within this unrestricted aristocratic ethos.

The kings themselves sometimes turned away from the pursuit of war to that of philosophy. This represented the other side of the aristocratic ethos. The idea of the philosopher king or sage-king (*rajarsi*) who combines in himself wisdom as well as power was an alternative to the hierarchical principle of two powers. In the nature of the case, the idea remained a rare ideal. On the other hand, the imperial ideal and the sacrifices designed to help the king to realise it became a permanent part of the Hindu political tradition, and this made the priest a ritual assistant to the king. A class of bards recounted the exploits of the kings and sought to preserve their names and genealogies. This bardic tradition came to constitute history and antiquity (*Itihasa Purana*). Some modern scholars have argued that there was a conflict between the kings and the priests. Conflicts there must have been between kings and priests and so much is attested by ancient texts. But one can hardly speak of any organised, continued or general conflict. In fact, neither of the two castes had an organisation which could ensure such a conflict.

Samiti still functioned in the later Vedic age as a reference in the *Chandogya* suggests. *Sabha* continued as the king's court. The administration of the state depended on the regular collection of taxes called *Bhaga* and *Bali*. Tax collectors were permanent officials called *bhagadugha*. The army had its own regular commander called *Senani*. The king was kept informed by couriers designated *Palagala*. The household was under the chamberlain or *ksatta*. *Ugras* were armed members of the king's retinue acting as policemen. The villages largely governed themselves under their headmen called *gramani*. Where the realm was large enough to have provinces, the king appointed a kinsman of his to the office of the governor.

The 'imperial'and internecine conflicts and wars of the later Vedic kings as recounted in the bardic tradition may sound unreal but their interest in philosophy and patronage to philosophers started a greater tradition. Kings like Asvapati of Kekaya, Pravahana Jaivali of Pancala, Janasruti Pautrayana, Ajatasatru of Kasi and Janaka of Videha are avid teachers or students of *Brahmavidya* in the *Upanisads*. *Dharma* was the king of Kings.[4] It was revealed to and proclaimed by the Brahmaned by the Brahman while Ksattriya maintained it. The two constituted the twin pillars of Vedic polity. The 'sacred marriage' of spiritual authority and temporal power ensured a law-abiding government which in turn ensured public safety and a just order.[5] This pristine order was corrupted towards the end of the Vedic age by the growth of aristocratic pride and priestly cupidity. Traditionally the *Mahabharata* battle destroyed the flower of ancient chivalry and thus began the Kali Age.[6]

From the sixth century B.C., we see an intense conflict between monarchies and between monarchies and republics. Behind this conflict lay the phenomenon of a declining and effete aristocracy, in the republics as well as the monarchies. These Ksattriyas, proud of their ancient lineage, engaged in duelling and fighting, romancing, hunting and gambling, remind one of European mediaeval chivalry. They fought according to a code, and honour was dearer to them than life or victory. They lost ground increasingly to new parvenu princes who captured power with the help of mercenary and professional soldiery and councilors who followed the new science of politics concerned with the realities of power rather than conventional tradition. The rise of cities and commercial wealth certainly made the hiring of soldiers and officials possible. Upstart adventurers with hired assistants ultimately succeeded in destroying the traditional aristocracy, which reminds one of the rise of the New Monarchy in the 15th century in Europe at the expense of traditional chivalry.

Bimbisara, Prasenajit and Udayana are historical examples of the heroic and aristocratic rulers, chivalrous and generous, virtuous and romantic. Ajatasatru, though not an upstart by birth, is said to have acted like a bastard and certainly followed the principles of the new Realpolitik. He destroyed the old aristocratic republic of the Licchavis. Vidudabha was treated like a bastard and reacting like one wreaked vengeance on the republican Sakyas, a kind of cruel nemesis for their pride of caste. Mahapadma Nanda and Candragupta Maurya whom the *Puranas* dub as Sudras and base-born finally eliminated the ancient Kasttriya ruling families and not only rescued the country from endemic anarchy but also created a state capable of resisting the invasions of powerful states beyond the Indian frontier. For a time, India became politically and militarily respected and enjoyed political security and peace. The age of the rise and fall of the First Magadha Empire remains the real classical age of India when her basic philosophies and sciences, institutions and ideals were formulated in the *sutras* and in the original and now largely lost *samhitas* and similar works. The creative age of Indian political science lies entirely in this period the Greeks were favourably impressed by the Maurya empire and described the people as truthful and just, law-abiding, and loyal, free and brave. The period of the *sutras* saw the emergence of the two distinct conceptions of *rajadharma* and *dandaniti*. The former looked upon governance as the performance of a socially given and codified duty by a ruler for whom the problem of acquiring and maintaining power did not arise. *Niti* on the other hand, concentrated on governance as the acquisition and expertise of power. Since popular contentment was a source of strength for the ruler, *Niti* oriented itself towards the conception of a welfare state, which is best illustrated by the *Arthasastra.*

Vast and orderly, the Maurya empire was no despotism. By necessity and choice, life was largely autonomous in the countryside. Taxation was mild, crime infrequent. But the state supervised affairs indefatigably. It had an efficient intelligence and courier service and insisted on detailed records and periodical inspections. There was a regular bureaucracy and departmental organisation where officials were often organised into supervisory boards. Councils discussed affairs at the local as well as the central level. Provinces were placed under princes of the royal blood. Villages were looked after by the elders and royal officers called *Gopa* and *Sthanika.* Towns were governed by a body of municipal officers. Civic regulation about sanitation and cleanliness, markets and traffic was quite strict. The state looked after the cleaning of the forests, the needs of irrigation, and the requirements of widows, orphans and destitutes. Life was kept in regular order without too much interference. The state was strong and enlightened but not despotic. The people enjoyed security and prosperity along with freedom.

From about the middle of the second century B.C., there is a dramatic change of scene. The country is now repeatedly overrun by foreign invaders—Bactrians, Scythians, Parthians and Kusanas. Following the Hellenistic, Roman and Chinese traditions brought into country by these Central Asian invaders, the character of the monarchy began to change. Kings now claimed divinity and assumed high sounding titles raising them above their fellowmen. A new ruling class came into existence and began to share administrative and economic power with the rulers. The traditional system of social classes was badly shaken and distorted and the *Smrtikaras* felt the social order threatened. They invoked the notion of social miscegenation or *varnasankara* as the determining phenomenon of the day. A new emphasis on rigidity and orthodoxy was the reaction to the current mixture and multiplication of social groups. The position of women suffered under the conditions of insecurity and the impact of male-dominated invading groups. The age of marriage was lowered and consequentially restrictions placed on women's opportunities of Vedic study. The *Vedas* were preserved ever more jealously from the ineligible classes. At the same time, a more anthromorphic religion arose to meet the need of the foreigners recruited to Indian culture. Anthromorphic deities and images acquired importance and so did the notion of the saving grace of God. Mahayanic Buddhism and Puranic Hinduism both exhibited these tendencies fully.

Two factors, however, checked this mounting wave of Central Asian influences. The cultural vitality of the people captivated the conquerors who were quickly and wholly Indianised. Economic prosperity continued to grow on account of the new contacts with other countries. Thus political anarchy was compensated by economic and cultural expansion and a new refinement of urban civilisation. The rise of polished literature, patronised by kings and merchants, of rational philosophical systems and of science abreast of international standards attested to this phase of progress in civilisation. All these tendencies reached their culmination in the Gupta period.

The Gupta empire was essentially an empire of Aryavarta which left out the Uttarapatha and Daksinapatha. The trans-Indus region tended to move out of the Indian into the Iranian and Central Asian spheres of influence. The decline of political power, thus, had the direct consequence of contracting the boundaries of Indian society. The Gupta emperors claimed the majesty of the divine *lokapalas*. They were themselves educated and accomplished and patronised learned men, saints, poets and artists. It is the brilliance of the poets and artists of the age which has made the Gupta period memorable. New temples and monasteries were built and art reached a distinctive refinement of style. The prosperity of the age is attested by its abundant gold coinage. Fa-hien speaks of the mildness of the rule, of the small incidence of crime and light punishments. There is ample evidence of religious toleration and of the growth of science and learning. Tradition remembered the age of Vikramaditya as a golden age.

From the middle of the fifth century, the danger of invasions from the north-west loomed large again and the cultural fabric created under a century of peace stood threatened. For a time, the empire was able to withstand the danger successfully by adopting a vigorous policy of frontier defense. It was still able to produce some heroic rulers and warriors. The end of the century, however, saw a reversal of fortunes. The struggle for succession made the empire ineffective and the Hunas appeared like a terrible scourge. A wave of destruction swept through the empire and a great age passed.

Although the post-Gupta age saw many brilliant courts and powerful dynastic empires, the extent, stability and prosperity of the Gupta age were not recovered. Dynastic wars were frequent and a new aristocracy claiming to stem from Rajput clans came on the scene. It has been suggested that these clans owed their origin to the impact of the Hunas or of the aboriginal tribes in central India and Rajasthan. While this remains a surmise, there is no doubt of the emergence of new ruling groups which sought to legitimise themselves as Ksattriya clans.[7] The character of the monarchy tended to change as a result. The kinsmen of the ruler of the clan as such began to claim special rights and the practice of assigning revenues to officials in lieu of services coupled with the growth of nobles and conquered rulers as vassals of the king created a near-feudal system. Sovereignty came to be regarded as a privilege arising from the circumstances of birth and closely connected with the right of collecting taxes over an area and exercising police functions in it. While in theory sovereignty remained importable and was quite distinct from property or land-owning, in practice a good deal of confusion was bound to arise. The most important consequences of this system were the increase of burden on cultivators and traders by the multiplication of imposts and tolls and the decrease in the cohesion of the army. The army of the king largely came to consist of the levies brought by his vassals. These soldiers owed their loyalty to the vassals primarily and the vassals had only a personal bond with the ruler. The 'dynastic armies', thus were very fragile and insatiable in structure. Defeats and victories were decided by single battles as if wars were nothing but personal combats. The political structure ceased to be a deep-rooted and stable structure in which the people participated. If became a system of many small princedoms owing temporary allegiance to the precarious power of a suzerain.[8] It became just a dynastic matter at the top. In course of time, the top came to be managed by rulers of foreign origin who refused to be converted as in the Scythian period. The state informed by a wholly different to the traditional thus, came to be hostile or at best indifferent to the traditional social and cultural order.

The Character of the State

The state was expected to promote public 'good and happiness' (*hitasukha*) through the adoption of a policy ultimately backed by force (*danda*) but in accordance with Right (*dharma*). Although the ends which the state ultimately promoted, formed part of the general scheme of human ends (*purusartha*) as conceived in the social system, the direct objectives of its policy were defined as *dharma* and *artha*. *Dharma* stands in a manner reminiscent of Plato for justice as well as for the social allocation of roles and duties. *Rajadharma* as political obligation is part of *dharma* in the wider sense and is constituted by the duty of conforming to and supporting the traditionally conceived socio-ethical order. *Artha* stands for interests and utilities, for power and goods. Although objectively seen, the contents of *dharma* and *artha* would seem to overlap, their distinction arises from the way in which each is given to us. *Dharma* is transcendently given. It cannot be apprehended by mere instinct, perception or reason. *Artha,* on the other hand, is what is desired directly or indirectly. For example, one may fight to protect oneself or to gain glory. One would then be pursuing *artha*. On the other hand, one may give up one's life or fight out of a sense of duty, which would be part of *dharma*. *Dharma* as the Law is primarily revealed but practically known through tradition, especially the sacred tradition (*Trayī*). *Artha* comprising economic and administrative affairs is known through the imperial sciences of *Varta* and *Dandaniti*. The belief in *dharma* as a perennial moral order to be followed in practice tended to orient the traditional political system towards stability and conservatism especially since *dharma* was believed to be ultimately accessible through revelation and its details authoritatively formulated in the *smrtis*. Thus formally there could be neither doubt nor question about the content or validity of the system of *dharma*. Learned Brahmanas and their councils (*pariṣad*) constituted an authentic source of decisions about the interpretation of *dharma*. The legislative activity of the ruler was required to be wholly subordinated to the code of *dharma* thus formulated and interpreted. The state, thus, was checked from attempting to play a 'progressive' or 'revolutionary'role. 'Revolution' was, therefore, conceived to be synonymous with either anarchy or the re-establishment of order after anarchy. In fact, the prevalent view was that the order to *dharma* is periodically undermined and then resuscitated. History shows a tendency, not towards progress, but towards the decline of virtue, though in the long run it follows a cyclical pattern.

Originally, however, in the Vedic period, the idea of Ṛta or *dharma* was more the idea of a general divine or 'natural' law rather than a formulated code. For long the attempts to decode Ṛta were only in terms of ritual symbolism which was added to diverse social ceremonies. In due course, these were themselves codified and conceptual explanations added. This process of the codification and interpretation of the *dharma* went on slowly for millennia and in its course did include not only the elaboration but also the modification of laws. Consequently, despite the conservative orientation of the ancient political system, the socio-legal system which it sought to maintain itself, underwent a slow change through a process of adaptive interpretation. Nevertheless by the early mediaeval period, the *smṛti* tradition came to exercise sometimes an almost paralysing and cruel grips on the political functioning. The Yadavas of Devagiri or the Senas of Bengal are examples of this.

It is true that there were some thinkers who denied the reality of any transcendent or revealed order. They tended to be matcrialistic and hedonistic and exalted the king as the sole source of law and justice. The school of thought was hostile to brahmancial orthodoxy and did influence some sections of political thought which tended to look upon religion and morality as merely conventions to be taken note of by the ruler. This Lokayata positivism tended to encourage the non-metaphysical tendency of the *Arthasastra* and also its characteristic amoral or 'Machiavellian' doctrine of *raison d'etat*. This tended to produce a conflict between the *Dharmasastra* and the *Arthsastra* in which the latter was ultimately wiped out as a rational theory leaving behind only the ideas of expediency and customary.

The brahmanical tradition of *dharma* was opposed by the Sramanic tradition which sought to hark back to the original idea of *dharma* as an imponderable and universal moral law which was to be apprehended not in terms of ritual symbolism but by one's own purified intuition. Such an appeal to one's own self (*paccattam*) and the disregard of established orthodoxy constituted a tradition of moral and social reform to which belonged not only Buddha and Mahavira but many later saints from time to time. The spiritual authority of these reformers enabled them to create new communities, especially religious but they did not essay the more difficult task of radically altering the traditional social order. By and large, Buddhist and Jaina rulers remained conservative in their social policy. Asoka was undoubtedly an exception but there was none to emulate him conspicuously. It should, however, be remembered that Asoka like Buddha appealed to the universal and essential idea of *dhamma* as the standard by which current distortions or natural deviations may be judged and corrected. This was not formally disputable within the tradition and hence the authority of the ruler to act in accordance with the idea of reform also could not be disputed. The really disputable thing was the claim of brahmanical orthodoxy to have the monopoly of interpreting the *dharma*. That is why Manu following Asoka lays all the stress on the position of the Brahmanas who were at the very time giving the lie to Manu by assuming royal authority through engineering a political revolution.

The peaceful co-existence of rival interpretations of *dharma* made the state catholic and tolerant, a feature which has attracted wide attention. The freedom opinion and worship were rarely challenged and the philosophical and religious literature of ancient India, which is full of diversities, bears eloquent testimony to this freedom as do the copious records of benefactions unhampered by sectarian consideration.

If the brahmanical privilege provided too narrow a base for the understanding of *dharma,* the appeal to personal intuition would appear to have been too variable. Under the circumstances, it is not surprising that the actual rules evolved by each locality, community and corporation were treated as valid laws for them to the extent they were consonant with morality. Actually operative laws must have depended far more on this free creativity and variability of 'local' tradition than on the supposedly Procrustean bed of canonical law.

This leads us to what may be called the free or 'democratic' ethos of the ancient polity. Despite western deprecation, a host of Indian historians proved during the national movement that democratic institutions were a real and significant part of the ancient political tradition. Elective kingship, popular assemblies, and republican constitutions were known in the Vedic and early post Vedic times. In classical polity too, royal power was not absolute but limited in a variety of ways. The king was required to keep the people pleased and to ascertain their opinions through their assemblies and leaders. Councils existed at all levels. Procedures of debate and voting were well developed, although consensus was the ideal usually striven after. The consent and judgment of the elders were generally sought. Corporate bodies of diverse kinds existed, villages and towns, guilds and castes being the most important. They had their own councils and leaders. Their traditions were respected and this ensured their autonomy.

Nor was his democratic ethos, this spirit of governance by consultation and consensus a mere looseness of grip; for administrative mechanisms adequate to the governance of vast territorial empires had been successfully devised. This democratic spirit was essentially the spirit of autonomy (*svarajya*), of respect for law which was not the fiat of any man however high but a just norm discoverable by the wise leaders of any corporate group. It did not give any concession to the spirit of license (*Kamakara*) but only recognised the right of a community to discover and follow its corporate law and tradition. The success of democratic institutions in contemporary India certainly tends to disprove the contention of those who regarded such reconstructions as merely patriotic fabrications. The tradition of democratically managing social affairs through village and caste *pancayats* did, in fact, survive long centuries of militaristic and feudal misrule. This democratic ethos, however, was based on the traditional solidarity of the community, not the rights of the individual. The whole of our contemporary emphasis on individualism and rights has a wholly modern western origin. The whole conception of man as a social animal whose rational being is exhausted by social roles and relations and of society as a system of competing individuals and classes is alien to the Indian tradition for which man is a spiritual being characterised by moral reason, individual identity being inseparable for social roles, and classes being essentially co-operative.

Since social being is not an externally given reality, the nature and meaning of social or political institutions cannot be comprehended simply by noticing their formal features. It is only in terms of the interpretation put on them by the social psyche for which they primarily exist, that they can be adequately understood. Thus the transportation of western political forms to India does not ensure any real transference of the institutions concerned. For this reason, it is necessary to relate political institutions to their underlying moral ideas and the general social and cultural milieu. It will be short-sighted, indeed, to assume that the western political tradition has been appropriated in India simply by institutional imitation and class-room teaching. The examination of political reality in India necessarily passes into the historical examination of its tradition. Now what is perennially important about the ancient political tradition is its philosophy, not the ephemeral laws and forms it threw up from time to time.

According to the *Arthasastra,* Anviksiki or philosophy illumines all the sciences (*vidyas*). This recognition should be pondered over by those modern critics who accuse the ancient Indian political tradition of being unphilosophical. As a matter of fact, they fail to see that knowledge was conceived as a hierarchy of sciences in ancient India. *Nitisastra* being concerned with the strategy of managing empirical behaviour, could not itself be philosophical but it presupposed philosophy. Philosophy was basically metaphysical and cosmological. As rational reflection over revealed knowledge, it came next to *trayi,* though in its methodological aspect as the logic of statements (*nyaya*) and imperatives (*mimamsa*) it took precedence in the order of principles and training. As *adhyatmavidya,* of course, it depended on the *agama* and showed that the understanding of man (*brahmavidya*). Since the macrocosm (*brahmanda*) and the microcosm (*pinda*) were held to be in correspondence, it was believed that the empirical order of human behaviour (*vyavahara* or *adhibhutam*) is to be understood in terms of inner psycho-ethical phenomena (*abhidharmatah, adhyatman*) which can be understood only in terms of their cosmic ground or ultimate value (*paramarthatah*), Trayi and *Anviksiki,* thus, are superior in the hierarchy of knowledge to *Varta* and *Dandanīti*. The former are concerned with foundational and intelligible principles while the latter deal with empirical and behavioral realities which they seek to control, something entirely different from philosophical reflection moving towards vision (*theoria*) and inner freedom. Nevertheless, since the whole of social life is based on the manner in which the self and the non-self are mutually related in consciousness proper philosophical understanding tends to influence social attitudes, values and modes of action. Philosophy as faith helps right action which in turn helps the rise of wisdom. The content of faith insofar as it includes the norms of action and the corresponding institutions of practical life, though adumbrated in *Trayi,* is formulated in the *Dharmasastra* which, again, is presupposed more proximately by the *Arthasastra*. The political tradition of ancient India is thus not confined to *Dandaniti* to *Arthasastra* but is extended over all the four *vidyas* mentioned by Kautilya. It includes by implication political philosophy as well as political science.

Basic Philosophy

The essential idea of the ancient political tradition of India may be said to have lain in the conception of an appropriate union of two principles viz., wisdom and power. In the Vedic age, this idea was imaged as the dual deity Mitra-Varuna and was sought to be institutionalised as the twin offices of Purohits and Rajanya, Brahman and Ksattra. The *Varna* system provided a social expression and safeguard to this idea by placing the Brahmana above the Ksattriya as the authoritative exponent of traditional sacred wisdom but reserving the exercise of power as a privilege for the Ksattriya. In the post-Vedic age, the basic ideal came to be understood in due course as the unity of *Dharma* and *Nīti*. *Dharma* stood for justice as such and for the traditionally conceived social order. What has been called Natural Law in the West is possibly the best equivalent of *Dharma*. *Nīti,* on the other hand, was conceived as Policy or the system of means employed in the exercise of power. *Dharma* was codified and interpreted by the Brahmanas. *Niti* was basically Ksattra-vidya, the prudence of the ruler and his administrative counselors and assistants. The separation and co-ordination of the Brahmana and the Ksattriya was thus again brought into play, but, unfortunately, this no longer served as an effective practical device because the *Varnas* had become hereditary and their functions had ceased to be uniquely characteristic.

Within *Dharma* and *Nīti* severally also an inner duality was sought to be harmonised. *Dharma* included *sadharana dharma* as well as *varnasrama-dharma,* general morality as well as specifically codified and institutionalised social ethics. The perception of *Dharma* thus required moral intuition as well as access to tradition. Only in terms of a wisdom which was at once pure in its intuition and well informed in its perception of social content could *Dharma* be adequately apprehended and interpreted. Similarly *Niti* comprised a basic quality of intelligence and force, which is implicit in the very pharase *danda-niti.* Just as in the case of *Dharma,* emphasis was to be placed on its conventional rather than rational side, similarly in the case of *Niti,* emphasis was placed on prudence and expedience rather than on force or the will which is its psychic source. Indeed Kalidasa expresses scorn at the idea of mere *niti* as sheer cowardice, mere bravery as sheer barbarism. "*Kātaryaṁ Keyalā nītiḥ Sauryaṁ śvāpadaceṣṭitam*". (*Raghu,* 17.47).[9]

Right governance thus requires the regulation of force by intelligent policy by moral reason. Only those who have a pure character and high wisdom can act as lawgivers. Only those who respect the law and are at the same time gifted with prudence and determination can act as rulers. The former can only be obtained within a living tradition of moral and spiritual wisdom. Rulers of the right kind can only be obtained through right education "*Vinayo rajyamulam*"

(*Arthasastra*). The union of disinterested wisdom with effective power in society can result only from a mode of education which teaches individuals self-government within. To restrain the senses and subordinate the mind to higher reason, this is the path of self-government or spiritual education called *Yoga* and vividly described in the *Kathopanisad* and the *Gīta.* Without it, there cannot be produced any *Brahmarsi* or *Rajarsi* or *Dharmika Cakravartin,* nor any 'sacred marriage' of *Brahman* and *Ksattra.* Unless philosophy as the search of wisdom is well established as the most valued activity in a society, the possibility of its being well-governed does not arise. At the same time, virtue in the original sense, as *vīrya,* must also be cultivated. That is why *Brahmacarya,* 'the tending of Brahman', is held to confer both wisdom and manly prowess.

Unfortunately the ancient *Varnas* were corrupted into hereditary castes, the ancient formulations of *dharma* and *niti* became covered into systems of conventions, the ancient institution of *Brahmacarya* simply fell into disuse, and philosophy became otherworldly. As a result, Indian polity was perverted from its high moral purpose into a petty game of self-seeking; a situation in which rulers and politicians cannot possibly stake their all in the event of a serious foreign invasion.

G.C. Pande

REFERENCES

1. *Nighantu,* 2.3. includes them among twentyfive '*manusya namani.* Yaska mentions several interpretations of "*Gandharvāḥ pitato deva asurā rakṣāṁsītyeke Catvāro Varnā niṣādah Pancamah ityaupamanyavah*" (*Nirukta,* 3.8). Some modern linguists have suggested that *panca* originally may also have had the sense of 'all'.
2. *Hindu Polity.*
3. J.P. Sharma, *Republics in Ancient India.*
4. *Br. Up.* quotd supra.
5. Coomarswami, *Spiritual Authority and Temporal Power*
6. Modern scholarship regards it as an age of progress based on the introduction of iron.
7. Cf. B.D. Chattopadhyaya, *IHR.* Vol III. No. 1, pp. 59ff.
8. Cf. D.C. Sircar, *The Emperor and Subordinate Rulers.*
9. This reference was pointed out to me by my friend Dr. S. C. Pande of the Deptt. of Sanskrit, University of Allahabad.

Social and Political Thought and Institutions

A civilisation may be known by its ideals and the means by which these are sought to be realised. No observer of the complicated picture of ancient and medieval Indian polity can fail to note the ideals which were affirmed. He will find them voiced in adages and maxims as numerous as their companions, the witty formulae that embody the essence of statecraft. The ideals were common to all regions, and were shared by learned and illiterate alike. Our treatises on law and politics contain principles popularised through the epics and the *Purāṇas*. The essence of good manners and good policy reached the uneducated by such means, while the worldly wisdom of these texts fed the compilers of fables and less juvenile handbooks. The great popularity of *Cāṇakya-nīti,*[1] that great pool of wise sayings on 'good policy', proves that techniques of managing any social or political question were not the perquisite of courtiers.

Translation blurs the wording in which the ideals are carried, and obscures the function and purpose of the social and political organs. Our texts, too, answer questions which we should not ask, and ignore problems which we tend to think inescapable, used as we are to a non-Hindu traditional society. Western writers sought to see familiar elements in an Oriental setting; some Indian patriots again have either followed that example or idealised the material at their disposal. The relation of ideals and theory to practice cannot be ignored; but we concentrate rather on the former, since the legacy of the past, both to present-day India and to the world at large, consists rather in the peculiar balance she achieved and in her view of life as it should be lived, a view which has, in large measure, outlived experiments and survived failures. Now that Indians have migrated in such numbers to countries which might never have expected them in the heyday of classical Indology, a need has arisen to know the virtues, and also the limitations, of men and women of Indian stock, and to estimate what they can, and what they will not, contribute to their new environments.

Traditional Indian values must be viewed both from the angle of the individual and from that of the geographically delimited agglomeration of peoples or groups enjoying a common system of leadership which we call the 'state'. The Indian 'state's' special feature is the peaceful, or perhaps mostly peaceful, coexistence of social groups of various historical provenances which mutually adhere in a geographical, economic, and political sense, *without* ever assimilating to each other in social terms, in ways of thinking, or even in language. Modern Indian law will determine certain rules, especially in relation to the regime of the family, upon the basis of how the loincloth is tied, or how the turban is worn, for this may identify the litigants as members of a regional group, and therefore as participants in its traditional law, though their ancestors left the region three or four centuries earlier. The use of the word 'state' above must not mislead us. There was no such thing as a conflict between the individual and the state, at least before foreign governments became establishment, just as there was no concept of state 'sovereignty' or of any church-and-state dichotomy. Modern Indian 'secularism' has an admittedly peculiar feature: it requires the state to make a fair distribution of attention and support amongst all religions. These blessed aspect of India's famed tolerance (Indian kings so rarely persecuted religious groups that the exceptions prove the rule) at once struck Portuguese and other European visitors to the west coast of India in the sixteenth century, and the impressions made upon them in this and other ways gave rise, at one remove, to the basic constitution of Thomas More's *Utopia*.[2] There is little about modern India that strikes one at once as Utopian: but the insistence upon the inculcation of norms, and the absence of bigotry and institutionalised exploitation of human or natural resources, are two very different features which link the realities of India and her tradition with the essence of all Utopias.

Part of the explanation for India's special social quality, its manifest virtues and compensating shortcomings, lies not in any prudent decisions by any men or groups of men, but in the traditional concept of the society in which *prajā* (the subjects) and *rājā* (the ruler) were the two principal elements, one might say, polarities; and part again lies in the fact that, though the ruler was a guardian of morals, the 'cause', as it was put, 'of the age', the power of penance was immeasurably more vigorous than any services the state could perform—even granted the fact that the prerogative of corporal or capital punishment (*danda*) served also as a penance for the guilty, and granted, too, that it was in theory one of the king's tasks to see to it that penances were actually performed. Ideals were expressed in terms of ethics, and are related, some to people in general, and some, more specialised, to the principal classes, in particular the brāhmans, whose inherited religious and magical powers, and responsibility for the spiritual and even material welfare of the state, marked them out for respectful treatment, financial patronage, and, if they were suitably conscientious, cramping taboos. Special ideals were naturally developed for the *rājā,* the key figure in leadership, whether he was a head of a clan, or an emperor.

The 'twice-born' to whom we shall return, reached, according to Manu (vi. 92), supersensory bliss by obeying a tenfold 'law', which was a mixture of moral and intellectual requirements. Hārita,[3] who goes into greater detail, gives the constituents of *śila* (good conduct) as 'piety, devotion to goals and ancestors, mildness, avoidance of giving pain, absence of envy, sweetness, abstention from injury, friendless, sweet speech, gratitude for kindnesses, succouring the distressed, compassion, and tranquillity'. *Dharma,* a term we shall discuss, in its wider sense of a general moral ideal (it is also used of a 'law' as such), requires of every man truthfulness, abstention from stealing, absence of anger, modesty, cleanliness, discernment, courage, tranquility, subjugation of the senses, and (right) knowledge.[4] This attitude towards moral qualities and forms of behaviour introduces us to the fact that equilibrium rather than equality, peace rather than liberty, were the fundamental ideals. These notions can be interpreted partly as an escape from, and partly as an attempted insurance against the primeval chaos which was supposed to lurk in the background, the chaos which was believed to justify indirectly, and positively to require, the state itself.

Unseen benefits hereafter and prestige in this life were not to be attained merely by moral qualities and good behaviour. The quality of absolute 'goodness' consists also in the study of the Vedas, austerity, pursuit of knowledge, purity, control over the organs of the body, performance of meritorious acts, and meditation on the soul. These properly belong to brāhmans or brāhmanised classes, but the opposite, the state of 'darkness', is demonstrated by covetousness, sloth, cowardice, cruelty, atheism, leading an evil life, soliciting favours, and inattentiveness,[5] and these were not confined to the upper classes. A similar arrangement of ideals is found in the maxim that one falls from caste (i) by not observing what is laid down (in law or custom), (ii) by observing what is prohibited, or (iii) by not bringing the senses under control.[6] Civilised life required that all three sources of 'fall' should be eliminated—an object no individual's power could achieve. The leading themes are well evidenced in that distinctively Indian, if non-brāhamanical, sect, Jainism, which combines venerable age and longevity.

The ideal Jaina householder is characterised by spiritual virtues, namely a spiritual craving, tranquility, aversion from the world, devotion, compassion, remorse, repentance, and loving-kindness; and by social virtues, namely non-violence, abstention from unrighteous speech (of which lies and slander are illustrations), abstention from theft or unrighteous appropriation (including embezzlement), chastity, avoidance of covetousness, and non-attachment. Since many Jainas have been commercially minded the significance of these virtues is apparent. How the social and personal intermingle is revealed in these standard characteristics of the Jaina householder: possessing honestly earned wealth, eulogistic of the virtuous, wedded to a well-guarded spouse who is of the same caste but of a different patrilineage, apprehensive of sin, following the customs of the locality, not denigrating others (particularly rulers), dwelling in a secure house (affording no temptations to in-dwellers or strangers), avoiding evil company, honouring elders, eschewing states of calamities, eschewing occupations that are reprehensible according to family, local, or caste customs, economical and making a right use of his income, of controlled diet and balanced aims (following righteousness (*dharma*), wealth (*artha*), and physical pleasure (*kāma*), the three *purushārthas* or aims relevant to this life, in due proportion), charitable to monks and the afflicted, mindful of his dependants, and victorious over the organs of sense.' We find throughout that the most reprehensible misdeeds are theft and adultery, and a commentary on Indian ethics could be woven on these items alone. Insistence that women must not be exposed to even a nominal risk of unchastity, the requirement that marriage should subserve the family's interest and not primarily that of the spouses, and the disfavour in which anything resembling 'courting' before marriage is held, have developed an attitude towards women, and a level of expectation on the part of women themselves, which set special limits to Indian social behaviour and give a peculiar quality to Indian life. Concern for the chastity of their womenfolk has, at least in the last millennium, been at the summit of every Indian family's prime concerns, and when hatred boiled over, the females were the immediate targets. Obedience to rulers, as such, we do not find amongst the typical virtues: but it is inculcated elsewhere. Avoidance of sin and social disgrace was a primary obligation, while duty to the ruler was secondary and dependent upon the first, for the ruler's function was to facilitate such avoidance. Respect for the caste-system is implicit in the scheme outlined. 'honestly earned wealth', 'reprehensible occupations' are terms referred to an established, if theoretical, apportionment of activities amongst the castes (*jāti*). To search for social and political ideals anterior to the caste-system would be fruitless.

No Indian ideal could be inconsistent with *dharma,* 'righteousness'. This word tends to bring cosmology down into touch with the mundane details of private law.[8] One who follows his *dharma* is in harmony, and attains bliss, though it remains doubtful how far his contemporaries' behaviour should guide him in his understanding of his *dharma.* Without *dharma,* in however etiolated a form, fertility, peace, civilised life are considered to be imperilled. *Dharma* is in one sense natural, in that it is not created or determined (though in practice in obscure cases its exponents determine what its sense is), and in another it is always to be striven for, *dharma* is unnatural in that to achieve it one must put forth uncongenial efforts of self-control, irrespective of popular reactions. If *dharma* (as contrasted with positive litigation) only in part resembles natural law it is nevertheless a code of moral obligations to which the uninstructed nations (*mlecchas*), innocent of brāhmanical learning, cannot attain. *Dharma,* indeed, means duty (*kartavyatā*), and the study of *dharma* involves a discovery of the duties of individuals, groups, and, among them, their political leaders. For *dharma,* in the sense which predominates in political theory, is an abstraction of *seva-dharma,* the 'own *dharma*' of each caste and category of person. As D.H.H. Ingalls, the Harvard scholar, has nearly put it, the 'essentially isolationist society' recognised a religious sanction behind an infinite variety of personal laws. Perhaps the categorisation and tendency to division was overdone in the writings, but they are faithful to the essential character of that society. Nominate the man, state his age, caste, and status, and one can be told what his *dharma* is. He deviates from it at his peril, his spiritual peril in any case, his physical or financial peril too if the king is as alert to deviations as he ought to be. But this is not to suggest that *dharma* was 'natural law' in the European sense; the ruler's conduct could not be tested by reference to *dharma* and invalidated thereby, and, though it justified, it could not delimit his administrative authority.

Adharma (unrighteousness) is the forerunner of chaos. Man has a natural tendency to decline into chaos. In one myth chaos required the invention of kingship and the appointment of a semi-divine king. *Dharma* and kingship are thus inseparable. *Dharma* derives linguistically from a root meaning 'to hold'. A loose hold is no hold. *Dharmas* vary according to the person's *varna* (his 'quality', class, or 'caste') and his *āśrama* (state of life, or status). *Varna* was acquired by birth (a principle nowadays under attack), *āśrama* was optional, though the family lost prestige if the *samskāras* or sacramental ceremonies were neglected by which entry into the essential stages was prepared for and celebrated. Every *dharma* had the king as its protector; and law could not, as a set of practical requirements, effectively demand anything that was not at the same time morally and legally binding.[9] Unrighteous government, illustrated by the fall of the mythical king Vena, is understood, but the point of the myth is that miracles are needed to dissolve the obligation of obedience. Texts evidencing the theory that a wicked king could be put to death by his subjects[10] are rare and uncharacteristic, *Varnāśrama-dharma* is nominally encyclopedic, comprehensive; laying the king, noble, commoner, citizen, and peasant under an apparently equal burden of obligation to a common complex ideal. If the subjects rebelled they did so because the king's duty to protect their *dharmas* was being neglected, and because his own life, conflicting with *dharma*, predicated their welfare from a religious point of view. Chaos could be forestalled by rebellion, but our texts do nothing either to encourage or to justify such an attitude. The effort concentrates on making the reigning king a success.

. Some illustrations of *dharma's* 'hold' are needed or we cannot grasp what was expected of king. The *varna* of the brahman would limit his freedom to associate, to male, to dine; it seeks to number the occupations he may pursue-to study, to each, to officiate at religious ceremonies (including the *samskāras),* and to advise and, if necessary, to chide rulers. To trade (especially in certain goods) and especially to lend at interest are forbidden, except in time of distress. And the brahman's *dharma* demands at least a minimum of classical education. The *varna* of the sudra, at the other end of the scale of 'clean' castes, also delimits. Not being one of the twice-born, as are the brahman and those who intervene between them, he does not study the Veda, and does not take the sacred thread which indicates initiation; not may he teach Vedic studies or have social intercourse with the twice-born except upon the footing of service, whether in the house, the workshop, or the field. Ideally his very name should suggest a humble status and the higher castes are entitled to his labour—an ideal which, needless to say, the most numerous *varna* from time to time repudiated. We hear, accordingly, of 'good sudras' who were supposed to be degraded twice-born and generally copied the latter in their behaviour. Between brahman and sudra were ranked the warrior (kshatriya) and mercantile (vaisya) classes, upon a theoretical basis explained in terms of their objective qualities and tendencies. Anomalies abounded from the first and we meet the theory of 'mixed castes', sprung from unions between the four *varnas.* Distribution of functions between the *varnas* and the mixed castes was often in debate, both historically and throughout our literature.

The brahman's ancient hereditary function as a teacher (*guru*) of the other castes is not dead. To this day brahmans are from time to time approached to resolve problems and act as 'confessors' by other castes; and a careful anthropological survey of a remote village in Madhya Pradesh, the abode for several centuries equally of brāhmans and non-brāhmans, both occupied in agriculture, revealed the strange fact that when the economy suddenly changed, due to improvements in communications and markets, large number of the brāhmans, but not of the other classes, took to teaching and other intellectual pursuits. Students of Western medieval literature know of the 'gymnosophists' whom Alexander the Great and his companions found in northern India. These made an impression on the Greeks and earned a not able place for the ascetics in the Alexander romance and its many derivative contributions to Western culture. They spoke fearlessly to kings, telling them their *dharma,* and their status as teachers (they were ostentatiously naked) depended on their utter indifferences to the world and contempt for death. The Jewish heroes of Masada, before committing suicide, as the Romans scaled the last wall, reminded themselves that they must not be inferior in faith to the poor Indians (whom they believed to be polytheists at that).[11]

The ideals of the *dharma-śātra,* the 'science', or rather 'teaching' of righteousness, proceeded far beyond these classifications. Marriage was a prime concern. Marriage between *varnas* was lawful provided that it was in the hypergamous form, the husband having the higher caste. The ideal marriage for a brāhman was in the form of a gift of the bride, along with her dowry, to the bridegroom summoned for the purpose; that for the kshatriya was by capture or in the love-match which, to the minds of some moralists, masked too often a mere education; while marriage by purchase, deprecated as barely suited to the furtherance of *dharma,* was left to the sudras. Ideals out-lived facts, both in marriage and in occupations. Brāhmans are found functioning as money-lenders or soldiers; sudras are actually found occupying thrones (an eventuality pathetically deplored in many texts). Intercourse with a woman other than one's wife was a sin; yet the keeping of concubines persisted (never, though, to the total exclusion of marriage) amongst well-to-do classes until very recent times.

The *dharmas* of a Vedic student (brahmacāri) were naturally not relevant to a śūdra youth. The principal *āśrama* of the *grihastha* (householder), the upon which in practice all the others depended, was reached by all ideally at marriage, which should be celebrated soon after the completion of a young man's academic training (if any) and would signalise his entry into full social responsibility. Marriage was the one *āśrama* which was nearly obligatory. Religion and social pressure made it virtually unavoidable. Procreation of at least one son was recommended, and better of two, so that at least one might go to Gayā and perform the efficacious *śrāddha* there which would secure perpetual bliss for deceased ancestors. If an *aurasa* (legitimate) son could not be expected, the mature make ought to provide himself and his paternal ancestors with a substitute by one of the approved methods of adoption. Spiritual responsibility towards the ancestors and the right to inherent their property were ideally inseparable.

No survey of the social order can neglect the slaves, for whom, as a social class, curiously, the *varnāśrama-dharma* (which calls them biped chattels) makes little or no room, satisfied, we note, to provide that a brāhman could not be enslaved unless he lapsed from the status of *sannyāsī,* or renunciate. This, the last *āśrama,* was in theory available to every former householder who chose to retire from the world, but in practice it became a title to live on charity, from which, naturally, only a lunatic would be likely to defect. Slaves were not, in the ideal view, a division of society, though they were a fact. In the status and fate of slaves, especially the 'born' slave, some would see a dark feature of Indian social ethics.[12] Yet even an extreme example of their situation has its dharmic aspect. A young female orphan, selling himself into slavery in return for her keep, would acknowledge that if she committed suicide as a result of her keeper's chastisement she would commit a dreadful sin.[13] On the footing that it is a charity to buy children as slaves in times of famine, the residual right to commit, or to threaten to commit, suicide seemed properly subject to limitation by contract.

The politically most significant branch of *dharma,* to which we shall devote attention, was that relating to the *rājā*. Preferably a kshatriya, his *dharma* could be summarised as 'to conquer and to protect'. To fix him with his responsibilities there must be a state. This existed (and could survive) when, according to traditional theory, there existed each of the seven constituents, the so-called *saptānga,* of that organism. There were the king himself, a minister of official class, a capital city, a rural area or inhabited tract, a treasury or revenue administration, an army, and at least one foreign ally. It was recognised that since all the constituents of the state no one could be aggrandised at the expense of others without endangering the organism. Mention of the state calls into play the two sciences of *dharma* and *artha*. The last word means politics and economics, and Kautilya's *Arthaśāstra* is in fact the sole substantial treatise on the art of public administration.[14] The passages dealing with the king's duties and powers in the *smritis* of Manu and Yājnavalkya, for example, were influenced by *arthaśāstra* learning. Wherever the two sciences conflicted the ruler was expected to follow righteousness rather than politics, and the cunning inculcated by the latter was supposed to be at the disposal of the former.

Politics, sarcastically called the *khattavijjā,* or 'kshatriyas' science', i.e. unrestrained opportunism, by the Buddhist writers, subsumed a minimum of righteousness in any scheme upon the basis that the end justifies the means. The ideal and the righteous king is insistently overdrawn in our sources, a fact telling its own story. It is claimed that, however kings came to exist as phenomena (a question to which we return), the function of a king is divinely predetermined. 'The kshatriya he (the Creator) commanded', says Manu,[15] to protect the people, to bestow gifts, to offer sacrifices,' to study the Vedas, and to obstain from attaching himself to sensual pleasures.' The last has a aomical sound, for a frame a negative precept as if it were a positive one betrays the historical state of affairs rather plainly.

For the king's role an education of some intensity was recommended, and no doubt required. 'Command of armies, royal authority, the office of a judge, and sovereignty over the whole world he alone deserves who knows the Veda science', says Manu elsewhere.[16] 'Let him act with justice in his own domains—Punishment (*danda* strikes down a king who swerves from his duty—with rigour chastise his enemies, behave without duplicity towards his friends, and be lenient towards brāhmans.' The duties of a king are to protect the good like a father and to put down evil-doer with rigour. The fourteen 'faults' in a king which are epics point to are these: atheism, falsehood, hot temper, carelessness, procrastination, not seeing the wise, laziness, addition to the five pleasures of the senses, considering state matters by himself (without consulting competent ministers), taking counsel with those who do not know politics, not commencing that which is decided upon, not keeping state secret, not practising auspicious acts, and taking up undertaking in all directions at once.

In order to uphold *dharma* a bureaucracy was required, whose functionaries were suspected of corruption, for, as Kautilya puts it, who can tell whether fish in water are drinking? A plenitude of regal power was called for, and obedience to the king's orders was imperative, whether or not they were capricious (as the *Jātaka* tales would have us believe they frequently were). To complain even after obeying seems not to have been contemplated. 'The unrighteous man who does not obey the laws promulgated by the king, shall be punished and even put to death...." Whatever a king does for the protection of his subjects, by right of his kingly power, and for the best of mankind, is valid....' 'As a husband should always be respected by his wives....a monarch should always be respected by his subjects, even though he be a bad ruler'. It is through devotion (or austerities in previous lives) that kings have acquired their subjects; therefore the king is lord; the subjects of a king must obey his commandments, and (as if from a father) they derive their substance from him.' [17]

The king was surrounded pomp and demonstrated conspicuous consumption. His consecration symbolised the dependence of the state for its crops and cattle upon the king's existence and attributes. Fertility, power, success were typified by the *rājā*, and a large share (ideally one sixth) of the produce of the lands (except those of brāhmans and deities) and of every productive occupation was not begrudged to him. Unproductive persons such as ascetics shared with their king their spiritual merit. He was like eight deities himself, and to some thinkers he appeared to have been created out of their attributes. He should shower benefits like Indra who showers rain (Indra and the king are often equated in the texts); he should extract taxes as the sun sucks up moisture; he is to penetrate everywhere with his spies like the wind; with the rod of chastisement (*danda*) he is to control all his subjects as Yama, the deity of death, subdues all in the end; he must punish the wicked as Varuna binds sinners with his rope; he is to gladden his subjects by shining upon them as the full moon gladdens men; he is to visit criminals with his anger and destroy wicked subordinates as fire burns all; and he is to support his subjects as the earth supports all creatures.[18]

Dharma upheld the king with the aid of superstitious symbolism, but its requirements from him were very practical and detailed. The *rājā* was viewed as the apex of a broad-based pyramid of authority, judicial and administrative. A family's patriarch, with recognised powers of coercion, ruled his household according to the ideals which we have reviewed. If he failed, relations would attempt to coerce him. There might be some debate whether custom permitted his acts. Social and moral misdeeds, and many crimes besides, were dealt, with by a similar machinery. A father might fine his wives and servants, and, where delay in bringing the crime to the notice of an official might result in a failure of justice, a husband was authorised to slay an adulterer.[19] A fiction of delegated authority left the men on the spot with a large responsibility for keeping the peace, suppressing crime, and compensating injured persons. There can be no doubt but that the stifling atmosphere of the smaller of the extended families out of which Hindu society was made up credited many personal problems which remained quite unknown, until a dramatic explosion (such as a daughter-in-law's suicide) drew public attention to latent evils.

In pre-classical time the *rājā* led in war and administered criminal justice; the *danda* was wielded to repel invaders, to acquire territory, and to execute or mutilate criminals. The notion that he was the foundation of all human justice came later, and until modern times the distinction persisted between the military and police power on the one hand and jurisprudence and the *sāstric* learning of the brāhmans (rather than professional administrators as such) on the other. Regulations, therefore, proposing to coerce an erring father would rely upon what corresponded to public opinion. If a compromise was impossible an eccentric could be brought under the ban of the village, the district, and eventually the state, which, slow to awaken and usually keen to delegate responsibility to local officials, was dreadful when aroused.

The maintenance of discipline therefore began in the home, and if that failed, higher forces, summoned *ad hoc,* could be brought to bear. The books speak of *pūga, śreni,* and *gana* tribunals, and these antiquated names refer, *inter alia,* to local, lay courts. The books suggest that the members should be impartial. The notion of *ius strictum* was totally absent. The aim, even today, outside the regular courts, is to effect reconciliation.[20] Not even the king desired to blind justice, come what might. *Dharma,* as a guide to the solution of disputes, had a built-in equity. What was abhorred by the public could not be *dharma.* Rule-of-thumb decisions were avoided and mutual adjustment was favoured even at the cost of repeated adjournments, a fact which the theory of the *śāstric* tests, however, by no means brings out. These envisage an ideal court and ideal conditions for discovering the truth, and then a flexible legal system fit to cope with it. Many of the legal rules of the *dharma-śāstra* seem vague, or frankly provide the judge with alternatives; the bald prescription of harsh punishment for offenders masks a system in which much wrongdoing was accounted for by groups interacting in an extra-legal manner.

Securing property-rights, repressing deviations from caste regulations, the king and his deputies were engaged for much of their time with actual or imaginary complaints against transgressions of the social order. Blessings awaited the king who so occupied himself. Instances might be a projected marriage between *jātis* not yet regarded as socially equal; a claim that a market price had been fixed unconscionably high; a claim that a sect should have an endowment comparable with that granted to rival sects; or a complaint that a caste had in a public meeting determined to assume an arrogant title. In all hearings which were judicial an ancient maxim came into play, that the four feet of *vyavahāra* (litigation) were *dharma*, *vyavahāra* (court practice), *charitra* (custom), and *rājā-śāsana* (royal decree). The latter in order overruled the former, a principle which speaks for itself. These were originally sources of law, but the notion that the king could not overrule *dharma*, in its transcendental sense, grew as time went on, and medieval commentators and even some late *smriti* sources saw the maxim as referring to methods of proof, and twisted the words accordingly.

In keeping order at home, forestalling attacks from abroad, planning attacks upon neighbouring kings, and finding his own level within the *mandala,* or circle of rulers amongst whom the theory of statecraft found his natural allies and opponents, assistance was available to the king from various quarters. Trained personnel abounded in the corps of officials. Their titles do not much interest us. The departments of state, headed by that of the *purohita* or family priest of the *rājā*, included those responsible for war and peace, the treasury, the elephant corps, registry and archives, forts, markets and prostitutes (an important source of royal income). There was a *mantriparishad,* or council of ministers, to whom the king might have recourse. Promotion to such a council was within his gift, but unfortunately removal from it was nearly impossible. The ideals of unquestioning loyalty to a righteous king and his family produced ministerial houses with hereditary ties to the sovereign. Such ministers were set up with fiefs in lieu of salary, they took no oaths of loyalty, and there were no reciprocal agreements; thus they could become troublesome subordinates, feudatories (without a true feudal system) capable of becoming kings in their turn. According to the recommendations of the texts on statecraft these ministers were to be selected for their knowledge, abilities, and character, and were to be tested by agents *provocateurs;* but there was nothing but loyalty to prevent their intriguing with junior members of the royal family, and even offering their support to a foreign king. The king was obliged to consult ministers, especially those holding prestige, but he was never bound by their advice; responsibility for unpopular acts was therefore entirely his, and, as we have seen, the possibility of deposition was never entirely lost sight of.[21] The position of the hereditary minister was more comfortable than that of the king, for all the books' recommendation that he should be constantly spied upon; even a righteous king is warned by these same books to be ever on the alert and to trust no one. An unsuccessful traitor, had, however, a great deal to lose, for the king's revenge would destroy him, family, dependants, and all.

The administration of justice, to which we have already alluded, was ideally the task of kshatriya judges advised by brāhman assessors; the books lay down the qualifications of the *sabhāsad* (judicial assessor), which are admirable by any standard. But in the villages all decisions would be taken by village councils; the villager would be bound by them because *dharma* required compliance with an agreement to which he was theoretically a party,[22] even if (as in the case of an untouchable) he had no right of speech at the meeting, and even if his opinion failed to win the general acceptance which always did duty for majority vote. The villager was theoretically present in his village parliament, and the *rājā*, his far-away 'father', was related by less tangible if definite religious ties. The *rājā*, not surprisingly, was required by the *śāstras* to take the local decisions seriously, and if they affected custom to inquire into and register them. The king's own orders, the *śāsanas* referred to above, were likewise recorded and put up in archives for future reference.

If the village could enact by-laws and the king promulgate regulations by decrec it would seem to follow that the society was progressive, moulding its laws and constitution to meet developments. On the contrary some observers emphasise the static nature of both. It was at one time supposed that *dharma* could disallow positive legislation, but this view has no foundation. Decrees emanating from the palace are actually contemplated by the *dharma-śāstra* itself. 'These goods shall not be exported' and 'Animals shall not be slaughtered on these days' are examples. The *artha-śāstra* actually authorises the aggressor to combine tactics, noble and ignoble, and the conflict between the transcendental and the expedient ends, with a distinct advantage to enlightened expediency. From successful treachery the king can purify himself by penance; by a failure in diplomacy he may lose his kingdom and inflict chaos upon his former subjects. In a war, or with reference to a projected war, the *dharma-śāstra* itself did not purport to chart the king's fiscal and administrative powers.

Dharma had thus an isolated existence of its own. It was not adjustable to suit opinion and occasion. We should look into its origins and relations with secular law more closely. In matters of detail, where the established ideals were not clear guides, the *śāstra* must needs follow custom.[23] As customs so recorded became antiquated the *śāstras*, or teachers, felt authorised to pass over many of the *smritis*, i.e. the immemorial maxims or oracular statements, which had accompanied the inspired philosophical and ethical material that made the greater *dharma-śāstra*, in particular that attributed to Manu, such splendid vehicles for law. Alternatively, they would interpret them if they remained them, in ways which would save their validity whilst insinuating a more contemporary meaning.[24] What was *dharma* was enunciated by the teachers, not the books, a jealously and successfully guarded privilege. Manu tells us that a committee of ten, of three, or, if need be, only one brāhman, properly qualified in point of character and learning, can give an authoritative and binding decision on a point of law, whether ritual or spiritual, or on judicial matters.[25] No appeal from such a decision is contemplated, though evidently the royal court acted as a supreme court of revision, where the best-qualified pandits could give a 'final' reading of the *śāstra* to meet the case. The state as such could not redefine *dharma* in any context. A custom, properly established, or a genuine *śāsana* might authorise a departure from *dharma* in a particular class of cases or a particular litigation, but then only if the court's attention was drawn to the former, and then without any bearing on the spiritual aspects of the question, in respect of which what was both 'right' and 'law' was immutable. Legislation by consent of the people did not exist, and the provision, which we have seen, that what the public abhorred could not be law, was of merely temporary and conditional effect. The *dharma-śāstra* from its very beginnings must have presupposed professional interpreters and a governmental machinery lacking jurisdiction to make more than *ad hoc* inroads upon it. This in turn presupposes a multiple, if 'isolation' society, far from the tribe or clan. What was best had been discovered by ancestors long ago, who had obtained it evidently from revelation; their insight and experience sufficed for their descendants; and it was thought that scholarship should be devoted to collating, systematising, and rationalising what had survived from the supposed corpus of injunctions. Debate was confined to the question whether current versions correctly appraised what the past had achieved.

Such a theory of society and its government left no room for progress in any modern sense. On the contrary the contemporary state of society was attributed to an inevitable decline, by stages, from a golden age. Apparently 'progressive' rules, such as that a girl could obtain an annulment of her marriage with an impotent man, preserved in ancient *smritis,* were held by the time of the *Smriti-chandrikā,* a thirteenth-century encyclopaedia of law, to belong to previous ages, and to be unavailable for the author's own period. The seemingly socialistic Directive Principles of the current Constitution of India would have astonished men of that age. Kautilya himself nowhere suggests that the resources of a region should be exploited to their utmost in the national interest, or that individuals should employ their earning power or their talents to their utmost limits. That the king should squeeze the peasantry to the limits of their capacity for regular payment was indeed recommended, but that was another matter. The principles of royal monopoly in numerous objects of production, and the regulation of market prices to avoid undue competition, indicate that the attainment of a balance was much more the object of policy than any adventure into the unknown. Individuals carried weight according to their membership of a group, and no group was independent. Hoarding, for example, was the function of merchant groups, who might live very economically, and to appropriate their hoards at his discretion, and so put the coins back into circulation, was a right of the *rājā*. In turn the *rājā* admitted responsibility for the occasional unfortunate (provided he was not an outcaste) who found himself or herself without support, and the *rājā* was the channel through which groups maintained their balance and those without groups to defend them were themselves protected.

Unduly successful claims upon the *rājā* for increasing the power or privileges of one group would drive the others into the hands of a rival for the throne. Since stability justified the state, the king was, as the *śāstra* interminably insist, bound to practice restraint, not least in forwarding those whom he favoured, for it was all too simple to exchange one *rājā* for another. We hear of puppet *rājās* whose seals authenticated their hereditary ministers' acts, and of conspiracies between notables which terminated in their favourite's being offered the crown.[26] Ultimately the system aimed at maximising the spiritual capacity of the individual as a member of a *contented* household, unambitious, protected from envy and unduly efficient competition, content with lawful acquisition, and relying upon the state for opportunities to put the good things of this world to the service of candidature for higher things in the next. The entire responsibility for this protect lay upon the king, a figure who has obtained less sympathy than he deserved.

The machinery of government was well suited to its limited aim. The *rājā* rested immune from unseen harm and his enemies' attacks if his subjects' welfare was secure, if castes kept to their functions, sages practised austerities, sacrifices were properly performed, nobles and leisures people roamed about gaily clad, merchants accumulated infinite wealth, and the toiling multitudes abstained from protest at the inequalities of life.[27] An army of spies informed him of maladjustments and plots. Which of the three conventional 'powers' of the king was the most essential, his strength of counsel, his material resources, or his personal energy? We have seen what were his conventional 'faults'. He needed each of these powers to perform his functions. The petty *rājā* needed neither elaborate espionage nor bureaucracy. He had his *parishad* or council, as later more extensive kingdoms relied on their *sabhā* or *samiti,* the assembly that represented local populations. In Vedic times the clan assembly advised the king on peace or war. Then women might actually be heard as counsellors, a possibility scarcely contemplated in classical times, when women had their own rights to property but only anomalously took upon themselves public responsibility.

In later times the king's deputy used to attend local gatherings and gave the royal assent to proceedings which often originated in the secretariat. The peace of small units was managed by the delicate interrelations between locally prestige-worthy families and the royal officials, from the village headmen to the district governors and tax-collectors, who were often the ministers to whom we have alluded already. These latter assisted in but did not necessarily take responsibility for local self-government. Checks and balances, threats of force, and more than anything the appearance of strength, kept people in their places. Officials were regulated by custom, and by *dharma* (if they were uncorrupt), under the ruler's oral or written instructions. The village assemblies were ruled by *dharma* in its most elemental sense, the conscience of the people understood through its customs.

Upon what did this obedience to the king rest? We have seen that in most ancient times his powers were circumscribed. Though a human fertility 'deity', he was, in his political aspects, more of an expedient that a necessity, so long as the tribe had not acquired for ·' .if dominion over strangers. But that people by that time puzzled over the king's powers is evident from the variety of explanations offered for their existence. According to Kautilya, when the king is making an eve-of-battle speech he should point out that he shares the fruits of the earth with his troops, and that he is, like them, an employee. But did anyone really believe that the king was appointed by his subjects or that he owed any of his powers to an agreement with or between them?

The *Mahābhārata,* rich in material on this subject, tells of a primeval king who took an oath to gods and sages that he would rule justly. But this was not a case of subjects electing their leader, nor of his making promises exclusively to them. What would be the outcome of breach of such a promise is not hinted at. It is true that at the consecration of each king a suggestion appears that he should be acclaimed, but elements of free choice are missing. The Vedic *ratnins,* who seem in very ancient times to have been kingmarkers, may have had no more than symbolic or ritual functions, and in any case indicate the humble suites of kings of a period too remote to serve any purpose in the discussion. Undoubtedly the ancient preference for prestige and natural leadership, when coupled with the later hereditary principle, must have enable the most worthy member of the royal stock to obtain the approval necessary for consecration, but an uneasy balance between the supreme power of the king and the goodwill of his most powerful supporters is visible in the torrents of advice poured on him by the *śāstras.*

That a king secure on his throne bears divinely sanctioned powers is evident. Constant reiteration of the theory that the king is the subject's servant, taking revenue as his wages, is coupled with the identifications with Indra of which we have made mention, and with the legendary origin of kingship from the intervention of the gods in a crisis. Prithu is said to have been created king by the gods, upon complaints by the sages, and he took an oath only to the gods. The people, in another legend, making compacts with each other, ask the god dharma to supply them with a king. Both these theories are found in the *Mahābhārata.* True, in Buddhist writings we have reference to the mythical king Mahāsammata, whose very name suggests compact, who, is keeping with the then fashion to place kshatriyas above brāhmanas, was appointed by consent of a public whose growing lawlessness required the kshatriya *varna* or their protection. But there is no suggestion, even in the Buddhist tradition, that the king's duties are fixed by the public, that it can interfere with his day-to-day business, or that any part of the public, such as the nobles, has a right to preferential treatment from him. The amalgamation of the ideas that a king must 'please' (*ranjayati*), and that his function exists by divine provision, ideas hardly reconcilable, shows that the themes were available for use as occasion demanded.

Yet no king could have functioned without the agreement of the people, ill organised as they were for expression of disagreement with him. Similarly, that religious aspect of kingship, admitted by all shades of opinion, was so pervasive that any state must have had someone able to contain it, and unlike some ancient societies India kept the religious and the political headship in the same person. In protecting *dharma,* and relieving or forestalling distress, the *rājā* lived out a role which gave rise to both these explanations.

This leaves open the questions where power resided, and what was its justification. Self-conscious in regard to aberrant customs, fruitful in expression of individual opinions and outlooks, tolerant of curiosities of faith or ethic, Indian literature provides no evidence that these problems were ever probable, and exemplifies at present (there may always be a dramatic discovery!) no specimen of a profound penetration into political philosophy. Perhaps the failure is to be explained by the lack of conflicts to which we referred at the head of this chapter. The kingly power was a trust, as it were, from the people; his religious status depended from his kingship. The trust was unconditional, and would have been meaningless without unbounded discretion. The divergent images suggesting that the king had rights against his subjects and they against him are misleading, and the concept that *dharma* reigned over all its merely uninformative. Power in fact stemmed from a state of affairs produced in a caste society; the state was a symptom or function of such a state of affairs. To maintain equilibrium, which caste cannot dispense with, detailed intervention in the nature of adjustment were required. An inherent characteristic was assumed to have an eternal meaning and purpose, and on this basis restraint were rationalised. No school of thought could doubt the transcendental expediency of kingship or the utter necessity of a state, the leader of which had the widest possible discretion subject only to revolution if the ultimate goals were prejudiced.

The goals themselves were a product of the rationalising of that caste society. We have seen them in connection with the ideals, conventionally phrased as *dharma, artha, kāma,* and, ultimately, *moksha,* 'release from rebirth', 'salvation', The possibility of pursuing one's *sva-dharma* was the test of the state; the vast authority of the *rājā* was justified by this narrow requirement alone. In modern terms this seems a high price to pay for a rather flimsy and speculative security. But we must remember that throughout Indian history until relatively recently the stoical patience of a people expecting nothing beyond subsistence and regarding prosperity as a temporary and delusory windfall moulded their goals and their requirements. By contrast, foreign ideals, still looked down upon in many quarters, make room for comfort, liberty, planning a career, and personality in this-worldly terms as an individual. The discovery in the *Arthaśāstra* of recommendations which are unethical by Indian standards is thus to be reconciled, for without *artha* (material advantage) *dharma* cannot be practised, nor *kāma* obtained, without which sons cannot be born to worship gods and ancestors, and thus *moksha* itself is in jeopardy. The need, psychologically, for *moksha* explained all aspects of the ancient Indian polity, in theory and in history; and with the decline of the desire for *moksha* we now find a redefinition of values, and a different conception of the state.

The background we have now surveyed may throw a welcome light on features of the Indian civilisation noticed elsewhere. A combination of *rājās* against foreign enemies or ideological opponents was hardly contemplated. Only an emperor could organise defence against such a foe. The advent of a new *rājā* was not feared as such, since even a foreign ruler was still a *rājā*,[28] and only the notion that he would convert the subjects to a different religion dissolved this recognition. Intrigue or competition between groups was innocuous in a society whose institutions were designed to prevent aggrandisement by groups, let alone individuals. The supreme social category was not the individual propelled by competitive self-interest.[29] Under the umbrella of the *rājā*'s gift of *abhaya* (security) tolerance caused no strain, bigotry could develop no inhuman aspects, enthusiasm were confined to individuals and leant towards personal immortality. Opinions which did not deny the fundamental requirements of *dharma* could flourish. Good behaviour or stereotyped attitudes were more important than opinions. Hypocrisy, self-deception, morals confined to the groups in which they were significant, an articulant rather than an integrated concept of society, these fitted a state in which dogmas had no absolute value, and there was no machinery to repress any but those who flouted the established order.

Similarly the system bred the notion that breaches of caste discipline, lapses from virtue, were not so much the fault of individuals as of the state, and that just as the king must restore the value of a cow which was stolen and not recovered, so he must punish adulterers; otherwise part of the guilt attaches to his own person. Underlying this concept is the fear (perhaps not unsupported by experience) that the removal of political authority turns every other man into a thief and a fornicator. India had a respect for order, custom, institutions, unaccompanied by any belief that these must be justified, without questioning the very assumption that there must be institutions. One could argue, and people did argue, that fraternal polyandry was congruent with *dharma,* but no one was so eccentric as to doubt for a moment that marriage and property were possible only in civilised political life, namely the state.

On the other hand India admitted the individual's right to try to leaven the lump in which fate had placed him. Hence the great importance of religious movements. These took the place occupied in the West by liberal movements in which political reforms and scientific advances came together. Another explanation, however, for the non-emergence in India of a popular striving for reform even in the face of gross exploitation, may be the theory, itself part of the system, that those who denied that the king was entitled to his revenue (on account of his ignoring their petitions) might properly decamp and live elsewhere. If grumbling could not keep revenue demands within practicable limits there was always this remedy. True, the migrants would soon be subject to a state like that which they had abandoned, but this possibility of migration, which remained well into the nineteenth century, excused an investigation of inherent weaknesses in the system.

Freedom of speech, provided the speech was not to the king's face, and freedom of movement were accepted; likewise freedom to agitate and propagate theories of an intellectual character, whether or not these had practical implications. Freedom of property, in the modern sense of the term freedom, or of choice of occupation and of way of life in a chosen environment, no one seems ever to have desired. Freedom to choose one's own direction seemed synonymous with insecurity,[30] with disorder and the dreaded state of affairs when the large fish swallow smaller fish, or, according to another explanation of the celebrated *mātsya-nyāya* (the maxim of the fish),[31] when people are roasted as fish are roasted on a spit. The ideals of the Indian peoples presupposed insecurity, from which political power rescued them. Against this background one sought one's soul's comfort by practising personal and social virtues; apart from that background, virtues were hardly to be aspired to. It is of interest that as soon as the fear of primeval chaos was actually removed, a taste for reform, for fundamental rights, and civil liberties actually made an entrance into the Indian mind, and, so far as recent history indicates, their continuance in India seems not unconnected with a firm intention not to relapse into it.

J. Duncan M. Derrett

REFERENCES

1. See e.g. (*Chanakya-rājā niti,* ed. Ludwik, Sternbach, Adyar, 1963, and the surprisingly original little handbook, *Laukikanyāyaślokāh,* ed. V. Krishnamacharya, Adyar, 1963.
2. J.D.M. Derett, 'Thomas More and Josephus the Indian', *JRAS,* Apr. 1962, pp. 18-34. The topic is pursued by the same at 'More's *Utopia* and Indian in Europe', *Moreana* (Angers), 5 (1965), 17-18; 'More's *Utopia* and Gymnosophy', *Bibl. Hum. Renaiss.* (Geneva), 27 (1965), 600-3; The Utopian Alphabet', *Moreana,* 12 (1966), 61-4.
3. Cited by Kullūka commenting on Manu ii, 6, Manu himself may be studied conveniently in the translation of G. Bühler, *Sacred Book of the East,* Vol. 25, 1886.
4. Yāijñavalkya iii, 66. Cf. the summary at Manu x. 63.
5. Manu xii. 31, 33
6. Yājn. iii. 219; cf. Manu xi. 44.
7. R. Williams, *Jaina Yoga,* 1963.Cf. Manu xii. 2-10.
8. The legal system based on *dharma* lives on in a spiritual sense, but its application in litigation ceased in India by virtue of the acts constituting the 'Hindu Code' (1955-6).
9. Note Manu vii. 13 (where *isteṣu* means, probably, 'topics provided for in the *śāstra*'): an important verse, poorly (as so often) expressed. The problem of the difference between 'law' as we understand it and Law as the *dharmaṣāstra* writers understood it is handed in *Festschrift für Otto Spies,* ed. W. Hoenerbach, Wiesbaden, 1967, pp. 18-41.
10. Visvarūpa on Yājnavalkaya i. 340. The general complexion of the status of 'subject' is handled in 'Rulers and Ruled in India', *Recueils de la Société Jean Bodin,* 22 (1969), 417-45; and the effect of these concepts

on principles of international law is handled in 'Hinduism and International Law; a Review of K.R.R. Sastry's Lectures at the Hague', *Indian Yearbook of International Affairs,* 15-16 (1966-7), 328-47. Both articles contain bibliographical indications. His subjects may kill a violent king: *Mahābhārata* xiii. 60, 19-20.

11. Josephus, *Bellum Judaicum,* vii, 341-57. Y. Yadin, *Masada,* London, 1966, p. 226.
12. Y. Bongert, 'Réflections sur le probleme de I'esclavage....', *BEFE-0,* 51 (1963), 143-94.
13. *Lekhapaddhati,* p. 44.
14. The text as well as the translation should be consulted now only in the versions of Prof. R.P. Kangle, to be modified by specialist discoveries published in the books of H. Scharfe (Wiesbaden, 1968) and (*cum grano salis*) T.R. Trautmann (Leiden, 1971).
15. i. 89.
16. xii. 100.
17. These passages are taken from Nārada's '*prak Irṇaka a* section.
18. Ghoshal, *History of Indian Political Ideas,* pp. 164, 273.
19. Vijñāneśvara on Yājñ, ii. 286.
20. *Report of the Study Team on Nyaya Panchayats,* Govt. of India, Ministry of Law (1962), which has a valuable historical section.
21. Manu vii. 111-12.
22. Manu viii. 219. Sec Derrett, *Religion, Law and the State in India,* London, 1968, Ch. 6.
23. N.C. Sen-Gupta, *Evolution of Ancient Indian Law,* 1953, esp. pp. 329-35, See also R. Lingat, *The Classical Law of India,* Berkeley, Cal. 1972, p. 2, ch. 2.
24. On the rolc of the jurist see *Etudes... Jean Macqueron,* Aix-en-Provence, 1970, pp. 215-24; Derrett, *Dharmaśāstra and Juridical Literature,* Wiesbaden, 1973, pp. 3, 52, 53,
25. xii. 110, 113.
26. Gopala, the founder of the Pāla Dynasty, and the Pallava Parameśvaravarman II are illustrations Derrett, 'Hindu Empires', *Recueils de la Société Jean Bodin,* 31 (1973), 565-98.
27. There is a telling quotation to a similar effect from *Mahābhārata* xii. 78. 9-17 by D. H. H. Ingalls, in 'Authority and Law in Ancient India', *in Authority and Law in the Ancient Orient,* Suppl. No. 17, *JAOS* (1954).

28. Pandits refer to the East India Company as *rājā* in their report referred to in (1817) *Morton's Montriou* 547, 548.

29. Varma, *Studies in Hindu Political Thought*... p. 189.

30. Spellman, *Political Theory of Ancient India*, p. 99.

32. This maxim migrated, like other scraps of Indian wisdom, and recurs in Talmudic literature (G.F. Moore, *Judaism*, vol. 2, pp. 114-15) whence, via. Spinoza at the latest, it finds a place in European political thought (S. von Pufendorf *De Iure Naturae et Gentium*, 11. ii. 3-5).

Kuḷyavāpa, Droṇavāpa and Āḍhavāpa

In the age of the Guptas, the popular units of the measurement of area in Bengal are known to have been the Kulyavāpa, Droṇavāpa and Āḍhavāpa. According to the Pāhāṛpur copper-plate inscription of the Gupta year 159 (=A.D. 479), 4 Āḍhavāpas made 1 Droṇavāpa, and 8 Droṇavāpas made 1 Kulyavāpa (Sircar, *Select, Inscriptions,* p. 347, n. 5). Since the introduction in the medieval period of the unit of measurement called Bighā (usually 80 square cubits), this one with its subdivisions has gradually ousted the older units and denominations from many parts of Bengal. But the Kulavāy (=ancient Kulyavāpa), Doṇ (ancient Droṇavāpa) and Āṛhā (ancient Āḍhavāpa) are still locally known in the eastern districts of Bengal and the adjoining western districts of Assam. It is however unfortunate that all the three denominations are not prevalent in the same locality, that the old relation of 1 Kulyavāpa=8 Droṇavāpas =32 Āḍhavāpas is totally forgotten, and that the Doṇ (=Droṇavāpa) which only is found in several places is different in area in different localities. The Kulavāy which is know from western Assam is equal to 14 Bighās, while the Āṛhā prevalent in the Mymensing, Sindha, Darji Bazu, Raydam, Susang, Hussenshahi, Nasir Ujial, Khaliajuri and Baukhanda *Parganās* of the Mymensingh District is equal to about 4-1/2 Bighās. The Doṇ is more widely distributed. In the Chittagong District the Doṇ is equal to about 21 Bighās; but in the Noakhali District it is equal to about 100 Bighās in Sandvip and to about 144 Bighās in the Shaista nagar *Parganā*. As pointed out long ago by Hunter in *A Statistical Account of Bengal,* this difference in the measurement of the same unit is due to the fact that the length of the measuring rod and also of the cubit is different in different localities. Usually a measuring rod was 14 cubits and a cubit 18 inches long. In Sandvip, however, the length of the cubit was 20 3/4 inches, while, in the Shaistanagar *Parganā,* that of the measuring rod was no less than 22 cubits. Now a days, 1 cubit=18 inches and 1 *nala* (measuring rod) =16 cubits, as standardised by the Government, have ousted the earlier lengths noticed by Hunter, and 1 Doṇ is now taken, according to the Government standard, to be equal to 76 Bighās in the Noakhali District. In the Rangpur District, where the ancient unit is lost but the name still survives, the Bighā is known by the name Doṇ. In the Hazradi, Kasipur, Nawabad, Barikandi, Joar Hussenpur, Kurikhai, Julandar, Balarampur and Idghar *Paraganās* of the Mymensingh District, the Doṇ is equal to about 17 Bighās, but in the Nikli, Juanshahi and Latifpur *Parganās,* it is equal to about 51 Bighās. Hunter does not refer to the Doṇ prevalent in other localities, e.g., in the Tipperah District. It will be seem from the above accounts that the actual area respectively indicated by the Kulyavāpa, Droṇavāpa and Āḍhavāpa in the Gupta age has little to do with that represented by the modern Kulavāy, Doṇ and Āṛhā, as they do not conform to the old relation of 1 Kulyavāpa=8 Droṇavāpas=32 Āḍhavāpas and as the Doṇ is now known to signify quite different areas in different localities. Apparently the area of all of them has changed in course of time, especially owing to the difference in the length of the cubit and the measuring rod in different localities. Attention in this connection may be drawn to the early practice of using a rod 4 cubits long for ordinary measurement but that of the length of 8 cubits for measuring Brahmadeya lands (Sircar, *Successors of the Sātavāhanas,* pp. 186n, 330n). But how can we have an idea about the original area of the Kulyavāpa, Droṇavāpa and Āḍhavāpa?

The words *Kulyavāpa, Droṇavāpa* and *Āḍhavāpa* indicate the area of land that was required to sow seedgrains of the weight respectively of one *kulya, droṇa* and *āḍhaka* (cf. *Amarakośa,* Vaiśyavarga, V. 10). Pargiter who tried to determine the area of a Kulyavāpa as known from the Faridpur plates (*Ind. Ant.,* XXXIX, p. 195 ff.) rightly pointed out that the staple food of Bengal is rice and the most important grain is paddy and that according to the *Raghuvaṃśa* (IV. 36-37) the usual practice especially in Central Bengal was to plant in the cultivated land the seedlings taken out from another field where the paddy seeds had been originally sown. This is the system followed in rice cultivation in many parts of Bengal even today. Pargiter therefore suggested that the Kulyavāpa indicated that area of land which was required to plant to seedlings of paddy seeds one *Kulya* in weight. Unfortunately the learned scholar did not know the actual weight of a *kulya* of grain. He had moreover to explain the passage *ashṭaka-navaka-nalen=āpavinchya* used in the Faridpur plates in connection with the measurement of a Kulyavāpa. He suggested that 1 Kulyavāpa of land was 9 *nalas* in length and 8 *nalas* in breadth, and further conjectured the length of a *nala* or measuring rod to have been 16 cubits and that of a cubit 19 inches. Accordingly, the area of a Kulyavāpa in Pargiter's calculation was a little above one acre (= $3\frac{1}{40}$ Bighās). The conclusion is however apparently conjectural. We have now to explain another expression *shaṭka-naḍair =apavinchya* used in connection with the measurement of a Kulyavāpa in the Pāhāṛpur copper-plate inscription, which would thus indicate an area only 6x6 *nalas*. It will be seen that an *ashṭaka-navakanala* Kulyavāpa would be much larger than a *shaṭka-nala* Kuylavāpa.

According to the Faridpur plates, the price of one Kulyavāpa of land was 4 *dīnāras* (gold coins) which, according to the Bāigrām copper-plate inscription (Sircar, *Select Inscriptions,* p. 343n.), were equal to 64 *rūpakas* (silver coins). Now the purchasing power of a Gupta Rupee was apparently much higher than that of our Rupee. From an analysis of the *Ain-i-Akbari,* Moreland (*India at the Death of Akbar,* p. 52) has shown that a Rupee of Akbar's time (1556—1605 A.D was equal to no less than six modern Rupees even in the estimate of 1912, *i.e.,* of a period to the First World War. The economic condition of eastern India of the Gupta age as noticed by Fa-hian who, in his dealings with the people of this region, never saw any coin but used only cowries, possibly suggests that the purchasing power of a Gupta Rupee was even higher than that of an Akbari Rupee. It thus seems to be probable that 64 Gupta Rupees were equal to no less than 640 modern Rupees in a quite moderate estimate It should also be remembered that the price of cultivable land depends much on that of its produce. When one Rupee was the proper price of eight maunds of rice (as is traditionally known to have been the case even during Shaista Khan's rule in Bengal), the price of land was undoubtedly much lower than it is today. Many parts of the Faridpur District are thinly populated and settlers may even now get land in those localities on incredibly easy terms. The inscriptions, again, speak of a fixed price of Government land for a large area (*vishaya*). It is therefore highly improbable that 64 Rupees would be the proper price of one acre= $3\frac{1}{14}$ Bighās of land in the Gupta age. That the Kulyavāpa indicated a much larger area can be demonstrated by another evidence.

According to a persistent tradition followed by the Bengali authorities on Smṛiti, such as Kullūka Bhaṭṭa (15th century), Raghunandana (16th century) and Panchānana Tarkaratna, 8 *mushṭis* or handfuls = 1 *Kunchi;* 8 *Kunchis* or 64 handfuls = 1 *pushkala; 4 pushkalas* or 256 handfuls = 1 *Āḍhaka;* 4 *Āḍhakas* or 1024 handfuls = 1 Droṇa. That this refers to the measuring of paddy is perfectly clear from the fact that the verse in question is quoted by Kullūka to explain the expression *dhānyadroṇa* in Manu, VII, 126. According to Panchānana Tarkaratna who has translated the *Manusaṃhitā* into Bengali and the Bengali compilers of the *Sabdakalpadruma, 1 Āḍhaka* = 16 or 20 modern Bengali seers, and 1 *Droṇa* = 1 maund 14 seers or 2 maunds. According to the lexicographer Medinīkara, 8 *Droṇas* (8192 handfuls) = 1 *Kulya.* A *Kulya* of paddy seeds would thus be equal to 12 maunds 32 seers or 16 maunds. These are the traditional weight of the *Kulya, Droṇa* and *Āḍhaka* as recognised by the Bengali authors, especially writers on Smṛiti who apparently relied on the authority handed down from old through a succession of preceptors. The traditional weight can moreover be tested by a measurement of 8192 handful of paddy for a *Kulya.* It should be noticed moreover that the scheme of 1 *Kulya* = 8 *Droṇa* = 32 *Āḍhaka* perfectly tallies with the other scheme of 1 Kulyavāpa =8 Droṇavāpas = 32 Āḍhavāpas. It is therefore clear that one Kulyavāpa of land required seedlings of 12 maunds 32 seers or 16 maunds of paddy.

Both the systems of planting seedlings and of sowing seeds are prevalent in Bengal, the first in some parts and the second in others. In some localities, *e.g.,* the Faridpur District, both the practices are followed. A cultivator of the Koṭālipāṛā region of the Faridpur District informs me that one maund of paddy seeds is required for 3 Bighās for sowing, while seedling of the same weight of paddy require 10 Bighās for planting. Seedlings of one *Kulya* (= 12 maunds 32 seers or 16 maunds) of paddy would thus require 128 Bighās or 160 Bighās of land for plantation. A Kulyavāpa was therefore originally equal to 128 to 160 Bighās, a Droṇavāpa to 16 to 20 Bighās, and an Āḍhavāpa to 4 to 5 Bighās. Even if we believe that the original calculation was based on the system of sowing seeds and not of transplanting seedlings, the position would be: 1 Kulyavāpa = 38 to 48 Bighās; 1 Droṇavāpa = $4\frac{1}{18}$ to 6 Bighās; 1 Āḍhavāpa = $1\frac{1}{8}$ to $1\frac{1}{2}$ Bighās. But this seems to have been hardly the case.

D.C. Sircar

8 South India

The Satavahanas held authority for about three centuries from 37 B.C. to 218 A.D. and this period is of supreme importance in the growth of the Neo-Aryan Civilisation in the south.

One remarkable feature relating to this dynasty is the maternal names by which the kings are known, Gautamiputra Satakarni, Satakarni, the son of Gautami; Vasishthiputra, Pulumayi, Pulumayi the son of Vasishthi; Gautamiputra Sriyajna Satakarni, etc. The same unusual custom will be noticed among some of the matriarchal kings of the far-eastern colonies also.

Placed strategically in the large area which geographically was the laboratory of relations between the Aryan civilisation of the north and the historic Dravidian Civilisation of the south, the Pratishthana Empire during the three hundred years of its existence can claim to have fulfilled its historical mission of establishing the cultural unity of India. The Mauryan conquest of the south was an extension of northern authority which no doubt was accompanied by a penetration of northern culture and ideas. But the Mauryan hold weakened after Ashoka and the influence of the imperial government was too short-lived to have brought the north and the south together in ideas. This was the historic mission of the Satavahanas and the geographical position of the Empire, placed as it was in the center of India, enabled them to fulfill it with success. The south India we see in the fourth century has been Aryanised in thought and ideas. The Pallava power at Kanchi is Sanskritic in its civilisation and even the Pandyas and Cheras have come fully into the composite structure of Hindu civilisation. The credit for this great transformation belongs to the Satavahanas.

Pratishthana their capital was one of the great centers of civilisation at the time, an imperial city whose glory is fully reflected in literature. It is the Paithan of Ptolemy, the capital of Sri Polemaios (Pulumayi). The great Gunadhya, the author of *Brihatkatha,* lived here and the story of the rivalry between Sanskrit and Paishachi (the dialect of the Barbarians) on which the story of *Brihatkatha* is itself based is a clear indication of the fight that was then taking place for the predominance of Sanskrit as the vehicle of civilisation and culture.

Under the Satavahanas Hinduism and Buddhism seem to have flourished equally. "In the first centuries of our era," says Grousset, "when northern India was being subjected in art as well as in polities to the domination of foreign peoples,—Greeks and Seythians,—Andhra has preserved inviolate as well as its political independence the tradition of Indian aesthetics." Amaravati, Goli, Nagarjunikonda had from the second to the fourth century A.D. become covered with stupas of which the sculpture serves as a link between the primitive Buddhist art of Sanchi and the Gupta workshops of the fourth to the seventh centuries. Religious establishments, temples, monasteries and *dharmashalas* were built all over the country both by royal bounty and by the munificence of private donors. The foreman of the artisans of Sri Satakarni is recorded in an inscription in Bhilsa topes as having made a grant. In the Nasik inscription which records the dedication of a great Buddhist cave monastery excavated at his own expense Ushavadata the donor speaks of his numerous charities to Brahmins also. Ushavadata, the pious Buddhist merchant also fed a hundred thousand Brahmins. Gautamiputra Satakarni who declares himself to be the sole protector of the brahmins records a benefaction for the Buddhists.

The Satavahanas were great excavators of eave temples and the magnificent temples of Ellora and Ajanta were the continuation of the Satavahana tradition to which all middle Indian dynasties in succeeding ages claimed historic relationship. The basic tradition in middle India is the Satavahana Empire, as in the North it is the Mauryan. From the point of view of historic continuity it is important to remember this primary fact, as up to quite recent times, the traditions flowing from the Satavahanas were living factors in Indian history, as we shall try to show.

The Satavahana Empire extended from sea to sea and virtually comprised the whole of south India excluding the Trairajya or the Chola, Pandya and Chera kingdoms in the extremity and in the north it included Bhilsa and a great portion of central India. Orissa was included in the direct domains of the Empire. Naturally with so vast a coast-line including many of the more important ports, trade and commerce flourished greatly within the Empire. Kalyan was the most important trade centre and we have the names of numerous merchant princes belonging to that place inscribed in the caves Kanheri and Junnar as having made generous contributions of a philanthropic nature. The extent of individual fortunes of the great merchants of this time may be judged from the fact that the Great Karli caves were excavated at the expense of a single pious Seth of Vaijayanti—a commercial town of great importance near the present Portuguese territory of Goa.

Another notable fact relating to the conditions within the Satavahana Empire was the facility of communications between its different parts. The grants made and recorded in many of the important places are by merchants living in distant parts of the Empire. Commerce which these monarchs specially encouraged and the influence which the great capitalist class of merchants undoubtedly exercised, involved the organisation of easy and peaceful communications, a tradition which a national system of pilgrimages which seem to have come into existence from the earliest times must have greatly strengthened. It was the emergence of Vakataka power in the Vindhya area somewhere about the middle of the third century that brought about the downfall of the Satavahanas. But an Empire so firmly established in its home domains does not break down with the fall of a dynasty. The Rashtrakutas and the Chalukyas in the Godavari valley and the Pallavas in the south, originally the viceroys of the Satavahanas, claimed succession to the Empire within their own territorial limits as the Vakatakas claimed it to the north of the Vindhyas. The Gangas and the Kadambas were also the inheritors of the tradition and as the Vijayanagar Emperors claimed in time to be Chalukya Chudamanis, or the crest-jewels of the Chalukya dynasty, and as the great kings of Gujarat equally elaimed succession from the Chalukyas the imperial tradition of the Satavahanas may be said to have been carried forward at least to the beginning of the seventeenth century.

The rise of the great dynasty of the Pallavas of Kanchi is shrouded in obscurity. A similarity of names led earlier historians to the hasty conclusion that the Pallavas and the Pahlavas were racially related. This is but another example of the tendency of European historians to believe that anything good in India must have had a foreign origin. Dr. Krishnaswamy Aiyangar, the doyen of Indian historians, after a careful and searching examination of evidence states:

> "We do not meet with the form Pahlava in connection with the Pallavas of Kanchi in any record of their time....The word as applied to Pallavas in the first instance seems to be a translation of the Tamil word Tondaiyar and Tondaman and this finds confirmation in some of the copperplate charters which do bring in tender twigs of some kind in connection with the eponymous name Pallava. This undoubtedly is a later use of the term but gives the indication that even at that comparatively late period the traditional notion was that they were not foreigners such as the Pahlavas would have been. In all the material that has been examined there is nothing to indicate either the migration of a people or even of a family that might have ultimately raised itself into a dynasty from the northwest, so that the assumption of a connection between the one set of people and the other rests upon the mere doubtful ground of a possibility whereas the translation or adaptation of a southern word into Sanskrit is very much more than a possibility as indeed a word like Dravida or Dramida would clearly indicate."

We have in fact in Rajashekhara the distinction between Pahlava and Pallava clearly made and emphasised. The Pallavas seem to have been the governors of the Satavahanas on the southern marches. With the breakup of the Pratishthana Empire they assumed their independence and when Samudragupta marched to the south they were well established in Kanchi, the ancient capital of Tondamandalam and of the great dynasty of Cholas. Vishnu Gopa mentioned in Harishena's inscription as having been conquered by Samudragupta was a Pallava king. But the greatness of the Pallavas was still to come, as the Cholas, though driven out of their capital, were still powerful and the Pandyas had maintained their independence and authority even against the Satavahanas.

An equally important succession State to the Satavahanas were the Chalukyas, the great bearers of the imperial tradition in north Deccan. The Chalukyas though claiming descent from the Solar dynasty were a local family which rose to power gradually and established themselves after a continuous period of fight with the Rashtrakutas who seem to have become the rulers of this territory during the declining years of Satavahanas. In any case the inscriptions definitely establish the fact that Jayasimha, the first important Chalukya king, defeated Indra the son of Krishna of the Rashtrakuta family, and founded his dynasty.

Between them, the Pallavas and the Chalukyas dominated south Indian history for over a period of three hundred years.

The redaction of the texts which may be said to have ended in the Gupta period and its great importance to national development have already been alluded to. From the point of view of religion the movement was even more significant. The re-written Puranas and the *Mahabharata* provided the people of India with a mythology, a corpus of unexampled heroic poetry, a rich system of popular ethics and a religious literature for the masses, catholic enough to include the worship of all creeds inside Hinduism. In fact by the sixth century Buddha himself had been included among the *avataras* of Vishnu and proclaimed an orthodox god entitled to worship by Hindus. The *Matsya-Purana* includes Buddha among the *avataras* and the passage is quoted by early writers. In the *Bhagavata-Purana* also Buddha is mentioned as an *avatara* of Vishnu and *Brahmanda* prescribes a festival for the anniversary of Buddha where it is declared that the image of Buddha should be worshipped in a particular manner on that day. Even in south India from an inscription of seventh century we know that Buddha was counted as an *avatara.*

In fact one of the great contributions of the Gupta religious revival is this emphasis on the doctrine of *avataras.* The theory of *avataras* goes back to pre-Buddhist times. Some of the *avataras* were known and worshipped as such in time of Panini, but it is in Patanjali (c. 150 B.C.) that we have a definite allusion to Krishna being an *avatara* of God and not merely a deified human being. The doctrine of *avatara* is simple enough and is stated with the greatest clarity in the *Gita* itself. "When religion declines and evil-doers are to be destroyed, I shall be born, at different periods" says Krishna. According to the now universally accepted doctrine of the Hindus, whenever the state of human society requires to be regenerated, divinely inspired men are born for the purpose. They are *avataras* but only men with such part of divine power as is required for the purpose in hand. Vishnu as the protector is the God of *avataras* and of his incarnations only Krishna is identified with him, while his other human forms like Rama Dasharathi, Bhargava Rama and Balarama though entitled to worship are not equated with God himself.

The doctrine of incarnation was interpreted elastically from the very beginning. Thus the Puranas include such Rishis as Kapila, Dattatreya, and Vyasa as *avataras* of Vishnu; also others who have worked for the re-establishment of *Dharma* are often locally elevated to semidivine dignity on the same score. The *avatara* doctrine had also advantage of providing the worshipper with personal gods, without his having in any way to break with the general body of Hindu thought which emphasised the impersonal aspect of Godhead and insisted on the doctrine of *Neti* (not like this). The unknowable *nirguna* God becomes knowable when it takes human forms and the compromise between the rigidity of Hindu philosophic thought and the popular demand for devotion to personal gods was easily effected by the doctrine of *avataras.*

If the Puranic and *Mahabharata* redactions provided Hinduism with a magnificent religious literature for the common people, it also brought to prominence a sacred text, the *Bhagavad Gita,* which was soon to become the scripture par excellence of the intelligentsia. The *Gita* is embedded as a dialogue in the first battle *parva* of the *Mahabharata* and is an essential part of the great epic. Even Rudolf Otto, who set out to find the "original *Gita*", comes to the conclusion that "the *Gita* in its entirety was not dovetailed into the epic at some late period: rather was the original *Gita* a genuine constituent of the epic when it became Krishnaized...The remainder of the material......consists of individual dotrinal treatises". The *Gita* with the doctrinal treatises which is the *Upanishad* is what matters from the religious point of view and this is the great book which comes to prominence as a scripture of *Bhakti,* Action and Knowledge in the fifth century.

The importance of *Gita* in the doctrinal reorganisation of Hinduism cannot be overestimated. There it was in a single compendious book which could be learnt by heart, the entire doctrine of the great *Upanishads* discussed and stated in the clearest terms. Since its formation there is no book which has exercised so great an effect on Hindu thought, which is proved by the fact that the great Shankara commented upon it in the eighth century as an authoritative text to establish his doctrine of Advaita and others who followed him had equally to depend on the authority of the *Gita* to prove their doctrines. By the time of Al-Beruni the authority of the *Gita* was pre-eminent, for the Muslim author not only quotes the text at different places but places his reliance mainly on Krishna's sayings when he discourses on the Hindu view of God. The importance of the *Gita* through ages can be judged from the numerous commentaries produced in every part of India and what is equally significant, is the voluminous literature that is published annually in India as modern interpretation of the text.

The reorganisation of Hinduism was on a popular basis. But the Brahmanical mind which was ritualistic in regard to religion elaborated at the same time the great doctrines of Mimamsa. The Sutras of Sabara and Jaimini's commentaries on them are no doubt anterior to the Gupta redactions but the popularity of the system as a school of religious thought dates only with Prabhakara at the end of the sixth century. Kumarila who probably belongs to the seventh century was the other great figure of his school. As a system of philosophy Mimamsa, both according to Prabhakara and Kumarila, deals more with the technique of thought; than with thought itself. It is the unique case of system interested in the method of ascertaining validity and the rules of interpretation without attempting to search for ultimate knowledge. As a religion it is only concerned with rituals. The Mimamsaka lives in a world of self-revealed Vedas, and he is concerned only with the correct performance of the rites as laid down. This is the reason why Jaimini was himself attacked as an atheist, an accusation against which defence only leads us to the conclusion that God does not matter as the results of Vedic rites correctly performed are automatic and not dependent on any Divine will.

The Mimamsa doctrine which under its exponents Prabhakara and Kumarila gained great ascendancy among thinkers of Hinduism in the seventh and eighth centuries was in fact a protest against the Puranic religion of the people and was opposed both to Buddhist and Upanishadic thought. It excluded not only a personal deity to be realised either through *Bhakti* or through *Yoga,* but also fundamentally clashed with teachings of Buddha. It was Shankara—the protagonist of Advaita—who prevented this barren ritualism from becoming a national religion and provided Hinduism with a corpus of philosophic doctrines, which has endured so long against the attacks of Islam and Christianity.

Shankara is generally placed in the eighth century. Born of a Nambudri family on the west coast of south India at Kaladi in the present State of Travancore, Shankara came to northern India after his education and propounded in different places his doctrine of Advaita Vedanta which he traced to ancient Upanishadic teachings, especially to Badarayana's *Brahma-sutra*. He buttressed his views further by a commentary on the *Bhagavad-Gita,* extracting from its teachings the essence of his Advaita. Armed with a philosophy which claimed to be in the true tradition of Upanishadic teaching and a body of religious beliefs which gave a higher vision of religious reality, Shankara met the scholastic teachers of the age, both the doctors of Mimamsa and the Acharyas of Buddhism. His contest with Mandana Mishra, who was the leading exponent of the school of ritualism is famous in Indian tradition. The accusation hurled against Shankara by the Mimamsakas was that he was a concealed Buddhist. This is undoubtedly true to the extent that like the Buddhists he was opposed to the system of mechanical rituals which claiming Vedic authority usurped the position of religion. Equally he was considered the strongest opponent of their creed by the Buddhists and the decline of Buddhist philosophical schools in India is attributed rightly to his influence.

It is appropriate that the great movement which provided Hinduism with a catholic philosophy and a conception of God which was acceptable to the highest thought of every sect should have had its origin in south India. From very early periods, powerful theistic schools following Shiva and Vishnu, both philosophical and devotional, existed in south India. Tamil Shaivism especially was a theological doctrine of great importance. The literature of this school assumed great spiritual authority between the third and the seventh century A.D. The *Tiruvachakam,* or the holy writ of Manikkavachakar, may be considered the most characteristic classic of the Tamil Shaivites and its importance to Indian religion has not been fully recognised. While it is undoubtedly devotional, its philosophic forms have close affinity with the orthodox doctrines of Hindu philosophy.

The Vaishnava movement of the Alvar saints which is contemporaneous was also devotional. The *Nalayiram* or the "Four thousand" which contains the hymns of the saints is accepted as a canonical scripture by the Tamil Vaishnavites. In fact the period immediately preceding the arrival of Shankara on the scene was one of notable spiritual and philosophical activity in the south. It is obvious that Shankara's thought was greatly influenced by his upbringing in the south. His own devotional hymns in Sanskrit, addressed to Shiva, Vishnu and Devi, which are still the most popular of all the devotional literature in Sanskrit, clearly indicate that the Philosopher of the Absolute also recognised the great value of devotion and religion.

Shankara was not merely a philosophical thinker reconciling a bold and original system with the doctrines and traditions of the past, thereby providing Hinduism with a philosophical background, but also a practical reformer. He purged the worship of the Devi of objectionable features which had crept into it from the practices of the Tantriks. The Samayachara form of worship of the goddess claims Shankara as its originator and undoubtedly the most famous hymn of this form of worship, the *Saundarya Lahari* or "the waves of beauty" is his composition. It may however be added that the followers of left-handed *marga* of the worship of Devi also claim *Saundarya Lahari* as their text and are able to find interpretations suitable to their creed in it.

The main organisational work that Shankara undertook was the establishment of the four great Mathas, at Badari in the north, high up in the Himalayas, at Puri in the east, at Dwarka on the west coast, off Jammagar and at Sringeri in the south. These pontifical seats were to be occupied by Shankaracharyas, who were to maintain unpolluted the teaching of Advaita and to maintain the ascendancy of Upanishadic thought. It is undeniable that these great monasteries together with their subsidiary institutions, also under religious teachers sometimes assuming the title of Shankaracharya, have helped to maintain the orthodoxy of Shankara's teachings and the hold of Hinduism on the people.

Connected with the establishment of these pontifical seats is the reorganisation of the monastic orders which is also associated with Shankara's name. The Dashanami Sannyasis claim their spiritual descent from him. A body of trained missionaries who would carry far and wide the teachings of the Master was necessary if the movement initiated by Shankara was to succeed. India always had its wandering religious teachers, but apart from the monks of Buddhism and Jainism, these Sannyasis do not seem in earlier times to have been attached to any monastic order. They were the disciples of individual Gurus. Shankara organised them into a regular body, and it is permissible to argue that the wide acceptance of his creed all over India was in a measure due to this reform.

The doctrines of the new school were popularised by the very large number of temple colleges which came into existence at this about which allusion has already been made. These colleges which gave free higher education on a large scale were predominantly religious and from inscriptional evidence it is clear that Buddhist thought was rigidly excluded from them. While in Nalanda and other Buddhist universities Hindu systems were freely studied and discussed, in the temple colleges of the Hindus a more narrow view was upheld and the curricula made no provision for the understanding of the doctrines which had for so long a time held sway in India. In the reorganisation of Hinduism these colleges played a great part.

The "disappearance"of Buddhism from the Indian scene is one of the facts of Indian history which have puzzled European thinkers. It is an undoubted fact that by the ninth century Buddhism had ceased to be a vital religion in India. No doubt in isolated centres like Nalanda it existed as philosophical schools up to a much later time, but actually as a religion of the people it disappeared by the beginning of the ninth century. The movement had in fact started much earlier for early in the seventh century Hiuen-Tsang had noted its decay in many important centres. But its virtual disappearance after having so profoundly influenced Indian thought for over thirteen centuries requires explanation. The reason is that gradually Buddhism and Hindusim became indistinguishable. Those who accused Shankara of being *Prachchhanna Bauddha* or a concealed Buddhist were in a measure right. Not only did the philosophical concepts of the Madhyamika school find echoes in Advaita, but Shankara by his fight against the Mimamsakas broke down the barriers between the Buddhist laity and Hinduism. Buddhist temples like the famous Jagannath temple of Puri became Hindu temples and with the laity accepting Hinduism recruitment to the monasteries became more and more difficult. As Eliot, the historian of Buddhism, says: "The line dividing Buddhist laymen from ordinary Hindus became less and less marked, distinctive teaching was found only in the monasteries: these became poorly recruited.... Even in the monasteries the doctrine taught bore a closer resemblance to Hinduism than the preaching of Gautama and it is the absence of the Protestant spirit, this pliant adaptability to the ideas of each age which caused Indian Buddhism to lose its individuality and separate existence".

In short it may be said that by the end of the tenth century Hinduism had asserted its universal supremacy in India, reorganised its popular doctrines, provided itself with a higher philosophy which found general acceptance among the intellectual classes and absorbed into its fold the religion of Buddha. From Kashmir to Cape Comorin, the worship of Shiva, Vishnu and Devi prevailed and the background of philosophy accepted without question the main doctrines of Paramatma, Jivatma, Maya and reincarnation in a society organised on the basis of caste and the Dharmashastras.

The Age of Imperial Kanauj

The Age of Imperial Kanauj begins with the repulse of the Arab invasion of the mainland of India in the beginning of the eighth century and ends with the fateful year A.D. 1001 when Mahmud defeated Jaipal near Peshawar.

This Age saw the rise and fall of three great Empires in the country: of the Rashtrakutas, founded by Dantidurga (c. A.D. 733-757) and his successor, Krishna I (c. A.D. 757-773), which dominated the south till its collapse in the year A.D. 974; of the Palas in the East, its zenith under Dharmapala (c. A.D. 770-810), and its partial revival for a short period at the end of the tenth century; of the Pratiharas of the west and north, founded by Nagabhata I, which reached its zenith during the reigns of Mihira Bhoja (c. A.D. 836-885) and Mahendrapala (c. A.D. 885-908), decayed on account of the catastrophic blows dealt by the Rashtrakuta raids, but retained a shadowy imperial dignity to the end.

Kanauj or Kanyakubja, the imperial city of Ishanavarman, dominated Madhyadesha, the heartland of India. It was the coveted prize of the three imperial powers racing for all-India supremacy. Ultimately it passed into the hands of the Prathihara Gurjareshvaras about A.D. 815; remained the metropolis of power till A.D. 950, and continued to be the most influential centre of culture till A.D. 1018 when it was destroyed by Mahmud of Ghazni.

By inheritance Kanauj was the home of Indo-Aryan traditions. In the post-vedic ages the region from Hardwar to Unnao, near Lucknow, was known as Aryavarta. Later with the spread of Indo-Aryan culture, first, north India, and then the whole country, came to be called by that name. The original Aryavarta, then come to be known as Brahmavarta, with accretions, was called Madhyadesha during this age.

In the seventh century the kings of Bengal and Malava destroyed the power of Kanauj, then in the hands of the descendants of Ishanavarman. On the ruins of the Maukhari kingdom, Sri Harsha built his short-lived empire of Madhyadesha. During his forty-two years' rule (A.D. 606-647), Kanauj grew into the foremost city of India. Sri Harsha, however, could not create a hierarchy pledged to support his imperial structure. He left no able successor. His empire was dissolved soon after he died.

For more than half a century thereafter, the history of Kanauj is wrapt in obscurity. At the end of it, Yashovarman, a great conqueror and the patron of Bhavabhuti and Vakpati, is found ruling Kanauj. Both Yashovarman and Lalitaditya of Kashmir joined hands against the inroads of the Arabs and Tibetans. But the allies soon feel out and Lalitaditya destroyed the power of Yashovarman.

The Classical Age of India closed with the reign of Yashovarman. This Age opened with one Indrayudha on the throne of Kanauj, which had retained its metropolitan and symbolic importance as the capital of India. And the stage was set for the triangular struggle for it between the Rashtrakutas of the south, the Pratiharas of Gurjaradesha and the Palas of Bengal.

The first great conqueror to emerge on the scene, with the Age, was the Rashtrakuta Dantidurga. He was succeeded by his uncle Krishna I, the builder of Kailasa temple of Ellora. In a reign of fifteen years, he added to the empire what are the modern states of Hyderabad and Mysore.

About the same time, Gopala, elected to the position of a chieftain, consolidated Bengal. His son Dharmapala (c. A.D. 770-810) led his conquering army through the whole valley of Ganga; reduced the ruler of Kanauj to a puppet; held courts at Kanauj and Pataliputra.. For long the commanded he allegiance of most of the kings of the north.

There was ferment also in the west. In A.D. 712 the Arabs conquered Sindh. About A.D. 725 Junaid, its governor, under the orders of Caliph Hasham of Baghdad, sent an army for the conquest of India. It overran Saurashtra, Bhillamala, the capital of Gurjara (the Abu region) and reached Ujjayini.

Then arose an unknown hero, Nagabhata by name; possible he belonged to a branch of the royal Pratihara family of Bhillamala, the capital of Gurjaradesha. Nagabhata fought the invading army, flung it back, destroyed it.

During Nagabhata's time Dantidurga with his conquering army swept over the north, captured Ujjayini, where the Pratihara, his fortunes temporarily eclipsed, played the host to the conqueror.

Vatsaraja, the son of a nephew of Nagabhata I, styled "the pre-eminent among valiant Kshatriyas", waxed strong and entrenched himself in a strong position in north India. He, however, suffered a disastrous defeat at the hands of Rashtrakuta Dhruva and had to take refuge in some inaccessible region.

Undaunted by reverses, the next ruler, Nagabhata II, consolidated the territory while comprised Marwad, Malava and modern North Gujarat. Having secured a base, he entered the race for all-India supremacy with the Pala kings of Bengal and the Rashtrakutas of the south.

Dharmapala marched on Kanauj, removed Indrayudha from its throne and installed Chakrayudha. Nagabhata II in his turn, marched against Chakrayudha, overthrew him and made Kanauj his capital. Soon after Rashtrakuta Govinda III invaded Kanauj and inflicted a defeat on Nagabhata which however, did not cripple his strength. Ultimately Kanauj passed in to the hands of the Pratiharas. About A.D. 815 it became the capital of the Pratihara empire.

In c. A.D. 834 Nagabhata II died. Ramabhadra, his son and successor, was in his turn, succeeded in c. A.D. 836 by Mihira Bhoja.

When he came to the throne, Mihira Bhoja, then a youth, was faced with a grave situation. Under the feeble rule of his father Ramabhadra, the power and prestige of the empire had suffered. Its outlying parts had become independent. Even Gurjaradesha the homeland was in open revolt. The imperial possessions extended no further than Kanauj and a small area surrounding it. Only a few of his fathers' feudatories stood loyal to the new ruler.

The first act of the young ruler was to restore his authority over his homeland, raise the morale of the allied clans of Gurjaradesha, and make them into a compact and invulnerable hierarchy. He did this with such success that the tenacity and vigour of the hierarchic dynasties survived more than a thousand years after the fall of the empire. Many of the Rajput rulers who surrendered power in the great integration of A.D. 1947-48 were descendants of the feudatories and generals of Mihira Bhoja.

The career of Mihira Bhoja, pieced together from stray references by modern scholars, was a great factor in making Kanauj a radiating centre of political and cultural activities which made for the integration of life.

Sometime after A.D. 836, Mihira Bhoja conquered Sarasvata-*mandala* in the Nepal Terai. By A.D. 876 he inflicted a crushing defeat upon the Pala king Narayanapala and annexed part of the Pala kingdom, particularly Bihar, within his dominion. The Rashtrakutas were now engaged elsewhere, so Bhoja pressed towards the west till he conquered practically the whole of modern Gujarat. The expansion of the power of the Arabs of Sind had been checked earlier. This period saw the power reduced to insignificance. It is almost certain, that this was due to Mihira Bhoja. The Muslim travellers however, have left accounts of the greatness of the Gurjara kings particularly Bhoja (Baura).

Bhoja probably died in A.D. 888. At the time of his death, the banner of the Ikshvaku Gurjareshvaras flew over an empire larger than that of Sri Harsha, if not that of the Guptas. The empire rested on the strength of regularly paid standing armies, the loyalty of the hierarchs and the support of popular enthusiasm.

The Age of Imperial Kanauj saw a vast religious and central resurgence in the country, of which the Puranas were the gospels. It harmonised the beliefs and practices of most of the cults which accepted it as the final source. The temple architecture, which began with the majestic Kailasa of Ellora and developed into the exquisite beauty of Chandella Dhanga's Shiva temple at Khajuraho, was its symbol. The cult of *tirthas* as a fundamental institution of religio-social significance strengthened the unity of India, carrying forward the consciousness that Aryavarta was the inviolate land of *Dharma*. The sweeping movement of the spirit was led by Shankaracharya, the prophet of the Age and the intellectual architect of ages to come.

It was an age of catholicity. The different creeds joined hands to respect each other. The gods of differing cults were all worshipped; Shiva was worshiped with his whole family, and so were the Trimurtis, the Panchayatana and the Matrikas. The kings generally patronised all religions and different rulers of the same dynasty are known to belong to different religious persuasions. Even the Arab traders were found happily settled in some parts of the country.

Though the Pala kings were its great patrons, Buddhism was on the decline since the days of Harshavardhana. Its disappearance from India during this period was hastened by the growing unpopularity of the Tantrik practices which it had adopted, by the Puranic pantheon accepting Buddha as an avatara of Vishnu and adopting several of its practices and beliefs, and above all by the evangelical triumphs of Shankaracharya.

The Pratihara Emperors formed the spearhead of this religio-cultural upsurge. Some of them, like Mihira Bhoja, worshipped Bhagavati as their guardian deity; others Vishnu and Shiva. They were of the people and did not stand away from their hopes, aspirations and traditions. Like the Gupta Emperors, they received the full co-operation of the Brahmanas, who, through their intellectual achievements and religious and social influence, could maintain a sense of identity between the dominant minorities and the people.

The Puranic Renaissance gave added sanctity to the Dharmashastras. In this Age, learning tended more and more to live on the past, the commentators and the writers of digests took the place of the law-givers. Of them, the most outstanding was Medhatithi, who wrote a commentary of the *Manu-smriti*.

The spirit of the Age found expression in relating *Varnashrama-dharma*, which was dynamic, to the virile concept of Aryavarta. Aryavarta, says Medhatithi, is not limited to geographical boundaries; it is not confined to the four corners of India; it is so called because the *Mlechchhas*, though they frequently invade the country, are not able to abide in it. No sanctity attaches to Brahmavarta as such; it would be *Mlechchhadesha* if the *Mlechchhas* subjugated it and lived there. Impurity does not attach to the land, but to the people. *Varnashrama-dharma* is a dynamic and expansive social organisation to be maintained and spread. Aryavarta extended wherever the dharma is enforced and maintained.

This concept did not remain a mere theory; it was in active operation. The culture having come to dominate India was on a march to wider expansion. Indians crossed the frontiers and established kingdoms, carrying religious, literary and cultural traditions with them to far off lands. In this way came into existence the Shailendra Empire in Java, Sumatra and Malay Peninsula (c. A.d. 778-13th century); the dynasty of Panduranga (c. A.D. 757-860) and Bhrigu dynasty (c. A.D. 860-895) in Champa, the dynasties of Jayavarman II (A.D. 802-877) and Indravarman (c. A.D. 877-1001) in Kambuja, the dynasty of Sanjaya (c. A.D. 732-928) in Central Java, and the dynasty of Sindok (c. A.D. 929-1007) in Eastern Java.

This dynamic outlook was followed in actual practice in India as would appear from the Arab chroniclers and the *Devala-smriti*. Even though converted to Islam, Brahmanas, Kshatriyas, Vaishyas and Shudras, who had been forced to do forbidden or unclean things, could be reclaimed by purification. A woman carried away by the *Mlechchhas* could become pure by isolation and abstention from food for three nights.

A king, says Medhatithi, has responsibility to maintain *dharma* in the land. He is under a paramount duty to resist foreign invasion at all cost. There can be no compromise with the invader: if his realm is invaded and is people massacred, the king must die fighting.

The king owes his position to no divine sanction but to the wishes of the people. He is only an instrument of maintaining *danda* or sovereignty which is based on the fundamental law propounded by the Dharmashastras. This law is above the king and is inalienable; nor would custom be permitted to override it. The king must submit to the ordinances of the *Smritis*. At the same time Dharmashastras are not to be rigidly interpreted. Equity is an equal authority with the Vedas, *Smritis* and *achara* for determining the right principle of law. "Satisfaction of the learned and the virtuous," says Medhatithi, "is a vital test; it may find what appears to be *dharma* as *adharma* and what appears *adharma* as *dharma*. When those learned in the Vedas feel that a thing is pure, it is to be deemed as pure."

Varnashrama-dharma of Medhatithi is a dynamic world force and not a static social order. A Brahmana can marry the daughter of a Kshatriya or a Vaishya. An adopted son may be of a caste other than the father's; a Brahmana can adopt even a Kshatriya boy. A Kshatriya and a Vaishya have the right to recite the Gayatrimantra. Brahmanahood is not acquired by birth alone.

A Shudra has the right to offer oblations to the fire, or to perform religious sacrifices, except the Vaivahika fire at marriage. He may not be competent to pronounce judgment according to the *Smritis*, but he can be one of the *sabhyas* in a court of justice. If any *Smriti*, says Medhatithi, takes away the right of a Shudra or lays down any prohibition, the injunction should be very strictly interpreted, and its scope is not to be enlarged by inferences from other texts. Those *Smritis*, which are in favour of the Shudras, should, therefore, he enforced. But these dicta are more in the nature of a protest against the growing rigidity of the social order and cannot be read as reflecting universal practice.

Medhatithi accords to women a position in refreshing contrast to some of the later authorities who wrote for the succeeding Era of Resistance. Women can perform all *samskaras*; only they should not recite Vedic mantras. At a partition an unmarried sister should be given one-fourth share of the dividing brothers.

A wife is obtained from God, not secured like cattle or gold in the market; a husband, therefore, has no ownership over his wife. Before the wife could be compelled by the husband to serve him, he must have the necessary qualifications, among others, a loving attitude towards her. Medhatithi condemns the dictum of Manu that one is to protect oneself even at the cost of one's wife; even princes should not forsake their wives says he. The practice of Sati, according to Medhatithi, is nothing but suicide, and as such, it is not permissible.

The position which the women occupied during this age, is also evidenced by other contemporary sources. The general level of their culture was high. Shilamahadevi, wife of the Rashtrakuta Emperor, Dhruva, enjoyed the privilege of granting large gifts without her husband's consent. Several queens of the Kara dynasty ruled in Orissa. Sugandha and Didda of Kashmir administered extensive kingdoms as dowager queens. There were learned women as well as women administrators. Avantisundari, the wife of the poet Rajashekhara, was an exceptionally accomplished woman. The poet quotes her thrice in the *Kavyamimamsa*. His *Karpuramanjari* was produced at her request and Hemachandra quotes three of her Prakrit stanzas. Ubhayabharati or Sarasvati, wife of Mandanamishra, who acted as an arbitrator in her husband's disputations with Shankaracharya, was a learned scholar herself.

We have a glimpse of social conditions of imperial Kanauj in the works of Rajasekhara, an ardent lover of Kanauj. Its women did not lag behind men in point of education. According to the poet, there were several poetesses in Kanauj. "Culture is connected with the soul and not with the sex" says the poet. The poet had met princesses and poetesses, daughters of prime ministers, courtesans and wives of court jesters who were well versed in science.

In the field of literature this Age cannot be compared with the Classical Age with its old masters like Kalidasa and Bhavabhuti. Under the influence of the rhetoricians external features of literature rather than literary beauty came into fashion; scholarship replaced poetic fancy; Sanskrit acquired a learned character.

Even kings, as we find from some notable instances, were highly educated; several of them were accomplished poets. Most of them were patrons of learning as well as authors. All branches of literature were assiduously cultivated.

There were *kavyas* in plenty; epics, romances and champus were composed in large number. Lexicography was cultivated; so were grammar, poetics, metrics and rhetorics. Anandavardhana wrote his famous *Dhvanyaloka*, propounding his famous theory of *Dhvani*. The favourite literary form of the Age was the drama though only one classical specimen survives in Vishakhadatta's *Mudrarakshasa*.

Literary activity in Sanskrit abounded even in the south. *Rigarthadipika* by Venkata Madhava, in the reign of Chola king Parantaka I, is one of the earliest of its kind in Sanskrit literature. Shaktibhadra contributed the drama *Ashcharyachudamani,* the first Sanskrit drama to be composed in the south, known so far.

Literature was also cultivated in Prakrit, Haribhadra being the greatest master of the period. There was a vast non-canonical literature in Pali and in Apabhramsha in which the works of several eminent Jain writers like Dhanapala, Pushpadanta, Kanakamara, Padmakirti and Svayambhu have survived. During this period, several works of great value were composed in Kannada and Tamil, forming landmarks in the development of these languages.

Philosophic literature was the Brahmanas. Of them all, Shankaracharya was the greatest. He provided a philosophic theory which undermined the barren ritualism of the Mimamsakas as well as the decadent Mahayana Buddhism and Jainism. He stood for monism; preached the superiority of *sannyasa* over ritualism. He purged many religious beliefs of their grossness. He was also a practical reformer. His organisational work, which brought cults, practices and rituals under the direction of the four great Mathas which he founded and which stood for his Vedantic monism, restored the cultural unity of the land. He also reorganised the monastic orders and infused a nobler sense of mission in them.

The *Bhagavata-Purana* was the culiminating point of the strong theistic movement started by the Alvars and Nayanmars in the south. It became the gospel of bhakti, the intense devotional ecstasy of the Alvars as well as the teachings of *Bhagavad Gita*. Its deep emotion and creative beauty saved the soul of India during the following Era of Resistance.

The last literary phase of the Age is represented by Rajashekhara, who lived in the reign of Mihira Bhoja, for he was the court poet and teacher of Mahendrapala and Mahipala. Rajasekhara's works give us a vivid glimpse of himself and the time. The poet was born in the family of Yayavaras, a family of poets. Though a Brahmana, he married into a Chahamana family and his wife, Avantisundari, was therefore a Kshatriya.

Rajasekhara had a partiality for Lata (South Gujarat). According to him, it was the "crest of the earth". Its people, however, hated Sanskrit, but spoke elegant Prakrit in a beautiful way. Its women were noted for their beauty and elegance of speech. Its poets possessed distinctive literary traits; and favoured the style called 'Lati'. Humour was its speciality.

The people of the region enclosed by the Ganga and the Yamuna, the centre of which was Kanauj, according to the poet, were the ornaments of the land. They liked new and elegant literary works. The composition of its poets was well constructed and their recitation was sweet like honey. To him the city was the centre of the universe; a sacred place; the home of the imperial Ikshvakus; a centre from where radiated power, fashion and culture.

The whole country, in this period, had a unit of culture. Sanskrit was the language of the cultured, spoken and understood among the educated throughout the country, but was most prevalent to the east of Banaras.

Mihira Bhoja was succeeded by his son Mahendrapala, a fearless military genius, who extended the empire of Mihira Bhoja adding to it the Karnal district in the Punjab, the Nepalese terai and the Rajshahi district of Bengal. In c. A.D. 910 he was succeeded by Mahipala who also like his father, was educated by the poet Rajashekhara.

Within a few years of Mahipala's coming to the throne of Kanauj, however, Indra III, the Rashtrakuta Emperor, marched to the north and occupied Kanauj. But he suddenly died, possibly in battle, and his army withdrew precipitately to the south. In A.D. 940, Krishna III reappeared in the north, overran Malava and Gurjaradesha, occupied Kalanjara and gave a shattering blow to the Pratihara empire.

The two raids of the Rashtrakutas had unfortunate results for the whole of India. Madhyadesha lay mauled and bleeding. The empire of the south tottered to a fall. The feudatories of both declared independence one after the other. The country was prostrate and defenceless, and the Aryavarta Consciousness was submerged by parochial sovereignties.

Out of the chaos, two powerful feudatories carved out independent kingdoms: the Paramaras of Malava and the Chandellas of Jejakabhukti. Kanauj, however, continued to remain the metropolis of culture, but its Emperor was no more than a shadow of his former self.

By about A.D. 974 the Empire of the Rashtrakutas was taken over by the Chalukya king, Taila II, a feudatory. A bitter and long drawn out war ensued between Taila II and Paramara Munja of Malava. Ultimately, Munja was captured and killed between A.D. 995 and 997. Taila followed him soon after in about A.D. 997.

In the fateful year A.D. 997 Abu-l-Qasim Mahmud, son of Sabuktigin, captured Ghazni, developed a marvellous striking power and turned his attention to India.

Ancient India ended. Medieval India began.

The *Mudrarakshasa*—the Web of Diplomacy

The *Mudrārākṣasa* of Viśākhadatta belongs to the imperial Gupta eta, but its subject is the technique of Mauryan diplomacy. We can accept it as throwing light on both periods, for it undoubtedly reads Gupta experience into a Mauryan context.

The central theme of the *Mudrarakshasa* is the Mauryan king's attempt to win over the chief minister of the deposed Nanda regime. Two masterminds, Chanakya (Kautalya) and Rakshasa, are pitted against one another. Kautalya has succeeded in installing the young Mauryan prince, Chandragupta, on the throne, but the structure of authority is still shaky. Stability evidently depends on harnessing the talents of Rakshasa (note the inclusion of his name in the play's title) to the service of Chandragupta Maurya. The schemes employed by Kautalya are elaborate, subtle, and amoral; they give a good idea of Mauryan-Gupta diplomatic intrigue. This purely political play is anything but politically pure. In its exclusive concern with politics, it differs from most Sanskrit dramas. the nuances of the more delicate sentiments of love find almost no place in the work. The plot is contrived and complex, but the dialectical development of the play is absorbing and the dialogue has a clarity and vigour befitting its theme. The ironic nature of the ultimate choice that confronts Rakshasa can be as readily appreciated today as it was in the day of the Gupta court. The *Mudrarakshasa* belongs to the category *nataka*; i.e., it fulfills a set of rigid structural requirements. For example, the major characters speak in classical Sanskrit, and the minor roles are expressed through Prakrit dialects.

In his introduction to the drama, M. R. Kale, the translator, sums up the important points in the plot's development: the acquisition of

Rakshasa's ring by Chanakya; the forged letter; the imprisonment of Rakshasa's friend Chandanadasa (who has been sheltering the family of Rakshasa the latter having fled the city); the faked rescue of Rakshasa's friend Shakatadasa from execution and the admission of Siddharthaka. Chanakya's spy, into the service of Rakshasa; the feigned quarrel between Chanakya and his prince; the arousing of suspicion in the mind of the Nanda prince, Malayaketu, against his minister Rakshasa, and the rupture of their relationship; the unjust murder of the five Mleecha (foreign) princes; Malayaketu's determination to wage war against Chandragupta; his defeat; the determination of Rakshasa to give himself up to the Mauryas in order to save his friend Chandanadasa; the report of the mysterious man in the grove about the imminent execution of Chandanadasa; and finally Rakshasa's reluctant consent to become Chandragupta Maurya's minister—with the consequent release of Chandanadasa (the perfect friend), the restoring of Malayaketu to his paternal territory, and the freeing of Chanakya for the life of an ascetic.

The play covers a year's time. The action does not begin until after the recital of a benediction and a contrivance that sets the stage of the intrigue to follow.

Manager: Enough of prolixity. I have been asked by the audience to present a new drama, 'Mudrarakshasa' by name, a composition by the poet Vishakhadatta, grandson of the tributary prince Vateśvaradatta and the son of Prithu, bearing the title of Maharaja. Surely, I too, who am now performing before an audience knowing the excellence of poetry, feel very great satisfaction. For,

Cultivation of seeds sown by even a foolish person when bestowed upon a good field bears fruit...

I will therefore first go home, and having called my consort, will commence singing with the inmates of the house....Holla, what do I see here? There seems to be a festival...

Here is a woman fetching water; here is one pounding aromatic herbs; and her is another stringing together garlands...

Well, I will call my wife and ask her.

O you, who are meritorious, who are an abode of expedients, who bring about the three objects of existence which are the cause of the stability of worldly life...come here quickly.

Actress (*entering*): Here am I, my lord. May your honour favour me with your command.

Manager: Lady, let aside for a moment the entrusting-with-my-command. Tell me—has our family been favoured by you by having invited venerable brahmans? Or have welcome guests come to our house, that there are these special preparations of meals?

Actress: My lord, the worthy brahmans have been invited by me.

Manager: Tell me for what reason.

Actress: Because they say the moon is to be eclipsed.

Manager: Lady, who says so?

Actress: Such, indeed, is the talk among the townsfolk.

Manager: Lady, I have spent some labour on the science of astronomy with its 64 branches; therefore let your preparation of meals in honour of the worthy brahmans proceed; as for the eclipse of the moon, you are deceived by some one. For see,

That well-known Ketu, the malignant planet, wishes perforce to attack the moon having the full orb; (Voice *behind the curtain*; who is he that, while I live, wishes to overpower Chandra?)—but the union (near) Budha [Mercury] saves him.

Actress: But my lord, who is this that, being a denizen of the earth desires to save the moon from the attack of the planet?

Manager: My lady, to tell you the truth, I too did not observe him. Well, being attentive again, I shall mark the manifestation of his voice. (Voice *repeats*—That malignant planet...)

Voice (*behind the curtains*): Ah! who is he that desires to attack Chandragupta while I am alive?

Manager: Ah, I see. It is Kautalya.

(Actress *gesticulates fear*.)

Manager: This is that Kautalya of perverse intellect, by whom the race of the Nandas was, perforce, burnt up in the fire of his wrath... He understands that there is to be an attack by the enemy on the moon-like Maurya who bears the same name [Chandra].

Let us therefore go away hence.

ACT I

Chanakya:.....The nine Nandas have been eradicated like so many heart-diseases of the Earth; sovereignty has been made firm-footed in the case of Maurya like a lotus-plant in a lake; and the two-fold well-deserved fruit of the two things, anger and love, has been equally meted out with a careful mind to the foe and the friend.

Or rather, so long as Rakshasa has not been won over, how can the race of Nanda be said to be extirpated, or what stability has been given to the sovereignty of Chandragupta? (*Thinking.*) O! how unsurpassable is the excellence of devotion of Rakshasa to the house of Nanda!...Noble, very noble, oh minister Rakshasa; praiseworthy, O learned brahman; well done, oh you Brihaspati-like minister, well done! For,

These [ordinary] people serve their lord (so long as he is) not deprived of his sovereignty, for the sake of gain...but rarely are to be found those blessed persons of your type, who undertake the responsibility of duty out of disinterested devotion, remembering past favours, even after the utter destruction of their master.

...(I) am making an effort, as much as I can, to secure him. How is that? In the first place this (has been done). A scandal is caused to be circulated in the world that poor Parvataka, our extremely obliging friend, has been killed by Rakshasa by means of a poison-maid (thinking that this would do harm to Chanakya)...I have also employed emissaries in various disguises and conversant with various places, dresses, languages, manners and modes of dealing, with the desire of knowing the people that are attached to or disaffected towards our side or that of the enemy...Thus then, nothing is wanting on our side. It is only Vrishala [Chandragupta], who, being a monarch entirely dependent on his minister, entrusts the responsibility of administering the kingdom to me, and always remains apathetic....

(*Enter a spy.*)

Spy:...there are three persons in the city who have already conceived affection and a great regard for Rakshasa...(one is) Jivasiddhi, by whom the poison-maid employed by Rakshasa was directed against king Parvateshvara.

Chanakya (*to himself*): This Jivasiddhi is but our spy. (*Aloud.*) Good fellow, who is the second man?

Spy: Your honour, the second man is a kayastha, also a friend of Rakshasa, Sakatadasa by name.

Chanakya (*with a smile, to himself*): A kayastha is a matter of small moment. Yet it is not proper to neglect even a small enemy...

Spy: The third man, the second heart as it were of the minister Rakshasa, is the chief of jewellers, Chandanadasa by name, and an inhabitant of Pushpapura, in whose house Rakshasa deposited his family and escaped from the town....

ACT II

(*Rakshasa's dwelling. Enter a snake-catcher.*)

Snake-Catcher (*to himself*): ...O, wonder! Seeing Chandragupta guided by the intellect of Chanakya, I consider the attempt of Rakshasa as futile; considering again (that) Malayaketu (is) aided by the counsel of Rakshasa, I look upon Chandragupta as almost deposed from his supreme power. For,

I consider the Royalty of king Maurya as stable, with her form tied down by the rope, in the form of the intellect of Kautalya; but that very Royalty I look upon as being snatched away by Rakshasa...

The bewildered goddess of wealth is surely tired by moving backwards and forwards through indecision between these two eminent ministers strongly opposed to each other in this case, like a female elephant in a large forest between two wild elephants...

(*Enter Rakshasa.*)

Rakshasa (*looking towards the sky, with tears in his eyes*): O venerable lotus-throned goddess, you are quite incapable of appreciating merits. For,

Tell me why you, having discarded His Majesty Nanda, though a source of delight, have become attached to his enemy, the son of Maurya? Why, oh fickle one, did you not vanish forever at that time, like the line of ichor-water disappearing at the death of a scent-elephant?...Or rather (why should I blame you?); the mind of elderly ladies, which by nature is as fickle as the edge of a kasha flower is averse to appreciate the merits of men...

(On reading a poem of the snake-catcher, Rakshasa realises that the charmer is in fact one of his spies. The spy relates the many reverses the Nandas have suffered.)

Viradhagupta, the spy: Minister, he [a pro-Nanda physician] had prepared a medicine mixed with powder of magical virtue for Chandragupta; but the villainous Chanakya happening to examine it, observed a change of colour in a gold plate, and said to Chandragupta—Vrishala, this medicine is poisoned; you should not drink it.

Rakshasa: He is a wily fellow indeed. What of the physician?

Viradhagupta: He was compelled to drink the same medicine, and died.

Rakshasa: ....And what news of Bibhatsaka?...

Viradhagupta: Minister,.... That wicked soul, the cursed Chanakya, entered the bed-chamber before Chandragupta's entry, when, the very moment, casting a searching look about, he noticed a line of ants with particles of food in their mouths issuing from some crevice in the wall, whence concluding that there were men hidden in the interior of the house, he ordered the bed-chamber to be set on fire. As it was burning, all those, Bibhatsaka and others, with their eyes obstructed by smoke, could not find the outlet through which they had previously arranged to make their exits, and being enveloped in flames, perished....

Rakshasa: Friend Viradhagupta, go on with the remainder of your tale.

Viradhagupta:...This is what has come to light.... Chandragupta has got angry with Chanakya ever since Malayaketu's escape. Chanakya, of course, in his extreme arrogance does not bear this, and pains the heart of Chandragupta with various acts of disobedience....

Rakshasa (*delighted*): Friend Viradhagupta, go again to Kusumapura in this very disguise as a snake-charmer. There lives a dear friend of mine, Stanakalasha by name, disguised as a bard. Tell him in my name that as Chanakya will be committing acts of disobedience, he should praise Chandragupta with stanza calculated to excite his jealousy....

ACT III

(*Kusumapura. The chamberlain comments on Chandragupta.*)

Chamberlain:...Make haste, friends. His majesty Chandragupta is at the gates. He.

Who being strong-minded, has resolved to bear aloft even in his prime of youth that very yoke of the earth, which though heavy was for a long time borne by his experienced and able father, who did not step amiss even on rough paths on account of his firm limbs; he stumbles on account of his youthfulness, but bears it lightly.

(*Enter the king.*)

Chandragupta (*to himself*): Sovereignty is, indeed, a source of great uneasiness to a king, who is intent on conforming to the duties of sovereigns. For,

...It is the advice of my esteemed minister that I should feign a quarrel with him and manage matters independently for some time. I accepted it with great difficulty as if it were a sin;...With my mind properly guided by his honour I am always independent. For,

In this world as long as a pupil acts in the right way, he experiences no check (from his preceptor); when, however, he strays from the proper path through infatuation, the preceptor becomes a goad to him; those good people therefore, who like to act according to instruction are always free from restraint; we for our part are averse to any independence beyond this.

(*Aloud to the chamberlain.*) How is it then that the festivities have not been commenced in Kusumapura?

Harlots accompanied by gay beaux skilled in free and clever talk do not grace the streets with their gaits slow on account of the weight of their plump hips; nor do the householders… partake, along with their consorts, in the desired festivities falling on the full-moon day.

Chamberlain: It is just this.

Chandragupta: What is that?

Chamberlain: My lord, this...

Chandragupta: Speak clearly.

Chamberlain: The Kaumudi festival has been prohibited.

Chandragupta: By whom?

Chamberlain My lord, beyond this I am not able to say.

Chandragupta: I hope the venerable Chanakya has not deprived the spectators of an exceedingly lovely sight.

Chamberlain: Sir, who else that loves life can transgress the command of Your Majesty?

(*Chandragupta exists, having ordered Chanakya brought before him.*)...

Chamberlain: This is the palace Suganga. Your Honour may gently ascend.

Chanakya: O, Vrishala [Chandragupta] is seated on the throne. Very good, very good.

The throne wrested from the Nandas, who treated with scorn even Kubera, has been occupied by Vrishala, the foremost among sovereigns; and it has been united with a worthy king. These good occurrences (brought about by me) produce a very great satisfaction in me.

(*Approaches Vrishala.*) Victory to you, Vrishala.

Chandragupta (*rising from his seat*): Venerable sir, Chandragupta bows to you.. (Falls at his feet.)

Chanakya (*taking him by the hand*): Rise, child ....Vrishala, why did you summon me?

Chandragupta: To bless myself with your honour's sight.

Chanakya (*with a smile*): No more compliments, please. Kings do not send for their officers without a purpose.

Chandragupta: Sir, what good has your honour in view in forbidding the Kaumudi festival?

Chanakya (*with a smile*): You have then summoned me to administer a reproof?

Chandragupta: God forbid, God forbid! No, not at all, only to make a respectful representation.

Chanakya: If so, the uncontrolled tastes of those who are to be respectfully treated ought by no means to be checked by a pupil.

Chandragupta: It is so; there is no doubt. But your honour never does a thing without having some object in view. So there is scope for my question....

Chanakya: Vrishala, listen. In connection with this topic writers on politics mention three kinds of administration: (1) that dependent on the king, (2) dependent on the minister, (3) and dependent upon both. Now what have you, who are entirely dependent upon your minister, to do with enquiring into the reasons of a thing—since I who am the responsible officer will alone act in this matter?

(*Chandragupta turns away face in anger.*)

(voices *behind the curtains.*)

First Bard: Whitening the sky with its ashen due that surpasses the brightness of kasha flowers, counteracting the impression of the elephant-hide-like space dark with clouds by means of the streaming rays of the moon, bearing the bright moon-light like a white garland of skulls and displaying its swans like beauteous smiles, may the autumnal season, thus unusually accoutred, remove your trouble, like the body of Shiva....

Second Bard: O best of kings, some universal sovereigns alone like you, who are for mysterious reasons created by the Creator the receptacle of pre-eminent valour, who by their peculiar might, subdue kings having a large force of rut-shedding elephants, and who are distinguished by their sense of self-esteem and pride, do not put up with the disobedience of their command, just as the lords of beasts who for some reason are created by the Creator as the store-houses of strength, who by their fierce vigour conquer the rut-shedding leaders of elephant-herds, and whose dignity and haughtiness are distinctly manifested, do not bear the breaking of their jaws.

Moreover,

A lord does not become a lord by the wearing of ornaments, etc. He is said to be a lord, like you, whose order is not slighted by others.

Chanakya (*to himself*): The first is a blessing describing the beauties of the autumnal season now set in, the form of the praise of a specific deity. What the other is, I do not understand. (*After reflecting.*) Ah, I comprehend it now. It is the design of Rakshasa. You are detected, vile Rakshasa. Be sure Kautalya is wide awake.

Chandragupta: Venerable Vaihinari [the chamberlain], let a hundred thousand gold coins be given to these bards.

Chamberlain: As your Majesty commands.

Chanakya (*angrily*): Stop. Vaihinari, don't go. Vrishala, why this large expenditure for so paltry a thing?

Chandragupta: (*in a rage*): Kingship is like bondage to me, when my course of action is thus checked in every case by your honour; it is not like kingship at all.

Chanakya: Vrishala, such evils are but the lot of those kings who do not apply themselves to their own duties. If you cannot bear them, apply yourself to your duties.

(*Chanakya tells the king that the prohibition of the festival was a deliberate defiance of the latter's order, and that—at this time—military exercises are more important than festivals. Then he tells Chandragupta of those who have gone over to Malayaketu.*)....

Chandragupta: If the causes of their discontent were known, why did not your honour promptly counteract them?

Chanakya: Vrishala, it was not possible to counteract.

Chandragupta: Why, owing to want of skill or to some purposes in view?

Chanakya: How could there have been want of skill? There was a special purpose in view.

Chandragupta: That purpose I want to hear now.

Chanakya: Hear it and bear it well in mind. With regard to the present matter (I have to observe that) there are two ways of dealing with discontented subjects, viz., favour or punishment. In the case of Bhadrabhata and Purushadatta who were dismissed from office, to show favour would mean to reinstate them. And if such people, who are careless of the discharge of duty on account of their addiction to vice, be restored to office, they would lead to destruction the whole body of horse and elephant, the main prop of the realm... The other alternative, too, had to be given up. For after our recent acquisition of the realm of the Nandas, had we inflicted severe punishment upon the influential persons who were our adherents, we should have been distrusted by the subjects who are yet attached to the family of the Nandas.... The present is thus the time for exertion and not for festivities....

Chandragupta: Sir, I have much to ask in this matter.

Chanakya: Vrishala, ask without reserve. I too have much to explain.

Chandragupta: Why did you allow Malayaketu, the cause of all this mischief, to escape?

Chanakya: In case he was not allowed to escape, there were two courses open—to punish him or to give him half the kingdom as promised. To have punished him would have given support to (the supposition) that the murder of Parvataka was an act of ingratitude perpetrated by us. On the other hand, had the promised half of the kingdom been given him, the only result of the assassination of Parvataka would have been the sin of ingratitude. For these reasons I suffered Malayaketu to escape.

Chandragupta: This is your explanation in this case. Then again you neglected to take proper steps against Rakshasa who was living here. What has your honour to say to this?

Chanakya:... If, therefore, he had been allowed to remain in this very city, he would have indeed caused great internal trouble. Whereas, if he were removed from the city, and then he caused disaffection abroad, it would be possible to manage him. He was therefore pulled off even as he lived here, like a dart rankling in the heart, and removed to a distance.

Chandragupta: Sir, why did you not capture him by force?

Chanakya: He is Rakshasa, mind you. Had we used violence against him, he would have destroyed many of our soldiers, or, found death himself—an unwelcome result in either case. See,

If being hard-pressed he were to meet with this end, then, O Vrishala, you would indeed lose so great a person as he is... He must be won over with stratagems like an elephant of the forest.

Chandragupta: We are unable to surpass your intelligence. But after all Rakshasa is more praiseworthy.

Chanakya (*in anger*): "Than you" I should supply. But it must not be so. O Vrishala, what has he done?

Chandragupta: If you cannot know it yourself, then hear it from me. He, a magnanimous soul,

Dwelt in the city, which had been captured by us, as long as he liked, planting his foot on our neck, and forcibly offered resistance to the proclamation of victory made by our forces....

Chanakya (*in anger*): Vrishala, you wish to lord it over me like a common servant.

My hand again runs to loosen the knot of hair though tied up....

. . .

(*Checking his pretended anger.*) Vrishala, enough of bandying words. If you think Rakshasa is superior to me, give him this sword. (*Throws down the sword, comments to himself on the king's foolishness, exits.*)

Chandragupta: Venerable Vaihinari, let it be proclaimed to the subjects that henceforward Chandragupta will rule independently of Chanakya.

Chamberlain (*to himself*): O, he calls him Chanakya, without any epithet of respect, and not as revered Chanakya. Alas! Authority has been withdrawn from him. But His Majesty is not to blame in this matter. For, it is the fault of the minister himself if the king does wrong (or does not respect the minister). An elephant comes to be censured as a vicious animal through the carelessness of the driver....

Chandragupta (*to himself*): My mind has, as it were, begun to enter the very cavity of the earth though I overstepped the limits of respectfulness by the command of his honour himself. Does not shame rend the hearts of those who wantonly slight their preceptors?

ACT IV

(*Rakshasa in conference with his aides. Eventually Malayaketu arrives to inquire after Rakshasa's headache—which will not leave until Nanda is restored.*)

Malayaketu: Sir, have you found out any weak point of the enemy?

Rakshasa: Yes.

Malayaketu: Of what nature is it?

Rakshasa: A ministerial one, what else? Chandragupta has fallen off from Chanakya.

Malayaketu: Sir, a weak point arising from the (loss of a) minister is no weak point.

Rakshasa: A difficulty arising from a minister may be no difficult in the case of other kings; but with Chandragupta it is so....

... The vile Chandragupta, however, is habitually dependent on his minister and is therefore like a blind man unfamiliar with the affairs of the world. How will he be able to resist us by himself?

The goddess of royalty stands with her legs rigidly placed on a king and on a minister when (both of them have) grown too powerful; being, as a woman, unable to sustain her weight she abandons one of them.

A king who entrusts everything to his minister, if drawn away from him, like a suckling child weaned from its mother's breast, will not be able to act even for a moment, his intellect not being unfolded on account of his inexperience of the affairs of the world.

Malayaketu (*aside*): I am glad that I don't depend on a minister for the management of my affairs. (*Aloud.*) Although it is so, still when there are many reasons for commencing hostilities success is certain in the case of one who carefully tries to find out some misfortune of the enemy and then assails him....

ACT V

(*Chanakya has arranged that the Nanda king should learn that it was Rakshasa that killed Malayaketu's father. The plot becomes exceedingly intricate and we are left with no doubts as to the competence and subtlety of Kautalya. At the end of the act Malayaketu confronts Rakshasa with the condemning evidence.*)

Malayaketu (*pointing to the forged letter, and a box of ornaments*): And what is this here?

Rakshasa (*tearfully*): The wanton play of fate. For,

It is the grand work of that fate, the frustrator of men's exertions, which, the accursed one, destroyed those kings who were the proper judges of men, and who, masters as they were, being grateful and of refined intellect, did not out of affection regard me as different from a son although there was the relation of servitude, which is subject to humiliation.

Malayaketu (*angrily*): You will deny it, calling it the sport of fate and not of your greed! Unrighteous man!

O ungrateful one, having employed the (poison) mind, dangerous by the use of virulent poison absorbed by her, you formerly consigned my father, disposed to trust you, to the domain of history. And now coveting the post of (the enemy's) minister, you have commenced, in order to work my destruction, to sell me off to the enemy like a steak of flesh.

Rakshasa (*aside*): This is a pimple on a boil. (*Stop his ears; aloud*.) God forbid, God forbid! I never set the poison-maid against Parvateshvara.

Malayaketu: Who then killed my father?

Rakshasa: Ask destiny.

Malayaketu (*angrily*): I should ask destiny, and not Kshapanaka Jivasiddhi?

Rakshasa (*aside*): What? Jivasiddhi too a spy of Chanakya! Alas! The enemies have captured my very heart.

Malayaketu (*in a rage*): Bhasuraka, give my order to Sekharasena thus: The five princes, Chitravarman of Kuluta, Simhanada, king of Malaya, Pushkaraksha, the Kashmira king, Sushena, king of Sindhu, and Meghanada of Persia, having formed a close friendship with Rakshasa, wish to gain Chandragupta's favour by designing against our person. Of these the first three covet my territory; they should be taken to a deep pit and buried with earth; the other two who wish to have my elephants should be killed by means of an elephant...(*to Rakshasa*): Go .... And serve Chandragupta with all your heart....

ACT VI

(*We learn that Chanakya has captured the Nanda forces. Rakshasa is in Pataliputra intent on rescuing his friend Chandanadasa. Chanakya has arranged for Rakshasa to hear that his loyal Chandanadasa is about to be executed.*)

ACT VII

(*Chandanadasa bids his wife and son farewell.*)

Chandanadasa: Dear wife, return now with your son. It is not proper to follow me further.

Wife (*weeping*): You leave, my dear, for the next world, not for a distant country.

Chandanadasa: Dear wife, I die for a friend's sake, and not for a personal crime. Grieve not therefore....

Wife: I shall be blessed if I follow my lord's feet (in death)....
(*Enter Rakshasa.*)

Rakshasa:...Here am I, the man for whose sake this person, though worthy of veneration, has incurred thy enmity, he who, the glorious one, saving another at the cost of his own life in these evil times of the Kali age in which the testes of the people are wicked, has rendered insignificant even the glory of Shibi, and who being pure in soul, has by his virtuous conduct eclipsed the course of conduct of the Buddhist saints....

(*Enter Chanakya.*)

Chanakya: Say, friend say,

Who bound with the skirt of his garment the fire red with the mass of its mighty flames? Who reduced the ever-moving wind to a state of stillness with snares? Who confined into a cage a lion with his mane still smelling of the rut-water of elephant? Who crossed by means of his arms the dreadful ocean, abounding in crocodiles and alligators?

Executioners: By your honour whose intellect is adept in statecraft.

Chanakya: No, no, say not so. Say—by fate, the inveterate foe of the house of Nanda.

Rakshasa (*aside*): This is the mean-minded—or rather noble-minded Kautalya.

The mine of all shastras, as the ocean is of jewels, with those merits we are not pleased, being simply jealous.

Chanakya (*looking at Rakshasa; joyfully, to himself*): Ah, here is the minister Rakshasa, by whom, the great-minded one,

The army of Vrishala and my own intelligence were seriously taxed for a long time with the heavy trouble of preparations, and of the devising of plans, which were the cause of protracted wakefulness. (*Removes his veil, approaches Rakshasa.*)

O minister Rakshasa, I, Vishnugupta, salute you.

Rakshasa (*aside*): "Minister" is a humiliating epithet now. (*Aloud.*) Vishnugupta, please do not touch me, polluted by the touch (of an executioner, a chandala).

Chanakya: O minister Rakshasa, these are not chandalas. This one is a royal official named Siddharthaka whom you have already seen. This other here too is a servant of the king, Samiddharthaka by name. Poor Shakatadasa also was made to write that forged letter by me, he knowing nothing (about its nature).... Those (your) servants, Bhadrabhata and others, the letter written in that way, that Siddharthaka, those three sets of decoration, that your friend Bhadanta, the man you saw in the old garden, and the trouble of the merchant, all these, oh valiant one, were devices of mine through my desire for Vrishala's union with you.

(*Enter Chandragupta*.)...

Chandragupta (*approaching Chanakya*): Venerable sir, Chandragupta bows to you.

Chanakya: All your desires have been accomplished. Salute, therefore, his honour, your prime minister.

Rakshasa (*aside*): He has established the relationship.

Chandragupta (approaching Rakshasa): Sir, Chandragupta bows to you....

Sir, just think—What have I not conquered in the world, when his honour and your honour are, as gurus, wide awake in the proper use of the six expedients?

Rakshasa (aside):...In this world a minister, although dull-minded, is sure to rise to an exalted position when he has to serve a proper person who is ambitious, whereas a minister, though of unerring policy, falls in the manner of a tree on the bank of a river when he has to deal with an unworthy master....

. . .

Chanakya:...If then you really wish to save Chandanadasa's life, accept this weapon (the badge of ministerial office)....

. . .

Unloose every tie except that of horses and elephants; having fulfilled my solemn declaration, I will now simply tie up my hair....

Valmiki, Vyasa and Kalidasa

Valmiki, Vyasa and Kalidasa are the essence of the history of ancient India; if all else were lost, they would still be its sole and sufficient cultural history. Their poems are types and exponents of three periods in the development of the human soul, types and exponents also of the three great powers which dispute and clash in the imperfect and half-formed temperament and harmonise in the formed and perfect. At the same time their works are pictures at once minute and grandiose of three moods of our Aryan civilisation, of which the first was predominatingly moral, the second predominatingly intellectual, the third predominatingly material. The fourth power of the soul, the spiritual, which can alone govern and harmonise the others by fusion with them, had not though it pervaded and powerfully influenced each successive development any separate age of predominance, and did not like the others possess the whole race with a dominating obsession.

It is because, conjoining in themselves the highest and most varied poetical gifts, they at the same time represent and mirror their age and humanity by their interpretative largeness and power, that our three chief poets hold their supreme place and bear comparison with the great world names, Homer, Shakespeare and Dante.

It has been said, truly, that the *Ramayana* represents an ideal society and assumed, illogically, that it must therefore represent an altogether imaginary one. That argument ignores the alternative of a real society idealised. No poet could evolve entirely out of his own imagination a picture at once so colossally so minute and so consistent in every detail. No number of poets could do it without stumbling into fatal incompatibilities either of fact or of view, such as we find defacing the *Mahabharata*. This is not place to discues the question of Valmikis age and authorship. This much, however, may be said the after excluding the Uttarakanda, which is a later work, and some amount of interpolation, for the most part easy enough to detect, and reforming the text which is not unfrequently in a state of truly shocking confusion, the *Ramayana* remains on the face of it the work of a single mighty and embracing mind. It is not easy to say whether it preceded or followed in date Vyasa's epic, it is riper in form and tone, has some aspects of a more advanced and mellow culture, and yet it gives the general impression of a younger humanity and an earlier, less sophisticated and complex mind.

The nature of the poem and much of its subject matter might at least justify the conclusion that Valmiki wrote in a political and social atmosphere much resembling that which surrounded Vyasa. He lived, that is to say, in an age approaching the present disorder and turmoil, of great revolutions and unbridled aristocratic violence when the governing chivalry, the Kshatriya caste, in its pride of strength was asserting its own code of morals as the one rule of conduct. We may note the plain assertion of this standpoint by Jarasandha in the *Mahabharata* and Valmiki's emphatic and repeated protest against it through the mouth of Rama. This ethical code was, like all aristocratic codes of conduct, full of high chivalry and the spirit of *noblesse oblige,* but a little loose in sexual morality on the masculine side and indulgent to violence and the strong hand. To the pure and delicate moral temperament of Valmiki, imaginative, sensitive, enthusiastic, shot through with rays of visionary idealism and eternal light, this looseness and violence were shocking and abhorrent. He could sympathise with them, as he sympathised with all that was wild and evil and anarchic, with the imaginative and poetical side of his nature, because he was a universal creative mind driven by his art sense to penetrate, feel and re-embody all that the world contained; but to his intellect and peculiar emotional temperament they were distasteful. He took refuge therefore in a past age of national greatness and virtue, distant enough to be idealised, but near enough to have left sufficient materials for a great picture of civilisation which would serve his purpose,—an age, it is important to note, of grandiose imperial equipoise, such as must have existed in some form at least since a persistent tradition of it runs through Sanskrit literature.

In the framework of his imperial age, his puissant magination created a marvellous picture of the human world as it might be if the actual and existing forms and materials of society were used to the best and purest advantage, and an equally marvellous picture of another non-human world in which aristocratic violence, strength, self-will, lust and pride ruled supreme and idealised or rather colossallised. He brought these two worlds into warlike collision by the hostile meeting of their champions and utmost evolutions of their peculiar character types, Rama and Ravana, and so created the *Ramayana,* the grandest and most paradoxical poem in the world, which becomes unmatchably sublime by disdaining all consistent pursuit of sublimity, supremely artistic by putting aside all the conventional limitations of art, magnificently dramatic by disregarding all dramatic illusion, and uniquely epic by handling the least as well as the most epic material. Not all perhaps can enter at once into the spirit of this masterpiece; but those who have once done so, will never admit any poem in the world as its superior.

My point here, however, is that it gives us the picture of an entirely moralised civilisation, containing indeed vast material development and immense intellectual power, but both moralised and subordinated to the needs of purity of temperament and delicate duality of action. Valmiki's mind seems nowhere to be familiarised with the high-strung intellectual gospel of a high and severe Dharma culminating in a passionless activity, raised to a supreme spiritual significance in the *Gita,* which is one great key-note of the *Mahabharata.* Had he known it, the strong leaven of sentimentalism and feminity in his nature might well have rejected it; such temperaments when they admire strength, admire it manifested and forceful rather than self-contained. Valmiki's characters act from emotional or imaginative enthusiasm, not from intellectual conviction; an enthusiasm of morality actuates Rama, an enthusiasm of immorality tyrannises over Ravana. Like all mainly moral temperaments, he instinctively insisted on one old established code of morals being universally observed as the only basis of ethical stability, avoided casuistic developments and distasted innovators in metaphysical thought as by their persistent and searching questions dangerous to the established bases of morality, especially to its wholesome ordinariness and every gayness. Valmik; therefore, the father of our secular poetry, stands for that early and finely moral civilisation which was the true heroic age of the Hindu spirit.

The poet of the *Mahabharata* lives nearer to the centre of an era of aristocratic turbulence and disorder. If there is any kernel of historic truth in the story of the poem, it records the establishment of those imperial forms of government and society which Valmiki had idealised. Behind its poetic legend, it celebrates and approves the policy of a great Kshatriya leader of men who aimed at the subjection of his order to the rule of a central imperial power which should typify its best tendencies and control or expel its worst. But while Valmiki was a soul out of harmony with its surroundings and looking back to an ideal past, Vyasa was a man of his time, full of its tendencies, hopeful of its results and looking forward to an ideal future. The one might be described as a conservative idealist advocating return to a better but departed model, the other as a progressive realist looking forward to a better but unborn mode. Vyasa, accordingly, does not revolt from the aristocratic code of morality; it harmonises with his own proud and strong spirit and he accepts it as a basis for conduct, but purified and transfigured by the illuminating idea of the *nishkama dharma.*

But, above all, intellectuality is his grand note; he is profoundly interested in ideas, in metaphysics, in ethical problems; he subjects morality to casuistic tests from which the more delicate moral tone of Valmiki's spirit shrank; he boldly erects above ordinary ethics a higher principle of conduct having its springs in intellect and strong character; he treats government and society from the standpoint of a practical and discerning statesmanlike mind, idealising solely for the sake of standard. He touches in fact all subjects, and what ever he touches he makes fruitful and interesting by originality, penetration and a sane and bold vision. In all this he is the son of the civilisation he has mirrored to us, a civilisation in which both morality and material development are powerfully intellectualised. Nothing is more remarkable in all the characters of the *Mahabharata* than this puissant intellectualism; every action of theirs seems to be impelled by an immense driving force of mind solidifying in character and therefore conceived and outlined as in stone. This orgiastic force of the intellect is at least as noticeable as the impulse of moral or immoral enthusiasm behind each great action of the *Ramayana*. Throughout the poem, the victorious and manifold mental activity of an age is prominent and gives its character to its civilisation. There is far more of thought in action than in the *Ramayana,* far less of thought in response; the one pictures a time of gigantic creative ferment and disturbance; the other, as far as humanity is concerned, an ideal age of equipoise, tranquillity and order.

Many centuries after those poets, perhaps a thousand years or even more, came the third great embodiment of the national consciousness, Kalidasa. There is a far greater difference between the civilisation he mirrors than between Valmiki's and Vyasa's. He came when the daemonic orgy of character and intellect had worked out and ended in producing at once its culmination and reaction in Budhism. There was everywhere noticeable a petrifying of the national temperament, visible to us in the tendency to codification, philosophy was being codified, morals were being codified, knowledge of any and every sort was being codified; it was on one side of its nature an age of scholars, legislators, dialecticians, philosophical formalisers. On the other side, the creative and aesthetic enthusiasm of the nation was pouring itself into things material, into the life of the senses, into the pride of life and beauty. The arts of painting, architecture, song, dance, drama, gardening, jewellery, all that can administer to the wants of great and luxurious capitals, received a grand impetus which brought them to their highest technical perfection. That this impetus came from Greek source or from the Buddhists seems hardly borne out the latter may rather have shared in the general tendencies of the time than originated them and the Greek theory gives us a maximum of conclusions with a minimum of facts. I do not think, indeed, it can be maintained that this period, call it classical or material or what one will, was marked off from its predecessor by any clear division such a partition would be contrary to the law of human development. Almost all the concrete features of the age may be found as separate facts in ancient India: codes existed from old time; art and drama were of fairly ancient origin, to whatever date we may assign their development; physical yoga processes existed almost from the first, and the material development portrayed in the *Ramayana* and *Mahabharata* is hardly less splendid than that of which the *Raghuvamsha* is so brilliant a picture. But whereas, before, these were subordinated to more lofty ideals, now they prevailed and became supreme, occupying the best energies of the race and stamping themselves on its life and consciousness. In obedience to this impulse the centuries between the rise of Buddhism and the advent of Shankaracharya became, though not agnostic and sceptical, for they rejected violently the doctrines of Charvaka, yet profoundly scientific and outward-going even in their spiritualism. It was therefore the great age of formalised metaphysics, science, law, art and the sensuous luxury which accompanies the arts.

Nearer the beginning than the end of this period, when India was systematising her philosophies and developing her arts and science, turning from Upanishad to Purana, from the high rarefied peaks of early Vedanta and Sankhya with their inspiring sublimities and bracing keenness to physical methods of ascetic yoga and the dry intellectualism of metaphysical logic or else to the warm sensuous humanism of emotional religion, before its full tendencies had asserted themselves, in some spheres before it had taken the steps its attitude portended, Kalidasa arose in Ujjayini and gathered up in himself its current tendencies while he foreshadowed many of its future developments. He himself must have been a man gifted with all the learning of his age, rich, aristocratic, moving wholly in high society, familiar with and fond of life in the most luxurious metropolis of his time, passionately attached to the arts acquainted with the sciences, deep in law and learning, versed in the formalised philosophies. He has some notable resemblances to Shakespeare: among others his business was, like Shakespere's, to sum up the immediate past in terms of the present: at the same time he occasionally informed the present with hints of the future. Like Shakespeare also he seems not to have cared deeply for religion.

In creed he was a Vedantist and in ceremony perhaps a Shiva-worshipper but he seems rather to have accepted these as the orthodox forms of his time and country, recommended to him by his intellectual preference and aesthetic affinities, than to have satisfied with them any profound religious want. In morals also he accepted and glorified the set and scientifically elaborate ethics of the codes, but seems himself to have been destitute of the finer elements of morality. We need not accept any of the ribald and witty legends with which the Hindu decadence surrounded his name; but no unbiased student of Kalidasa's poetry can claim for him either moral fervour or moral strictness. His writings show indeed a keen appreciation of high ideal and lofty thought, but the appreciation is aesthetic in its nature: he elaborates and seeks to bring out the effectiveness of these on the imaginative sense of the noble and grandiose, applying to the things of the mind and soul the same aesthetic standard as to the things of sense themselves. He has also the natural high aristocratic feeling for all that is proud and great and vigorous, and so far as he has it, he has exaltation and sublimity; but aesthetic grace and beauty and symmetry sphere in the sublime and prevent it from standing out with the bareness and boldness which is the sublime's natural presentation. His poetry has, therefore, never been, like the poetry of Valmiki and Vyasa, a great dynamic force for moulding heroic character or noble or profound temperament. In all this he represented the highly vital and material civilisation to which he belonged.

Yet some dynamic force a poet must have, some general human inspiration of which he is the supreme exponent; or else he cannot rank with the highest Kalidasa is the great, the supreme poet of the senses, of aesthetic beauty, of sensuous emotion. His main achievement is to have taken every poetic element, all great poetical forms, and subdued them to a harmony of artistic perfection set in the key of sensuous beauty. In continuous gift of seizing an object and creating it to the eye he has no rival in literature. A strong visualising faculty such as the greatest poets have in their most inspired descriptive moments, was with Kalidasa an abiding and unfailing power; and the concrete presentation which this definiteness of vision demanded, suffused with an intimate and sovereign feeling for beauty of colour and beauty of form, constitutes the characteristic Kalidasian manner. He is, besides, a consummate artist, profound in conception and suave in execution, a master of sound and language who has moulded for himself out infinite possibilities of the Sanskrit tongue a verse and diction which are absolutely the grandest, most puissant and most full-voiced of any human speech, a language of the Gods. The note struck by Kalidasa when he built Sanskrit into that palace of noble sound, is the note which meets us in almost all the best work of the classic literature. Its characteristic features of style are a compact but never abrupt brevity, a soft gravity and smooth majesty, a noble harmony of verse, a strong and lucid beauty of chiselled prose, above all, an epic precision of phrase, weighty, sparing and yet full of colour and sweetness. Moreover, it is admirably flexible, suiting itself to all forms the epic to the lyric, but most triumphantly to the two greatest, the epic and the drama. In his epic style Kalidasa adds to these permanent features a more than Miltonic fullness and grandiose pitch of sound and expression, in his dramatic and extraordinary grace and suavity which makes it adaptable to conversation and the expression of dramatic shade and subtly blended emotion.

With these supreme gifts, Kalidasa had the advantage of being born into an age with which he was in temperamental sympathy and a civilisation which lent itself naturally to his peculiar descriptive genius. It was an aristocratic civilisation, as indeed were those which had preceded it, but it far more nearly resembled the aristocratic civilisations of Europe by its material luxury, its aesthetic tastes, its polite culture, its keen worldly wisdom and its excessive appreciation of wit and learning. Religious and ethical thought and sentiment were cultivated such as in France under Louis XIV, more in piety and profession than as swaying the conduct; they pleased the intellect or else touched the sentiment, but did not govern the soul. It was bad taste to be irreligious, but it was not bad taste to be sensual or even in some respects immoral. The splendid and luxurious courts of this period supported the orthodox religion and morals out of convention, conservatism, the feeling for established order and the inherited tastes and prejudices of centuries, not because they fostered any deep religious or ethical sentiment. Yet they applauded high moral ideas if presented to them in cultured and sensuous poetry much in the same spirit that they applauded voluptuous description similarly presented. The ideals of morality were much lower than of old; free drinking was openly recognised and indulged in by both sexes; purity of life was less valued than in any other period of our civilisation. Yet the unconquerable monogamous instinct of the high-class Hindu woman seems to have prevented promiscuous vice and the disorganisation of the home which was the result of a similar state of society in ancient Rome, in Italy of the Reniascence, in France under the Bourbons and in England under the later Stuarts. The old spiritual tendencies were also rather latent than dead, the mighty pristine ideal still existed in theory—they are outlined with extra-ordinary grandeur by Kalidasa—nor had they yet been weakened or lowered to a less heroic key. It was a time in which one might expect to meet the extremes of indulgence side by side with the extremes of renunciation; for the inherent spirituality of the Hindu nature finally revolted against the splendid and unsatisfying life of the senses. But of this phase Bhartrihari and not Kalidasa is the poet. The greater writer lived evidently in the full heyday of the material age, and there is no sign of any setting in of the sickness and dissatisfaction and disillusionment which invariably follow a long outburst of materialism.

The flourishing of the plastic arts had prepared surroundings of great external beauty of the kind needed for Kalidasa's poetic work.

The appreciation of beauty in nature, of the grandeur of mountain and forest, the loveliness of lakes and rivers, the charm of bird and beast life had become a part of contemporary culture. These and the sensitive appreciation of trees and plants and hills as living things, the sentimental feeling of brotherhood with animals which had influenced and been encouraged by Buddhism, the romantic mythological world still farther romanticised by Kalidasa's warm humanism and fine poetic sensibility, gave him exquisite grace and grandeur of background and scenic variety. The delight of the eye, the delight of the ear, smell, palate, touch, the satisfaction of the imagination and taste are the texture of his poetical creation and into this he worked the most beautiful flowers of emotion and intellectual or aesthetic ideality. The scenery of his work is a universal paradise of beautiful things. All therein obeys one law of earthly grace; morality is aestheticised, intellect suffused and governed with the sense of beauty. And yet this poetry does not swim in languor, does not dissolove itself in sensuous weakness; it is not heavy with its own dissoluteness, heavy of curl and heavy of eyelid, cloyed by its own sweets, as the poetry of the senses usually is, Kalidasa is saved from this by the chastity of his style, his aim at burdened precision and energy of phrase, his unsleeping artistic vigilance.

As in the *Ramayana* and *Mahabharata*, we have an absorbing intellectual impulse or a dynamic force of moral or immoral excitement driving the characters, so we have in Kalidasa an intense hedonistic impulse thrilling through speech and informing action. An imaginative pleasure in all shades of thought and of sentiment, a rich delight of the mind in its emotions, a luxuriousness of ecstasy and grief, a free abandonment to amorous impulse and rapture, a continual joy of life and seeking of beauty mark the period when India, having for the time exhausted the possibilities of soul experience attainable through the spirit and the imaginative reason, was now attempting to find out the utmost each sense could feel, probing and sounding the soul-possibilities in matter and even seeking God through the senses.

The emotional religion of the Vaishnava Puranas which takes as its type the relation between the human soul and the Supreme, the passion of a woman for her lover, is already developing. The corresponding Tantric development of Shaivism may not yet have established itself fully; but the concretisation of the idea of Purusha-Prakriti, the union of Ishvara and Shakti, from which it arose, was already there in the symbolic legends of the Puranas, and one of these is the subject of Kalidasa's greatest epic poem. The *Birth of the War-God* stands on the same height in classical Sanskrit as the *Paradise Lost* in English literature; it is the masterpiece and *magnum opus* of the age on the epic level. The central idea of this great unfinished poem, the marriage of Shiva and Parvati, typified in its original idea the union of Purusha and Prakriti, the supreme Soul and dynamic divine legend was used esoterically to typify also the Nature-Souls'search for and attainment of God, and something of this conception pierces through the description of Parvati's seeking after Shiva.

Such was the age of Kalidasa, the temper of the civilisation which produced him; other poets of the time expressed one side of it or another, but his work is its splendid integral opitome, its picture of many composite hues and tones. Of the temperament of that civilisation the *Seasons* is an immature poetic self-expression, the *House of Raghu* the representative epic, the *Cloud Messenger,* the descriptive elegy, *Shakuntala* with its two ster love plays intimate dramatic pictures and the *Birth of the War-God* the grand religious fable. Kalidasa, who expressed so many sides and faces of it in writing, stands for its representative man and genius, as was Vyasa of the intellectual mood of Indian civilisation and Valmiki of its moral side.

It was the supreme misfortune of India that before she was able to complete the round of her experience and gather up the fruit of her millenniums of search and travail by commencing a fourth and more perfect age in which moral, intellectual and material development should be all equally harmonised and all spiritualised, the inrush of barbarians broke in finally on her endles solitary *tapasya* of effort and beat her national life into fragments. A preparation for such an age may be glimpsed in the new tendencies of spiritual seeking that began with Shankara and continued in later Vaishnavism and Shaivism and in new turns of poetry and art, but it found no opportunity of seizing on the life of the nation and throwing it into another mould. The work was interrupted before it had well begun; and India was left with only the remnants of the culture of the material age to piece out her existences even the little that was done afterwards, proved to be much; for it saved her from gradually petrifying and perishing as almost all the old civilisations of Assyria, Egypt, Greece, Rome, petrified and perished, as the material civilisation of Europe, unless spiritualised, must before long petrify and perish. That there is still an unexhausted vitality in her, that she yet nourishes the seeds of re-birth and renewal, we owe to Shankara and his successors and the great minds and souls that came after them. Will she yet arise anew, combine her past and continue the great dream where she left it off, shaking off on the one hand the soils and the filth that have grown on her in her period of downfall and futile struggle, and re-asserting on the other her peculiar individuality and national type against the callow civilisation of the West with its dogmatic and intolerant knowledge, its still more dogmatic and intolerant ignorance, its deification of selfishness and force, its violence and its ungoverned Titanism? In doing so lies her one chance of salvation.

The Muse of Kalidasa

Kalidasa, the most brilliant luminary in the literary firmament of the Gupta Age who has shed lustre on the whole of Sanskrit literature, is by common consent the greatest poet and dramatist that ever lived in India; and his works have enjoyed a high reputation and popularity throughout the ages. Yet, curiously enough, we know hardly anything about his life, and have no definite knowledge of the time when he flourished. As usual, numerous legends and anecdotes have gathered round his name, but they possess little historical value. These represent him as an idiot in early life who later became a great poet through the grace of goddess Kali, and died in Ceylon at the house of a hetaera. He is said to be one of the nine learned men (nine jewels) who graced the court of king Vikramaditya (or king Bhoja of Dhara). It is, however, almost certain that the different scholars who are referred to as his associates could not all have been his contemporaries. Most scholars regard as a historical fact his association with king Vikramaditya of Ujjain, and the deliberate change in the name of the hero of the *Vikramorvashiya* from Pururavas to Vikrama lends colour to it. Some regard this Vikramaditya as the ruler who, according to well established traditions, defeated the Shakas in B.C 58 and founded an era—the well-known Vikrama samvat—to commemorate this fact. Most modern scholars, however, do not believe that there was any king Vikramaditya in B.C. 58, or that Kalidasa flourished at so early a period. The general opinion seems to be that he lived at the court of a Gupta Emperor, most probably Chandragupta II, who was also known as Vikramaditya, and, having defeated the Shaka satraps, could well lay claim to the title Shakari which is associated with the Vikramaditya of tradition. The only definite data about the date of Kalidasa is that he must have flourshed after Agnimitra (c. B.C. 150), who is the hero of one of his drames, and before A.D. 634, the date of the famous Aihole inscription which refers to him as a great poet. If, as is held by competent scholars, some verses in the Mandasor Inscription of A.D. 473 indicate knowledge cf Kalidasa's works, the lower limit of his date may be fixed at about A.D 450. The theory that Kalidasa flourished in the Gupta Age is now generally accepted and is supported by various arguments, viz. that he borrowed from Ashvaghosha and Vatsyayana's *Kamasutra* and revised *Setubandha* of the Vakataka king Pravarasena II, that his works contain veiled allusions to the names of Gupta Emperors, that he knew of the Huna invasion, etc. But these are all mere conjectures which do not carry conviction. While it may be permissible to argue that "the balance of evidence suggests that the end of the fourth century A.D. is the most probable date of the poet," we must admit that the evidence adduced in support of it is neither definite, nor direct and decisive. The safest course is to hold that Kalidasa flourished some time between 100 B.C. and A.D. 450.

A close perusal of his works shows that Kalidasa was a pious Brahman of Ujjain and a liberal Shaiva by belief, who had acquired a knowledge of the various branches of Brahmanical learning and gathered vast experience by travelling far and wide throughout India. He shows his familiarity with the whole range of Vedic literature, the philosophical systems, especially the Sankhya and Yoga, the various works on Dharmashastra, the *Kamasutra,* Natyashastra, Vyakarana, Jyotishashastra, and even fine arts like music, drawing and painting. His versatile genius, his acquaintance with court etiquette, his shrewdness, his modesty, not without a due sense of self-respect, and his poetic talent are very well reflected in his works which are all permeated with a feeling of ease contentment "perfect satisfaction with the existing order of things".

The best known work of Kalidasa is his drama *Shakuntala.* This play is, by common consent, one of the best not only in Sanskrit literature, but in the literature of the world. Kalidasa has based the play on the story of Shakuntala as found in the *Mahabharata,* but he has breathed quite a new and vital spirit into it by introducing several slight but effective changes in the original and also by adding to it some altogether new characters and incidents of high dramatic power. Thus, for example, while the *Mahabharata* shows Kanva as having gone out merely for fetching flowers, etc., Kalidasa sends him, on a plausible ground, further away, thus postponing his return to the hermitage to an indefinite future. Similarly in the original we find Shakuntala herself narrating the story of her birth to the king and later on bargaining with him before accepting his suit. Kalidasa, with his dramatic instinct, has made Amasuya, a friend of Shakuntala, narrate Shakuntala's past (and that too with proper decorum), while the idea of bargaining has been altogether dropped, only to give us an exquisitely charming picture of the working of love in the heart of a young innocent maiden. The curse of the wrathful Durvasas, the loss of the ring, the scene of the fisherman and the concluding portion of the play, which charm the audience by creating alternately an atmosphere of suspense and relief, are products of Kalidasa's genius. By these dramatic touches, Kalidasa has created a magnificent edifice out of the brick and mortar supplied by the *Mahabharata*. He has succeeded, not only in rescuing the hero and the heroin from the crudities under which they labour in the original and bestowing on them the vital qualities required in a hero or a heroine worth the name but also in giving us a very fine portrait of an ideal king Dushyanta, and a bewitchingly transporting picture of the life of a truly Indian maiden in all the three important stages. A loving sympathy with nature forms the background of this play in which Kalidasa has also displayed his mastery in delineating sentiment, his wonderful skill in characterisation, construction of plots and creating dramatic situations, as well as his great lyrical gifts. The dramatic power and poetic beauties of this unique work have elicited the highest praise and admiration from scholars all over the world.

Before *Shakuntala*, Kalidasa had already composed two plays, the *Malavikagnimitra* and the *Vikramorvashiya*. The former is a court comedy wherein king Agnimitra falls in love with a maid in the service of one of his queens and, in spite of repeated obstacles on the part of the queen, at last succeeds in his project with the help of his friend, the Vidushaka. There can be little doubt that this is the first play composed by the poet as is apparent from the way in which he has in the prologue tried to plead on behalf of the new poem, *nava kavya*. In spite of several defects, the play bears the unmistakable stamp of Kalidasa's workmanship; and his authorship of it can hardly be doubted. The *Vikramorvashiya* is a fairy-tale of the love of a celestial nymph and a mortal. Mme de Willman-Grabowska considers this to be the last of Kalidasa's plays and remarks that "it already shows signs of commencing decline". Some hold that the play was very probably composed on the occasion of the installation of Kumaragupta as *Yuvaraja.* Welding together the elements of the ancient Vedic legend found in the *Rig-Veda* and the *Shatapatha-Brahmana* and its versions in the *Vishnu* and *Bhagavata Puranas* and possibly also in the *Brihatkatha,* Kalidasa has introduced therein several incidents and scenes of his own creation. In this play he seems to have concentrated more on characterisation than on plot-construction as he has done in the *Malavikagnimitra.* But the most debated portion of the play is Act IV where the hero, distracted by separation, gives vent to his feelings in short, sweet, and pathetic lyrics. These in themselves are exquisite, but they detract from the movement and dramatic power of the composition. But it is this very defect that constitutes for posterity the peculiar charm of the work and has won for Kalidasa such a high degree of popularity.

Kalidasa's genius shone with equal brilliance both in drama and in poetry or Kavya. His two Mahakavyas, *Raghuvamsha* and *Kumarasambhava,* and the lyrical poem *Meghaduta* are universally regarded as gems of Sanskrit poetry. The *Kumarasambhava* in eighteen cantos tells us the story of the birth of Kumara, the son of Shiva and Parvati, who led the celestial forces and vanquished the demon Taraka. Commentators like Mallinatha have commented only on the first eight cantos of this poem, and one of them has in clear terms recorded the belief that the poem was left incomplete owing to the curse of Parvati whose anger was provoked by the descriptions in Canto VIII. It is also evident that the later cantos are much inferior in poetic power and hence they are not regarded as the work of Kalidasa. It would seem, therefore, that Kalidasa left this work incomplete; for the title of *Kumarasambhava* requires that at least the birth of Kumara should be included in the poem. Kalidasa has displayed considerable skill in delineating the main characters and the poem contains several passages of enchanting beauty, such as the *Rativilapa,* the conversation between Parvati and God Shiva in the guise of a Jatila, the description of the Himalaya in Canto I, and of the sudden advent of spring in Canto III. The poet, however, has exposed himself to criticism at the hands of rhetoricians like Anandavardhana by indulging in what may be called sacrilegious description in the eighth canto.

In the *Raghuvamsha* the poet has set himself the onerous task of describing the varied incidents in the lives of several monarchs, who though possessed of some common characteristics, must needs have individuality of their own; and it must be admitted that he has achieved his purpose in a superb manner. The merit of *Raghuvamsha* as a Mahakavya is unquestioned and the Indian estimate of it is well reflected in the fact that our poet is pre-eminently known as *Raghukara* (author of *Raghuvamsha*). This poem, which is based on the *Ramayana* and some Puranas, describes in all thirty kings of the Solar race among whom Raghu appears to be singularly fortunate in having not only illustrious ancestors but also illustrious descendants for at least three immediate successor. That seems to be the reason why Kalidasa named his poem after Raghu. This poem as we have it, is evidently also incomplete, breaking off with the description of the lascivious Agnivarna. In spite of the reports of the existence of more cantos it is likely that Kalidas composed it only up to the end of the 19th canto and left it there owing to illness or death. This poem also, like its compeer *Kumarasambhava,* has several enchanting sections, the most appealing among them being the *Ajavilapa*.

Among the lesser poems of Kalidasa, the *Ritusamhara* is now generally accepted as his first work, though some have recently expressed doubts about his authorship of it. The neglect by rhetoricians and commentators and also its inferiority in some respects need not, however detract from its genuineness. Its subject is so simple and so devoid of opportunities for characterisation, etc. that it naturally failed to evoke much interest. It contains six cantos describing the six seasons bearing ample testimony to the poet's minute observation and love of nature.

The *Meghaduta* is, however, among the most fascinating little poems that ever came to be written in Sanskrit. In a little over a hundred verses the poet has displayed the vitality and versatility of his poetic genius. An imaginary Yaksha, separated from his beloved through his master's curse and maddened with pangs of separation at the sight of a cloud, requests this cloud to carry his message from Ramagiri—for that was where he was in exile—to Alaka, the abode of his beloved, and describes in detail the path it should follow and the various places of interest that it would traverse. The poet has chosen the Mandakranta metre and has thus given us a complete picture in each of the constituent verses. This poem has been variously called a lyric, an elegy or even a monody, though Sthiradeva would insist on calling it a Mahakavya, while Vallabhadeva would call it only a Khandakavya, Rama-giri, where three Yaksha was in exile, is now identified with

Ramtek near Nagpur. The story of Ashadha-Krishna Ekadashi, Yoginimahatmya, is said to be the source of the theme of this poem. This exquisite little poem has evoked the highest admiration of literary critics of all ages. According to a modern European writer "it is difficult to praise too highly either the brilliance of the description of the cloud's progress or the pathos of the picture of the wife, sorrowful and alone."

As to the comparative merits of the different poetical works of Kalidasa, the same critic observes: "Indian criticism has ranked *Meghaduta* highest among Kalidasa's poems for brevity of expression, richness of content, and power to elicit sentiment, and the praise is not undeserved.... To modern taste the *Kumarasambhava* appeals more deeply by reason of its richer variety, the brilliance of its fancy and the greater warmth of its felling.... Though inferior in some slight degree to the *Kumarasambhava,* the *Raghuvamsha* may rightly be ranked as the finest Indian specimen of the Mahakavya as defined by writers on poetics."

Kalidasa is "unquestionably the finest master of Indian poetic style", and his inimitable skill in the use of the simile has become proverbial. His charming and graceful diction, the refinement of his language and sentiments, his minute observations of man and nature, his innate sense of beauty, his masterly use of metaphors and other figures of speech, his elevation of thought and suggestiveness of expression have immortalised him, and as has been aptly expressed, his works will endure so long as human beings retain a taste for great literature.

Both in drama and poetry Kalidasa stands not only unsurpassed but even unrivalled. Nevertheless, many other poets and dramatists flourished during the age and some of them were not unworthy successors of the great poet.

(III) SHAKUNTALA

> "Wouldst thou the young year's blossoms and the fruits of its decline,
> And all by which the soul is charmed, entraptured, feasted, fed,
> Wouldst thou the earth and heaven itself in one sole name combine?
> I name thee, O Shakuntala, and all at once is said."
>
> —*Goethe.*

Goethe, the master-poet of Europe, has summed up his criticism of *Shakuntala* in a single quatrain; he has not taken the poem to pieces.

This quatrain seems to be a small thing like the flame of a candle, but it lights up the whole drama in an instant and reveals its inner nature. In Goethe's words, *Shakuntala* blends together the young year's blossoms and the fruits of its maturity; it combines heaven and earth in one.

We are apt to pass over this eulogy as a mere poetical outburst. We are apt to consider that it only means in effect that Goethe regarded *Shakuntala* as fine poetry. But it is not really so. His stanza breathes not be exaggeration of rapture, but the deliberate judgment of a true critic. There is a special point in his words. Goethe says expressly that *Shakuntala* contains the history of a development—the development of flower into fruit of earth into heaven, of matter into spirit.

In truth there are unions in *Shakuntala,* and the motif of the play is the progress from the earlier union of the First Act, with its earthly, unstable beauty and romance, to the higher union in the heavenly hermitage of eternal bliss described in the Last Act. This drama was meant not for dealing with a particular passion, not for developing a particular character, but for translating the whole subject from one world to another,—to elevate love from the sphere of physical beauty to the eternal heaven of moral beauty.

With the greatest ease Kalidasa has effected this junction of earth with heaven. His earth so naturally passes into heaven that we do not mark the boundary-line between the two. In the First Act the poet has not concealed the gross earthiness of the fall of Shakuntala: he has clearly shown, in the conduct of the hero and the heroine alike, how much desire contributed to that fall. He has fully painted all the blandishments, playfulness and flutterings of the intoxicating sense of youth, the struggle between deep bashfulness and strong self-expression. This is a proof of the simplicity of Shakuntala she was not prepared beforehand for the outburst of passion which the occasion of Dushyanta's visit called forth; she had not learned how to restrain herself, how to hide her feelings. Shakuntala had not know Cupid before; hence her heart was bare of armour, and she could not distrust either the sentiment of love or the character of her lover. The daughter of the hermitage was off her guard, just as the deer there know not fear.

Dushyanta's conquest of Shakuntala has been very naturally drawn. With equal ease has the poet shown the deeper purity of her character in spite of her fall,—her unimpaired, innate chastity. This is another proof of her simplicity.

The flower of the forest needs no servant to brush the dust off her petals. She stands bare; dust settles on her; but in spite of it she easily retains her own beautiful cleanliness. Dust did settle on Shakuntala, but she was not even conscious of it. Like the simple wild deer, like the mountain spring, she stood forth pure in spite of it.

Kalidasa has let his hermitage-bred youthful heroin follow the unsuspecting path of nature; nowhere has he restrained her. And yet he has developed her into the model of a devoted wife, with her reserve, endurance of sorrow, and the life of rigid spiritual discipline. At the beginning we see her self-forgetful and obedient to Nature's impulses like the plants and flowers; at the end we see the deeper feminine soul,—sober, patient under ill, intent on austerities, strictly regulated by the sacred laws of piety. With matchless art Kalidasa has placed his heroine on the meeting-point of action and calmness, of Nature and Law, of river and ocean, as it were. Her birth was the outcome of interrupted austerities, lest her nurture was in a hermitage, which is just the sport where nature and austerities, beauty and restraint, are harmonised. There is none of the conventional bonds of society there, yet we have the harder regulations of religion. Her Gandharva marriage, too, as of the same type; it had the wildness of Nature joined to the social tie of wedlock. The drama stands alone and unrivalled in all literature, because it depicts how restraint can be harmonised with freedom. All its joys and sorrow, unions and partings, proceed from the conflict of these two forces.

Shakuntala's simplicity is natural, that of Miranda of truly so. The different circumstances under which the two were brought up, account for this difference. Shakuntala's simplicity was not girt round by ignorance, as was the case with Miranda. We see in the First Act that Shakuntala's two companions did not let her remain unaware of the fact that she was in the first bloom of youth. She had learnt to be bashful. She also knew something of the world, because the hermitage did not stand altogether outside society; the rules of home-life were observed hero too. She was inexperienced, though not ignorant, of the outside world; but trustfulness was firmly enthroned in her heart. The simplicity which springs from such trustfulness had for a moment caused her fall, but it also redeemed her for ever. The trustfulness kept her constant to patience, forgiveness and loving kindness, in spite of the cruellest breach of her confidence. Miranda's simplicity was never subjected to such a fiery ordeal; it never clashed with knowledge of the world.

Our rebellious passions raise storms. In this drama Kalidasa has extinguished the volcanic fire of tumultuous passion by means of the tears of the penitent heart. But he has not dealt too long on the disease; he has just given us a glimpse of it and then dropped the veil. The desertion of Shakuntala by the polygamous Dushyanta, which in real life would have happened as a natural consequence of his character, is here brought about by the curse of Durvasa. Otherwise, the desertion would have been extremely cruel and pathetic and would have destroyed the peace and harmony of the whole play. But the poet has left a small front in the veil through which we can get an idea of the royal sin. It is in the Fifth Act. Just before Shakuntala arrives at court and is repudiated by her husband, the poet momentarily draws aside the curtain from the King's love-affairs. Queen Hamsapadika is singing to herself in her music room:

"O honey-bee, having sucked the mango blossoms in your search for new honey, you have clean forgotten your recent loving welcome by the lotus."

This tear-stained song of a stricken heart in the royal harem gives us a rude shock, especially as our heart was hitherto filled with Dushyanta's love-passages with Shakuntala. Only in the preceding Act we saw Shakuntala setting out for her husband's home in a very holy, sweet, and tender mood, carrying with herself the blessings of the hoary sage Kanva and the good wishes of the whole forest world. And now a stain falls on the picture we had so hopefully formed of the home of love to which she was going.

When the Jester asked, "What means this song" Dushyanta smiled and said, "We desert our lasses after a short spell of love-making, and therefore I have deserved this strong rebuke from Queen Hamsapadika." This indication of the fickleness of royal love is not purposeless at the beginning of the Fifth Act. With masterly skill the poet here shows that what Durvasa's curse had brought about had its seeds in human nature.

In passing from the Fourth Act to the Fifth we suddenly enter a new atmosphere; from the ideal world of the hermitage we go forth to the royal court with its hard hearts and crooked ways of love-making. The beauteous dream of the hermitage is about to be broken. The two young monks who are escorting Shankuntala, at once feel that they have entered an altogether different world, "a house encircled by fire". By such touches at the beginning of the Fifth Act, the poet prepares us for the repudiation of Shakuntala at its end.

Then comes the repudiation. Shakuntala feels as if she has been suddenly struck with a thunderbolt. Like a deer stricken by a trusted hand, this daughter of the forest looks on with blank surprise, terror and anguish. At one blow she is hurled away from the hermitage, both literal and metaphorical, in which she has so long lived. She loses her connection with the loving friends, the birds, beasts and plants and the beauty, peace and purity of her former life. She now stands along, shelterless. In one moment the music of the first four Acts is stilled.

O the deep silence and loneliness that then surround her! She whose tender heart had made the whole world of the hermitage her own folk, today stands absolutely alone. She fills this vast vacuity with her mighty sorrows. With rare poetic insight Kalidasa has declined to restore Shakuntala to Kanva's hermitage. After the renunciation by Dushyanta it was impossible for her to live in harmony with that hermitage in the way she had done before. She was no longer her former self; her relation with the universe had changed. Had she been placed again amidst her old surroundings, it would only have cruelly exhibited the utter inconsistency of the whole situation. A mighty silence was now needed, worthy of the mighty grief of the mourner. But the poet has not shown us the picture of Shakuntala in the new hermitage—parted from the friends of her girlhood, and nursing the grief of separation from her lover. The silence of the poet only deepens our sense of the silence and vacancy which here reigned round Shakuntala. Had the repudiated wife been taken back to Kanva's home, that hermitage would have spoken. To our imagination its trees and creepers would have wept, the two girl friends would have mourned for Shakuntala, even if the poet had not said a word about it. But in the unfamiliar hermitage of Maricha all is still and silent to us; only we have before our mind's eye a picture of the world-abandoned Shakuntala's infinite sorrow, disciplined by penance, sedate and resigned—seated like a recluse rapt in meditation.

Dushyanta is now consumed by remorse. This remorse is *lapasya*. So long as Shakuntala was not won by means of this repentance, there was no glory in winning her. One sudden gust of youthful impulse had in a moment given her up to Dushyanta, but that was not the true, the full winning of her. The best means of winning is by devotion, by *tapasya*. What is easily gained is as easily lost. Therefore, the poet has made the two lovers undergo a long and austere *tapasya* that they may gain each other truly, eternally. If Dushyanta had accepted Shakuntala when she was first brought to his court, she would have only added to the number of Hamsapadikas, occupied a corner of the royal harem, and passed the rest of her life in neglect, gloom and uselessness.

It was a blessing in disguise for Shakuntala that Dushyanta abjured her with cruel sternness. When afterwards this cruelty reacted on himself, it prevented him from remaining indifferent to her. His unceasing and intense grief fused his heart and welded Shakuntala with it. Never before had the king met with such an experience. Never before had he had the occasion and means of loving truly. Kings are unlucky in this respect; their desires are so easily satisfied that they never get what is to be gained by devotion alone. Fate now plunged Dushyanta into deep grief and thus made him worthy of true love—made him renounce the role of a rake.

Thus has Kalidasa burnt away vice in the internal fire of the sinner's heart; he has not tried to conceal it from the outside. When the curtain drops on the last Act, we feel that all the evil has been destroyed as on a funeral pyre, and the peace born of a perfect and satisfactory fruition reigns in our hearts. He has made the physical union of Dushyanta and Shakuntala tread the path of sorrow and thereby chastened and sublimated it into a moral union. Hence did Goethe rightly say that *Shakuntala* combines the blossoms of Spring with the fruits of Autumn, it combines Heaven and Earth. Truly in *Shankuntala* there is one Paradise lost and another regained.

The poet has shown how the union on Dushyanta and Shakuntala in the First Act as mere lovers is futile, while their union in the Last Act as the parents of Bharata is a true union. The First Act is full of brilliancy and movement. We there have a hermit's daughter in the exuberance of youth, her two companions running over with playfulness, the newly flowering forest creeper, the bee intoxicated with perfume, the fascinated king peeping from behind the trees. From this Eden of Bliss, Shakuntala, the mere sweet-heart of Dushyanta, is exiled in disgrace. But far different was the aspect of the other hermitage where Shakuntala—the mother of Bharata and the incarnation of goodness—took refuge. There no hermit girls water the trees, nor bedew the creepers with their loving sister-like looks, nor feed the young fawn with handfuls of paddy. There a single boy fills the loving bosom of the entire forest world; he absorbs all the loveliness of the trees, creepers, flowers and foliage. The matrons of the hermitage, in their loving anxiety, are fully taken up with the unruly boy. When Shankuntala appears, we see her clad in a dusty robe, face pale with austerities, doing the penance of a lorn wife, pure-souled. Her long penances have purged her of the evil of her first union with Dushyanta; she is now invested with a new dignity, she is the image of motherhood, gentle and exquisite. Who can repudiate her now?

The poet has shown here, as in *Kumarasambhava,* that the Beauty that goes hand with Moral Law is eternal, that the calm, controlled and beneficent form of Love is its best expression, that Beauty is truly charming under restraint and decays quickly when it gets wild and unfettered. This ancient poet of India refuses to recognise Love as its own highest glory; he proclaims that Goodness is the final goal of Love. He teaches us that the love of man and woman is neither beautiful, nor lasting, so long as it remains self-centred, so long as it does not yield fruit, so long as it does not diffuse itself over son and daughter, guests and neighbours.

The two peculiar principles of India are the beneficent tie of home life on the one hand, and the liberty of the soul abstracted from the world on the other. In the world India is variously connected with many races and many creeds; she cannot reject any of them. But on the altar of devotion (*tapasya*) India sits alone. Kalidasa has shown, both in *Shakuntala* and *Kumarasambhava,* that there is a harmony between these two principles, an easy transition from the one to the other. In his hermitage human boys play with lion cubs, and the hermit spirit is reconciled with the spirit of the householder.

On the foundation of the hermitage of recluses Kalidasa has built the home of the householder. He has rescued the relation of the sexes from the sway of lust and enthroned it in the holy and pure seat of asceticism. In the sacred books of the Hindus the ordered relation of the sexes has been defined by strict injunctions and laws. Kalidasa has demonstrated that relation by means of the elements of Beauty.

The Beauty that he adores is lit up by grace, modest and goodness; in its range it embraces the whole universe. It is fulfilled by renunciation, gratified by sorrow, and rendered eternal by religion. In the midst of this Beauty, the impetuous, unruly love of man and woman has restrained itself and attained to a profound peace, like a wild torrent merged in the ocean of Goodness. Therefore is such love higher and more wonderful than wild and unrestrained passion.

R.C. Dutt's Translation of the Epics

During the years 1898 and 1899, Mr. Dutt worked at what Professor Max Müller considered the almost impossible task of translating into English verse the kernel of the great Epics of ancient India. But Mr. Dutt was never deterred by the difficulty of any task which, after mature consideration, he took up. He went on with his work, and when the "Mahabharata" was completed, he presented to copy of it to the Oxford Professor. Professor Max Müller was so charmed and astonished with the result that he readily consented to write an introduction.

The "Mahabharata" appeared in August 1898, and exactly a year afterwards his "Ramayana" saw the light. In his luminous epilogues to these two works, Mr. Dutt explains both the scope of the Epics and the method pursued by him.

In the epilogue to the "Mahabharata" he wrote:

> The work went on growing for a thousand years after it was first compiled and put together in the form of an Epic; until the crystal rill of the Epic itself was all but lost in an unending morass of religious and didactic episodes, legends, tales, and traditions. The modern reader will now understand the reason why this great Epic—the greatest work of imagination that Asia has produced—has never yet been put before the European reader in a readable form. A poem of ninety thousand couplets, about seven times the size of the "Iliad" and the "Odyssey" put together, is more than what the average reader can stand; and the heterogeneous nature of its contents does not add to the interest of the work.

> But, although the old Epic has thus been spoilt by unlimited expansions, yet, nevertheless, the leading incidents and characters of the real Epic are still discernible, uninjured by the mass of foreign substance in which they are embedded, even like those immortal marble figures which have been recovered from the ruins of an ancient world, and now beautify the museums of modern Europe. For years past I have thought that it was perhaps not impossible to exhume this buried Epic from the superincumbent mass of episodical matter, and to restore it to the modern world. For years past I have felt a longing to undertake this work, but the task was by no means an easy one. Leaving out all episodical matter, the leading narrative of the Epic forms about one-fourth of the work; and a complete translation even of this leading story would be unreadable, both from its length and its prolixness. On the other hand, to condense the story into shorter limits would be, not to make a translation, but virtually to write a new poem; and that was not what I desired to undertake, nor what I was competent to perform.
>
> There seemed to me only one way out of this difficulty. The main incidents of the Epic are narrated in the original work in passages which are neither diffuse nor unduly prolix, and which are interspersed in the leading narrative of the Epic, as that narrative itself is interspersed in the midst of more lengthy episodes. The more carefully I examined the arrangement, the more clearly it appeared to me that these main incidents of the Epic would bear a full and unabridged translation into English verse; and that these translations, linked together by short connecting notes, would virtually present the entire story of the Epic to the modern reader in a form and within limits which might be acceptable. It would be, no doubt, a condensed version of the original Epic, but the condensation would be effected not by linking together those passages of the original which describe the main and striking incidents, and thus telling the main story as told that, in the passages presented to the reader, it is the poet who speaks to him, not the translator. Though vast portions of the original are skipped over, those which are presented are the portions which narrate the main incidents of the Epic, and they describe those incidents as told by the poet himself.

Accepting the dictum of Stopford Brooke—that prose no more represents poetry than architecture does music, and that translations of poetry are never much good, but at least they should always endeavour to have the musical movement of poetry and to obey the laws of the verse they translate—Mr. Dutt decided to render his translation into verse.

One of my greatest difficulties in the task I have undertaken has been to try and preserve something of the "musical movement" of the sonorous Sanskrit poetry in the English translation. Much of the Sanskrit Epic is written in the well-known *sloka* metre of sixteen syllables in each line, and I endeavoured to choose some English metre which is familiar to the English ear, and which would reproduce to some extent the rhythm, the majesty, and the measured sweep of the Sanskrit verse. It was necessary to adopt such a metre in order to transfer something of the truth about the "Mahabharata" into English, for without such reproduction or imitation of the musical movement of the original, very much less than a half truth is told. My kind friend, Mr Edmund Russell, impelled by that enthusiasm for Indian poetry and Indian art which is part of him rendered me valuable help and assistance in this matter, and I gratefully acknowledge the benefit I have derived from his advice and suggestions. After considerable trouble and anxiety, and after rendering several books in different English metres, I felt convinced that the one finally adopt was a nearer approach to the Sanskrit *sloka* than any other familiar English metre known to me.

It would be too much to assume that even with the help of this similarity in metres, I have been able to transfer into my English that sweep and majesty of verse which is the charm of Sanskrit, and which often sustains and elevates the simplest narration and the plainest ideas. Without the support of those sustaining wings, my poor narration must often plod through the dust, and I can only ask for the indulgence of the reader, which every translator of poetry from a foreign language can with reason ask, if the story as told in the translation is sometimes but a plain, simple, and homely narrative. For any artistic decoration I have neither the inclination nor the necessary qualification. The crisp and ornate style, the quaint expression, the chiselled word, the new-coined phrase, in which modern English poetry is rich, would scarcely suit the translation of an old Epic whose predominating characteristic is its simple and easy flow of narrative. Indeed, the "Mahabharata" would lose that unadorned simplicity which is its first and foremost feature if the translator ventured to decorate it with the art of the modern day, even if he had been qualified to do so.

For if there is one characteristic feature which distinguishes the "Mahabharata" (as well as the other Indian Epic, the "Ramayana") from all later Sanskrit literature, it is the grand simplicity of its narrative, which contrasts with the artificial graces of later Sanskrit poetry. The poetry Kalidasa, for instance, is oranate and beautiful and almost scintillates with similes in every verse; the poetry of the "Mahabharata" is plain and unpolished, and scarcely stoops to a simile, or a figure of speech unless the simile comes naturally to the poet. The great deeds of godlike king sometimes suggest to the poet the mighty deeds of gods; the rushing of warriors suggests the rushing of angry elephants in the echoing jungle; the flight of whistling arrows suggests the light of sea-birds; the sound and movement of surging crowds, the heaving of billows; the erect attitude of a warrior suggests a tall cliff; the beauty of a maiden suggests the soft beauty of the blue lotus. When such comparisons come naturally to the poet, he accepts them and notes them down, but he never seems to go in quest of them, he is never anxious to beautify and decorate. He seems to trust entirely to his grand narrative, to his heroic characters to his stirring incidents to hold million listeners in perpetual thrall. The majestic and sonorous Sanskrit metre is at his command, and even this he uses carelessly, and with frequent slips, known as *arsha* to later grammarians. The poet certainly seeks for no art to decorate his tale he trusts to the lofty chronicle of bygone heroes to enchain the listening mankind.

And what heroes! In the delineation of character the "Mahabharata" is far above anything which we find in later Sanskrit poetry. Indeed, with much that is fresh and sweet and lovely in later Sanskrit poetry, there is tittle or no portraiture of character. All heroes are cast much in the same heroic mould; all love-sick heroines suffer in silence and burn with fever; all fools are shrewd and impudent by turns; all knaves are heartless and cruel, and suffer in the end. There is not much to distinguish between one warrior and another, between one tender women and her sister. In the "Mahabharata" we find just the reverse; each hero has a distinct individuality, a character of his own, clearly discernible for that of other heroes. No work of the imagination that could be named, always excepting the "Iliad", is so rich and so true as the "Mahabharata" in the portraiture of the human character, not in torment and suffering as in Dante, not under overwhelming passions as in Shakespeare, but human character in its calm dignity of strength and repose, like those immortal figures in marble which the ancients turned out, and which modern sculptors have vainly sought to reproduce. The old Kuru monarch Dhritarashtra, sightless and feeble, but majestic in his ancient grandeur; the noble grandsire Bhishma, "death's subduer," and unconquerable in war; the doughty Drona, venerable priest and vengeful warrior, and the proud and peerless archer Karna have each a distinct character of his own which cannot be mistaken for a moment. The good and royal Yadhishthir (I omit the final a in some long names which occur frequently), the "tiger-waised" Bhima, and the "helmet-wearing" Arjun are the Agamemnon, the Ajax and the Achilles of the Indian Epic. The proud and unyielding Duryodhan, and the fierce and fiery Duhsasan stand out foremost among the wrathful sons of the feeble old Kuru monarch. And Krishna possesses a character higher than that of Ulysses; unmatched in human wisdom, ever striving for righteousness and peace, he is thorough and unrelenting in war when war has begun. And the women of the Indian Epic possess characters as marked as those of the men. The stately and majestic Queen Gandhari, the loving and doting mother Pritha, the proud and scornful Draupadi nursing her wrath till her wrongs are fearfully revenged, and the bright and brilliant and suny Subhadra, these are distinct images pencilled by the hand of a true master in the realm of creative imagination.

And if the characters of the "Mahabharata" impress themselves on the reader, the incidents of the Epic are not less striking. Every scene on the shifting stage is a perfect and impressive picture. The Tournament of the princes in which Arjun and Karna—the Achilles and Hector of the India Epic—first met, and each marked the other for his foe; the gorgeous bridal of Draupadi; the equally gorgeous coronation of Yudhishthr, and the death of the proud and boisterous Sisupala; the fatal game of dice, and the scornful wrath of Draupadi against her insulters; the calm beauty of the forest life of the Pandavs; the cattle-lifting in Matsyaland in which the gallant Arjun threw off his disguise and stood forth as warrior and conqueror; and the Homeric speeches of the warriors in the council is war on the even of the great contest—each scene of this venerable old Epic impresses itself on the mind of the hushed and astonished reader. Then follows the war of eighteen days. The first few days are more or less uneventful, and have been condensed in this translation often into a few couplets; but the interest of the reader increases as he approaches the final battle and fall of the grand old fighter Bhishma. Then follows the stirring story of the death of Arjun's gallant boy, and Arjun's fierce revenge, and the death of the priest and warrior, doughty Drona. Last comes the crowning event of the Epic, the final contest between Arjun and Karna, the heroes of the Epic, and the ends in a midnight slaughter, and the death of Duryodhan. The rest of the story is told in this translation in two books describing the funerals of the deceased warriors, and Yudhishthir's horse-sacrifice.

"The poems of Homet," says Mr. Gladstone, "differ from all other known poetry in this, that they constitute in themselves an encylopaedia of the life and knowledge, at a time when knowledge, indeed, such as lies beyond the bounds of actual experience, was extremely limited, and when life was singularly fresh, vivid, and expansive." This remark applies with even greater force to the "Mahabharata"; it is an encyclopaedia of the life and knowledge of ancient India. And it discloses to us an ancient and forgotten world, a proud and noble civilisation which has passed away.

For the rest, the people of modern India know how to appreciate their ancient heritage. It is not an exaggeration to state that the two hundred millions of Hindus of the present day cherish in their hearts the story of their ancient Epics. The Hindu scarcely lives, man or woman, high or low, educated or ignorant, whose earliest recollections do not cling round the story, and the characters of the great Epics. The almost illiterate oil manufacturer or confectioner of Bengal spells out some modern translation of the "Mahabharata" to while away his leisure hour. The tall and stalwart peasantry of the North-West know of the five Pandav brothers, and of their friend the righteous Krishna. The people of Bombay and Madras cherish with equal ardour the story of the righteous war. And even the traditions and tales interspersed in the Epic, and which spoil the work as an Epic, have themselves a charm and an attraction and the morals inculcated in these tales sink into the hearts of a naturally religious people, and form the basis of their moral education. Mothers in India know no better theme for imparting wisdom and instruction to their daughters, and elderly men know no richer storehouse for narrating tales to children, then these stories preserved in the Epics. No work in Europe, not Homer in Greece, or Virgil in Italy, not Shakespeare or Milton in English-speaking lands, is the national property of the nations to the same extent as the Epics of India are of the Hindus. No single work except the Bible has such influence in affording moral instruction in Christian lands as the "Mahabharata" and the "Ramayana" in India. They have been the cherished heritage of the Hindus for three.thousand years; they are to the present day interwoven with the thoughts and beliefs and moral ideas of a nation numbering two hundred millions.

The following extracts are from his epilogue to the "Ramayana":

> The "Ramayana," like the "Mahabharata," is the growth of centuries, but main story is more distinctly the creation of one mind. The "Mahabharata" grew out of the legends and traditions of a great historical war between the Kurus and the Panchalas; the "Ramayana" grew out of the recollections of the golden age of the Kosalas and the Videhas. The characters of the "Mahabharata" are characters of flesh and blood, with the virtures and crimes of great actors in the historic world; the characters of the "Ramayana" are more often the ideals of manly devotion to truth, and of womanly faithfulness and love in domestic life. The poet of the "Mahabharata" relies on the real or supposed incidents of war handed down from generation to generation in songs and ballads, and weaves them into an immortal work of art; the poet of "Ramayana" conjures up the memories of a golden age, constructs lofty ideals of piety and faith, and describes with infinite pathos domestic seenes and domestic affections, which endear the work to modern Hindus. As an heroic poem the "Mahabharata" stands on a higher level; as a poem delineating the softer emotions of our everyday life, the "Ramayana" sends its roots deeper into the hearts and minds of the millions in India.

And yet, without rivalling the heroic grandeur of the "Mahabharata," the "Ramayana" is immeasurably superior in its delineation of those softer and perhaps deeper emotions which enter into our everyday life, and hold the world together. And these descriptions, essentially of Hindu life, are yet so true to nature that apply to all races and nations.

There is something indescribably touching and tender in the description of the love of Rama for his subjects and the loyalty of his people towards Rama—that loyalty which has ever been a part of the Hindu character in every age. Deeper than this was Rama's duty towards his father and his father's fondness for Rama; and the portion of the Epic which narrates the dark scheme by which the prince was at last torn from the heart and home of his dying father is one of the most powerful and pathetic passages in Indian literature. The stepmother of Rama, won by the virtues and kindliness of the prince regards his proposed coronation with pride and pleasure, but her old nurse creeps into her confidence like a creeping serpent, and envenoms her heart with the poison of her own wickedness. She arouses the slumbering jealousy of a woman and awakens the alarms of a mother, till—

> "Like a slow but deadly poison worked the ancient nurse's tears. And a wife's undying impulse mingled with a mother's fears!"

The nurse's dark insinuations work on the mind of the queen till she becomes a desperate woman, resolved to maintain her own influence on her husband, and to see her own son on the throne, the determination of the young queen tells with terrible effect on the weakness and vacillation of the feeble old monarch, and Rāma is banished at last. And the scene closes with a pathetic story in which the monarch recounts his misdeed of past years, accepts his present suffering as the fruit of that misdeed, and dies in agony for his banished son. The inner workings of the human heart and of human motives, the dark intrigue of a scheming dependant, the awakening jealousy and alarm of a wife and a mother, the determination of a woman and an imperious queen, and the feebleness and despair and death of a fond old father and husband, have never been more vividly described. Shakespeare himself has not depicted the workings of stormy passions in the human heart more graphically or more vividly, with greater truth or with more terrible power.

It is truth and power in the depicting of such scenes, and not in the delineation of warriors and warlike incidents, that the "Ramayana" excels. It is in the delineation of domestic incidents, domestic affections jealousies, which are appreciated by the prince and peasant alike that the "Ramayana" bases its appeal to the hearts of the millions in India. And beyond all this, righteous devotion of Rama, and the faithfulness and womanly love of Sita, run like two threads of gold through in the eyes of the Hindus. Rama and Sita are the Hindu ideals of a perfect man and a perfect woman; their truth under trials and temptations, their endurance under privations, and their devotion to duty under all vicissitudes of fortune; form the Hindu ideal of a perfect life. And if trial and endurance are a part of a Hindu's ideal of man's life, devotion and self-abnegation are still more essentially a part of his ideal of a woman's life. Sita holds a place in the hearts of women in India which no other creation of a poet's imagination holds among any other nation on earth. There is not a Hindu woman whose earliest and tenderest recollections do not cling round the story of Sita's faithfulness, told in the nursery, taught in the family circle, remembered and cherished through life.

The ideal of life way joy and beauty and gladness in ancient Greece; the ideal of life was piety and endurance and devotion in ancient India. The tale of Helen was a tale of womanly beauty and loveliness which charmed the Western world. The tale of Sita was a tale of womanly faith and self-abnegation which charmed and fascinated the Hindu world.

The modern reader will now comprehend why India produced, and has preserved for well-nigh three thousand years, two Epics instead of one national Epic. No work of the imagination abides long unless it is animated by some sparks of imperishable truth, unless it truly embodies some portion of our human feelings, human faith and human life. The "Mahabharata" depicts the political life of ancient India, with all its valour and heroism, ambition and lofty chivalry. The "Ramayana" embodies the domestic and religious life of ancient India, with all its tenderness and sweetness, its endurance and devotion. The one picture without the other were incomplete; and we should know but little of the ancient Hindus if we did not comprehend their inner life and faith as well as their political life and their warlike virtues. The two together give us a true and graphic picture of ancient Indian life and civilisation; and no nation on earth has preserved a more faithful picture of its glorious past. To trace the influence of the Indian Epics on the life and civilisation of the nation, and on the development of their modern languages, literatures, and religious reforms, is to comprehend the real history of the people during three thousand years.

Professor Max Müller, in his introduction to Mr. Dutt's "Mahabharata," says:

> It is easy to see how round the nucleus of this war an immense mass of poetry, both popular and artificial, was accumulated, but it was not so easy a task to sift this enormous mass, and to extract from it what may have been the original story. This task has been boldly undertaken and carried through, as far as I can judge, with great success, by

> Mr. Romesh Dutt in his "Mahabharata" condensed into English verse. He has himself given an account of the principles by which he was guided in his work. He has, as much as possible, taken a number of verses of the original and rendered them faithfully into English. He has left out on the very largest scale, but he has not added; and the impression which his bold undertaking leaves on the reader, is certainly that something like what we here read in English may have been recited in India when the war between the Kurus and the sons of Pandu was first sung by the ancient bards of the country.
>
> As a mine of information the "Mahabharata" is inexhaustible, and will for a long time remain unexhausted. We are all the more grateful to Mr. Romesh Dutt for having given us a kind of photographic representation, a snap-shot, as it were, of the old poem—the longest poem, I believe, in the whole world—and having enabled students of literature to form for themselves some kind of idea of what our Aryan brother in India admired and still admire in the epic poetry of their country.

The translations were reviewed in most of the leading journals and reviews, and Mr. Dutt received many letters from distinguished literary men and his personal friends about them. He presented specially bound copies of both the "Mahabharata" and "Ramayana" to Queen Victoria, who in graciously accepting the present directed the following letter to be written to him:

Windows Castle, *8th March 1899.*

Dear Sir,—I have laid before the Queen the copy of your "Epic of Ancient India" which you have been good enough to offer for Her Majesty's acceptance. I am desired to express to you the thanks of Her Majesty for this interesting work—I am, dear Sir, yours very faithfully,

Arthur Bigge

From officials connected with the Indian Administration he received the following letters:

6th April 1900

Dear Mr. Romesh Dutt,—I am much obliged to you for sending me a copy of the epic "Ramayana" in English. The "Mahabharata," into which I occasionally dipped, was very instructive, as bringing before me the peculiar ideal which the Hindu race tried to cultivate and attain.

I was very glad to be able to allude to you in the recent debate in the House of Commons, as I shall always be glad to hear from one of your exceptional experience and moderation, and who, whilst anxious to improve British administration in India, does not depreciate its best work.—Believe me, yours truly,

George Hamilton.

My Dear Mr. Dutt,—I have to thank you for the handsomely bound volume of your work, "Epic of Ancient India," which you so kindly sent me. I will read it with utmost pleasure. Your labour and trouble in translating such a classical poem will be repaid, for it will bring home to many, who before were wholly ignorant of the fact, what Indian civilisation and literature were when we were comparative savages.—Believe me, yours truly,

George Hamilton.

Lahore, 25th April 1900.

Dear Mr. Dutt,—Let me thank you for the very dainty companion volume to that which I already possess. It has reached me by the last mail. The presentation of these ancient Epics, in a readable and therefore a condensed form, to European readers is in the nature of a public service. It acquaints English students with a good many of the bases of Indian history, thought, religions, and life, and helps to strip off the mask from the mysterious and sometimes almost unintelligible features of the past—Yours faithfully,

Curzon.

24th September 1898.

Dear Mr. Romesh Dutt,— Your letter has just reached me, and I hasten to say that it will give me much pleasure that you should dedicate to me your translation of the "Mahabharata." I am gratified by your wish to do so.—Believe me, yours very truly,

Ripon.

From the Lieutenant-Governor of Bengal:

3rd January 1901.

Dear Mr. Dutt,—The last mail brought me a beautiful copy of the new edition of your "Epics," and I hasten to thank you. The gift would have been complete with the author's signature, and I hope some day that may be added to it.

Your labour must be amply repaid; not yet have the great Indian epics been presented to the English in a form so winning. Everything that makes us know more of each other makes us like each other better, and I thank you for your share in this best of works.

With my best wishes for the new year, and renewed thanks for your beautiful gift,—Believe me, yours very sincerely,

J.Woodburn.

Amongst acknowledgments from men of letters the following will be of interest:

The Athenaeum, *27th June 1899.*

My Dear Sir,—I duly received your kind note, and today I have the pretty volume, for which pray accept my best thanks. I have hastily sampled the contents. I find everywhere musical and accomplished verse, which I shall read carefully and with interest when I get into the country. I will then write my impressions and thanks. I think it is doing a great service to English readers to familiarise them with the great Indian epics, which have been the delight of so many generations of mortal men, and for me in particular everything connected with India has especial interest. Thanking you again for your kind gift,—I remain, yours very truly,

Lewis Morris.

21st April 1899.

Dear Sir,—I can assure you that I am much honoured by your letter, and greatly gratified by having presented to me so charming a volume. It is certainly on the face of it one of the most graceful books of the time, and I congratulate you on the taste and judgment of its general form.

Absorbed as I am now with pressing matters, I have only been able to sip passages in leisure half-hours; but I am already much struck with the vigour and grace of your verses, and with the case and harmony of the rhythm. Like so many others, I am only a believer on trust of the merits of the "Mahabharata," and have never had the courage to face its immense cantos for myself. I shall read your work through with great expectation and interest, and will write to you again when I have so done.—Yours very truly,

Frederic Harrision.

Parkstone, Dorset, 1st March 1899.

Dear Sir,—I thank you very much for sending me your beautiful translation of the "Mahabharata," which I have heard much of, but have never before become acquainted with. If, as you say, your translation is almost a literal one, it is indeed great poem. I am surprised at the clear sequence of the story, which is in itself interesting, but more especially in the force and simplicity of the language and the beautiful, often poetical and lofty ideas.

I must also express my admiration of your beautiful, poetical, and rhythmical version in what is to you a foreign tongue. It is perfectly clear and harmonious, and is a pleasure to read; and I am sure that, if better known, it would become a favourite with English readers. I only regret that it has not been issued in a more worthy form, with better paper and a little more margin. You have showed excellent judgment in giving what you do translate in full, with brief connecting prose summaries. I think, however, you should give in notes, or in a glossary at the end, the meaning of the various untranslated Sanskrit words you introduce in your translation. Also the proper names are so numerous that I think, at the commencement of each book, the names of all the persons mentioned should be given, with their positions, titles, and relationships, as in the *dramatis persona* of a play. I should like to see a new edition, with illustrations of the chief scenes like that you have as a frontispices.

I seldom go to London now, but shall have great pleasure in receiving a visit from you here, should you ever be in the vicinity.—Believe me, yours very truly,

Alfred Wallace.

Parkstone, Dorset, *8th March 1899.*

My Dear Sir,—Very many thanks for the copy of the large edition of your translation of the "Mahabharata." It is very elegant and well worthy of the great poem, and I hope will have a large sale. I waited to finish reading the poem before writing to you, and I have also read the earlier books over again with even greater pleasure than at first. One wants to know the characters and all the chief ideas of such a poem before it can be duly appreciated, hence a second reading is necessary. I have noted, while reading, a number of places where I think the wording can be improved or the meaning better expressed, and also a few press error. I enclose you notes of all these, with new readings suggested in many cases, which I hope may be of use to you in correctiong for a new edition.

The "Story of Savitri" is the gem of the whole poem, and I cannot recall anything in poetry more beautiful, or any higher teaching as to the sanctity of love marriage. We have really not advanced one step beyond this old-world people in our ethical standards. How fine and lofty, too, is Krishna's exposition of a king's duties at the end of Book III. Draupadi's plaint and Dhritarashtra's kindness are also very fine, and the acceptance of slavery by these warlike princes on a point of honour is grand, though we may consider it excessive.

The least satisfactory part of the poem is the fact of Draupadi, after having accepted Arjun, becoming the wife of Yudhishthir. Considering her character, that seems very extraordinary. Was she married to Arjun or Yudhishthir? I cannot believe that she became the wife of five in common. I wish you had translated the main part of the wedding ceremony. Also the great game of dice, which must surely lend itself to some fine poetry. But, even as you give it, it is a grand poem.—Believe me yours very faithfully,

Alfred Wallace.

24th June 1899.

Dear Sir,—I thank you heartily for your gift of the interesting abridgment of the "Mahabharata," which you have been good enough to send me. I am reading it with much enjoyment, having long had a great curiosity to know something of the famous Indian Epic, and being debarred by my ignorance of Sanskrit from studying it in the original. You have rendered no small service to English lovers of primitive literature in enabling us to form an idea of the great Oriental parallel to the "Iliad."

If as I go on I find that any of the observations which occur to me in reading your spirited version seem worthy of being conveyed to you, I will write them to you.—Believe me, faithfully yours,

James Bryce.

As examples of the many criticisms to which the translations gave rise, we may quote the following from the *Jaurnal of the Royal Asiatic Society* (July 1899):

It should be judged as a literary effort, not as historical criticism. And as literary effort, it is certainly a very great success. A generous admiration for the original, and a warm sympathy with its tone, a striking command of vigorous and flowing and idiomatic English, a fine sense of rhythm, and a real power of poetic imagination have combined to render this selection just what it is intended to be—a most interesting and attractive way of introducing to English readers what the author considers to be the essence of the grand old Indian poem.

Classical Literature

The classical tradition in Indian literature is essentially secular. Religious scripture *(āgama)* and scholarly treatises *(śāstra)* are usually distinguished from 'literature' *(kāvya)*, the latter being both human and an art. 'Tradition' *(itihāsa)*, including 'antiquity' *(purāṇa)* and 'epic' *(ākhyāna)*, is distinguished from all three as the inspired words of ancient sages. In fact its simple heroic verse, lacking the style and figurativeness of *kāvya*, represents the narrative poetry of an age before the institutionalisation of literature as an art according to the conscious principles of criticism elaborated in the *Nāṭyaśāstra* (Treatise on Drama) and elsewhere. Tradition as extant is mostly not as antique as it purports to be, but it follows the archaic narrative style and continues to be a source of classical themes for 'literature'. On account of its aesthetic power, some critics allowed the great epic *Mahābhārata* to be 'literature' as well as 'tradition'. For our present purpose we too are interested in this 'true' epic derived from the bards *(sūtas)* of antiquity as well as in the 'artificial' epics of individual authors.

In Vedic scripture we find relics, preserved for the liturgy, of a still earlier phase (second millennium B.C) of epic poetry, celebrating especially the deeds of Indra but sometimes of human warriors, and of lyric in which, characteristically for India, natural phenomena are personified, such as the goddesses Dawn and Night and the gods Sun and Thunderstorm. A few dialogues suggest dramatic action, e.g. Purūravas and the nymph. In prose (mainly the somewhat later *Brāhmanas)* there are examples of story telling, terse and abrupt in style, such as Maṅu and the Fish and the various wars of the gods and demons. The story of Hariścandra and Śunaḥśepa is in mixed prose and verse.

The lay of the *Jaya* (Victory') was handed down orally for at least a thousand years after the battle celebrates (c.900 B.C) before becoming relatively fixed in writing as the *Mahābhārata*, 'Great Bhārata (Battle)'. A shadowy Dvaipāyana or Vyāsa is recorded first to have sung of this terrible struggle of his own time. Vaiśampāyana later elaborated the epic in 24,000 verses and C. 750 B.C. Lomaharṣaṇa and Ugraśravas are supposed to have recited the complete *Mahābhārata* in 100,000 verses. On metrical and other grounds, however, the text constituted in the Critical (Poona) Edition, which may approximate to the manuscripts of the fourth century A.D., includes additions down to that century, with a balancing nucleus of archaic verses producing an average date of composition not earlier than C. 100 B.C.

The theme of the *Mahābhārata* has been well summed up, by Rājaśekhara as the anger of the Pāṇḍavas, sons of Pāṇḍu. Pāṇḍu had been consecrated Emperor, in the Bhārata Dynasty, because his elder brother Dhṛtarāṣṭra was blind and so legally disqualified from ruling. But Pāṇḍu died first and Dhṛtarāśtra seized power, though claiming to act as regent for Pāndu's son Yudhiṣṭhira, who was made crown prince and later given a fief to rule. Yudhiṣṭhira formed a marriage alliance with Kṛṣṇa, leader of the Satvants, and then assumed imperial prerogatives. Dhṛtarāṣṭra's son Duryodhana, ambitious and envying Yudhiṣṭhira;s prosperity, challenged him to a gambling match, sure of victory through the trickery of an uncle. Yudhiṣṭhira loses everything, his kingdom, and finally his Queen Draupadi, who is publicly stripped as a slave by Duryodhana's brother, a humiliation she will never forgive. The elders intervene and arrange terms: Draupadi is restored but Yudhiṣṭhira and his brothers are condemned to twelve years' exile and a further year incognito. After enduring this, they enter the service of King Virāṭa of Matsya. From this base, Yudhiṣṭhira sends Kṛṣṇa as envoy to negotiate the restoration of a kingdom, but Duryodhana will not give up even one village and war becomes inevitable. Yudhiṣṭhira marshals his allies against a huge enemy army and the battle lasts eighteen days. The main events are single combats: finally, through the stratagems of Kṛṣṇa (deceit and foul blows contrary to the warriors' code), the Pāṇḍavas destroy their enemies and Yudhisthira becomes Emperor.

We should note the ethical questions raised by this story of a fratricidal war of succession with its bitter passions and terrible slaughter. Yudhisthira's claim was legally sound, but Duryodhana stood for the time-honoured right of the first born and his descendants. Yudhisthira lost his kingdom through deceit and regained it through deceit. The loss was accompanied by humiliating insult, generating an anger that only the blood of the enemy could quench. The *Mahābhārata* fascinated Indian historians, who tool it as a kind of model for this work, whilst critics argued about its aesthetic significance and dramatists and other authors reinterpreted it. Many held that the ultimate aesthetic experience produced by it was the calmed state arising from the renunciation of destructive worldly ambitions. Indeed in the extant *Mahābhārata* Yudhiṣthira finally abdicates, after hearing of the tragic death of Kṛṣṇa, and retires to the Himālaya, leaving the Empire to his brother Arjuna's grandson.

In contrast to the simple style of the *Mahābhārata*, with its refrains and repetitions and verse-filling epithets, *kāvya*, or literature as it developed gradually from about the fifth century B.C., becomes highly organised in form, richly adorned with figures of speech, taut in style, profuse in metres, and above all aimed at producing methodically a defined aesthetic experience in an audience, hearer, or reader. This trend, especially in metres, can be traced back to some of the lyrics of the Buddhist *āgama*, the *Tripiṭaka*, available in Pāli, which appear to reflect secular lyrics in the Māgadhi language of the Buddha's time. The *Tripiṭaka* was enriched by the art of certain poets and actors who, becoming Buddhist monks, applied it in praise of the Buddha (notably Vāgiśa), in describing mountains suitable for meditation (notably Kāśyapa) and in other unworldly themes. From about 400 B.C. onwards we find also dramatic dialogues in the *Tripiṭaka*, in verse with prose stage directions, showing the same new metrical art apparently extended to the stage.

Apart from some incidental discussions on genres, figures of speech, etc., in the *Tripiṭaka* and in grammatical and other works, the *Nāṭyaśāstra* of 'Bharata' (the mythical first 'Actor') is the oldest work of Indian literary criticism now available. It is the outcome of several centuries of theatrical practice by hereditary actors, from the fifth century B.C. or earlier down to about the second century A.D., no doubt at first handed down by oral tradition like the *Mahābhārata*. The purpose of drama is the amusement of the audience, but the 'joy' *(harṣa)* and solace given them is not left to chance by the actors but induced through a special technique or method of acting. The drama is an imitation of all the actions of the world, but the essential part of this is the emotions *(bhāvas)* which the characters are represented as experiencing during their actions. There are eight basic emotions: love, humour, energy, anger, fear, grief, disgust, and astonishment. These are not conveyed directly but by playing their causes and effects, the latter including other, transient, emotions. The audience, imagining the basic emotions in the characters through this acting, enjoys eight corresponding tastes *(rasa)*, in other words the perception of them, the aesthetic experience (not the emotional experience itself) correspondingly divided into sensitive (perception of love), comic, heroic, furious, apprehensive, compassionate, horrific, and marvellous. Besides being essentially enjoyable, the drama is incidentally instructive because it represents all kinds of actions, good and bad, and the ends or motives which inspire them.

According to the *Nāṭyaśāstra*, drama originated because of the conflicts which arose in society when the world declined from the Golden Age (Kṛta Yuga) of harmony. Thus a drama always presents a conflict and its resolution, and in construction, the conversion of a story into a 'plot', with its elements and conjunctions, is based on the single main action which ends the conflict. Each of the five 'conjunctions' (opening, re-opening, embryo, obstacle, and conclusion) of a full-scale play is bodied out with up to a dozen dramatic incidents and situations (its 'limbs' or parts), showing the characters in action; and, a large number of other dramatic devices were available to express the causes and effects of emotion through incidents related to the ultimate action. Among these devices, the discussion of the 'characteristics' of dramatic expression leads into the figures of speech and qualities of style in the language of drama. The *Nāṭyaśāstra* describes ten types of play, distinguished as history or fiction of full scale (five or more acts, implying as many nights' performance since the Indian theatre, though highly organised, is not rapid in movement). The remaining eight types, with from one to four acts only, are heroic, tragic, or comic plays, together with the satirical monologue, the street play, and three kinds of archaic play about the gods and demons. Secondary to all these is the four-act 'light play' as a fictitious sensitive comedy about a real character, whilst the solo *tāṇḍava* dance of Śiva and the delicate *lāsya* invented by Pārvati, as well as group dances *(piṇḍibandhas)*, may be introduced in drama where appropriate. The *lāsya* represents a story, or part of a story, and is regarded as the prototype of the profusion of independent popular ballets which has always accompanied the more serious and classical theatre of India.

Bhāmaha (fifth century A.D.?), the earlier individual critic whose work is available, extended the *Nāṭyasastra* analysis (*rasa* aesthetics, construction) to literature as a whole, setting out the genres as drama, epic, lyric, prose biography, and the (usually prose) novel. Then he takes up as his main problem literary expression and what makes it beautiful, which the Treatise on Drama barely touched on. The 'ornament' *(alankāra)* or beauty, which distinguishes literature from ordinary communication, consists in a kind of 'curvature' *(vakratā)*, i.e. artistic distortion, indirectness, figurativeness. Both the meaning and the language (derivation of words) must be 'ornament' and hence the definition of literature is '(beautiful) language and meaning combined' (this is urged against earlier writers who advocated one or the other only). The beauty of meaning is analysed into some three dozen 'figures' *(alankāras)*, simile, metaphor, etc., taken up from earlier writers but accepted by Bhāmaha only to the extent that each embodies 'curvature'. Bhāmaha, however, favours realism and rationalism in literature, though transmuted into art in this 'curved' way, and he devotes a chapter to epistemology and logic as applied to literature.

Daṇḍin (seventh century) adds to the genres *campū* or narration in mixed prose and verse, which became extremely popular later (like the biography it is intended for live recital before an audience). His main contention is that ten qualities of style (developed from the *Nāṭyaśāstra)* are the essential in literature, the combination of the ten giving the excellent *vaidarbha* or 'southern' style. The 'figures' are secondary. Vāmana defined style as 'a special arrangement of words' and carried this stylistics much further, analysing the qualities into language and meaning. Rudraṭa, on, the other hand, greatly increased the number of figures, classifying them as 'objective' (e.g. 'contrast'), 'comparative', 'exaggerative', and 'double-meaning'. He described the genres further, adding the 'short story' under the novel, and put forward a principle of 'harmony' *(aucitya)* between form and content.

His contemporary Ānandavardhana (ninth century) redefined the essential indirectness of literature as a kind of implication or suggestion, 'revealed' *(vyaṇgya)* as opposed to 'expressed' meaning, where the revealed might even be the opposite of the expressed (like an invitation hidden in a warning). As the *Nāṭyaśāstra* method already made clear, *rasa*, which it is the main object of literature to produce, is always the result of such implication, since the emotions are portrayed indirectly through their causes and effects.

Kuntaka (eleventh century) instead revived 'curvature' but reworked Bhāmaha's doctrine, reducing the figures to eighteen, mainly on the ground that whatever belongs to the subject-matter, rather than the expression, should be excluded and treated instead under *rasa*. Though literature is really 'indivisible', it may be theoretically analysed into six levels of expression, all of which have 'curvature', the phonetic, lexical, grammatical, sentential, contextual, and the work as a whole. The figures are found at the sentential level. The subject-matter is discussed in relation to the three higher levels, the underlying principle being the effective production of *rasa*, for which the source material is selected and modified. On stylistics, Kuntaka offers a new theory of 'natural' versus 'cultivated' (studied) style, either of which may be beautiful though the second is more difficult to succeed in, as Bāna, Bhavabhūti, and Rājśekhara did. Throughout, Kuntaka gives quotations and references from the literature and is in the best empiricist tradition of criticism: he is analysing literature, not setting up an abstract speculative theory. Mahiman (later eleventh century) on the other hand explained indirectness as 'inference' and sought 'middle terms' in the expressions studied by Ānandavardhana and Kuntaka, through which further meanings were inferred by readers.

Meanwhile, Udbhata (eighth century) is the first critic known to us (certainly not the first in fact) to develop the *rasa* aesthetics by adding a ninth *rasa*, the 'calmed', with 'calm' as its basic emotion. Rudraṭa added a tenth, the 'affectionate', and held that all the transient emotions might give rise to as many *rasas*, apparently following Lollaṭa who believed that *rasas* were innumerable.

Lollaṭa (early ninth century) and Daṇḍin thought that *rasas* were simply emotions 'increased'. Śaṅkuka maintained they were something quite different, but imitations of basic emotions (which again did not exist, but were inferred from their causes and effects being shown). Nāyaka (late ninth century) argued for a process of 'development' which replaced the often unpleasant emotions of individual people by an experience in the highest degree enjoyable and also socially generalised and enlightened (stopping the delusion of worldly emotions). Abhinavagupta (A.D. 1000) propounded the most widely accepted theory as to how the production of *rasas* actually works. Like Nāyaka, he makes *rasa* a transcendent, non-worldly, experience, which is even identical with the highest religious experience, transcending individual involvement and emotion as well as space, time, and particular circumstances. In an act of pure contemplation the spectator in the theatre forgets himself and attains a universality of outlook which is also the highest happiness. The 'calmed', consequently, appears as the supreme *rasa*.

Dhanañjaya (A.D. 1000, partly following Nāyaka) instead described *rasa* as a single continuum, with four zones of thought corresponding to phases of a favourable or hostile environment in which the flower of beauty bloomed. These occur in the sensitive, heroic, horrific, and furious, which may be followed by the comic, marvellous, apprehensive, and compassionate as secondary *rasas* giving rise to the same zones of thought.

Bhoja (eleventh century), in the wake of these discussions on the nature of *rasa*, maintained that ultimately there was only one *rasa*, the 'sensitive', since love, the 'queen' of the emotions, absorbs all the others into herself in the form of love of these: each is in fact a kind of love, love of its own special passion. In place of Abhinavagupta's universalisation, Bhoja finds in this sensitive *rasa* a supreme form of self-assertion, an aesthetic development of the primeval instinct of egoism in the individual soul. In his extensive works, treating all aspects of literature in relation to the sensitive aesthetic experience, Bhoja is the greatest Indian critic available to us, giving us the largest number of quotations and reference and showing a very fine taste in selection and comment.

Later critics are too often pedants, sometimes manufacturing their own examples to suit an abstract theory, but empiricism did not die out completely, whilst some of the new explanations of *rasas* are interesting. Nārāyaṇa, Dharmadatta, and Viśvanātha held, for example, that the 'marvellous' is the only *rasa*. In the age of religious revivals, Rūpa (sixteenth century) initiated a devotional theory of drama and wrote religious plays to exemplify it. On the other hand the anonymous *Natāṇkuśa* (fifteenth century) defended the old practice of the theatre against innovations in Keralā which slowed down the performance to the point of disintegration in order to allow greater scope for the virtuosity of individual actors. We must at lest mention a number of other critics between the tenth and the fourteenth centuries, to whose analysis of classical works, we owe so much of our enjoyment of them: Rājaśekhara, Sāgaranandin, Rāmacandra, Guṇacandra, Śaradātanaya, and Śingabhūpāla.

In the evolution of the very numerous and ever-changing popular theatrical genres of India, finally, Koḥala (second century?—known only from quotations) early noticed various musical plays, ballets, and *rāgakāvyas*, from the last of which such modern forms as *kathakali* eventually developed. Abhinavagupta noted a series of solo performances probably evolved from the *lāsya*, among which the *ḍombikā* was most characteristic. The modern so-called *bharatanāṭyam* is evidently descended from this, in which the dancer does not wear costume but impersonates in mime various characters in a story. Meanwhile the street play gave rise to *yakṣagāna* with its eastern (Āndhra) and western (Karnāṭaka) variants as well as the Tamil street play. We may recall here the social milieu of kāvya as described in the *Nāṭyaśāstra* and the *Kāmasūtra*, for 'classical' literature is not opposed to 'popular' and has usually sought a mass audience. The drama was contrasted with the *Veda* as being for the whole of society, *śūdras* (helots) included, and wealthy amateurs were responsible for patronising regular public festivals in the villages as well as the cities, with plays and other performances (modern *yakṣagāna* in the villages has substituted the box office and sale of tickets for the vanished patrons).

Of all the characteristics of *kāvya* discussed by the critics, the easiest to identify in the earliest period is the large number of new metres, organised on different principles from Vedic metres. These appear in the Buddhist lyric noted above and increase in number in the later parts of the Pāli Canon, where we begin to find them used for epic narrations as well. An important result of this use of originally lyric metres in epic is that an epic narration becomes a series of self-contained quatrains instead of a continuous series of running on lines.

The *Rāmāyana*, in Sanskrit, is traditionally ascribed to Vālmiki, whom Bhavabhūti and others call the 'First Kavi' (*kavi* meaning the 'author' of a *kāvya*). Although this epic, as we have it, is not as old as the first Pāli *kāvyas*, it is formally on the border line between *itihāsa* (such as the *Mahābhārata*) and *kāvya*, Metrically it is certainly latter than the *Mahābhārata* on the average and it shows a few of the new lyric metres just noted (though only at the ends of cantos). It is also more homogeneous, lacking completely the archaic rhythms of the earlier parts of the old Epic but also having far less apocryphal matter added after the first century A.D. The average date of composition seems to fall in the first century B.C.

If *kāvya* is defined by its power to produce aesthetic experience *(rasa)*, however, the *Rāmāyana*, with its unforgettable story of the conflicts of human passions, is certainly a *kāvya*. This story was reworked by 'Vālmiki' (if we apply the name to the author of the present text) from old traditions containing two or three probably separate legends in several versions (one is found in the Pāli Canon). In the *Rāmāyana* we thus find: (1) the palace intrigue at Ayodhyā by Queen Kaikeyi resulting in her stepson Rāma's exclusion from the succession to his father's throne and sentence to twelve years' exile and (2) Rāma, exile in the south, finds its inhabitants oppressed by the raids of demons *(rākṣasas)* from Laṅkā (Ceylon), the island fortress of the demon king Rāvana, and himself suffers the abduction of his wife Sitā by Rāvana; he raises an army (mostly of 'monkeys'), gaining allies, invades Laṅkā, kills Rāvana, frees Sitā, and returns home in triumph, the period of exile having elapsed and his noble stepbrother Bharata generously surrendering the throne to him. The legend or myth of Rāvana itself, with his victorious wars against the gods, may have been a separate source, as perhaps was that of the great 'monkey' hero Hanumant, son of the Wind God. Vālmiki's finest cantos are surely those of the palace intrigue, with the psychological study of the characters of Kaikeyi and her confidante. The apocryphal last book of the *Rāmāyana* adds a tragic ending: Sitā's new exile on suspicion of unchastity, when a captive, and final disappearance. This changes the main rasa to the 'compassionate', whereas originally the poem would be 'heroic', though with a considerable compassionate element resulting from Rāma's sufferings.

Prose story-telling in the Buddhist Canon is a little less heavy and abrupt than in the *Veda* but still full of repetitions and rarely ornamented except by the occasional insertion of a verse to emphasise a point. Humour and satire, however, abound. The novel, as an extensive prose fiction (running to hundreds of pages), seems to us to begin with Gunādhya's *Brhatkathā* ('Great Story') about 100 B.C. (the lost *Cārumati* of Vararuci may have been an earlier novel). Gunādhya's language was Paiśāci, closely related to the Pāli of the Buddhists, and both the milieu and the matter of the *Brhatkathā* were akin to those of the old Buddhist story telling. Unhappily Guṇāḍhya's text seems to be lost save for a few quotations, so that we have to reconstruct the narrative from the excessively free paraphrases in Sanskrit, Māhārāstri, and Tamil which superseded the archaic and forgotten language of the original. Though a fiction, the *Bṛhatkathā* is made to seem historical by giving its imaginary hero Naravāhanadatta a history father, Udayana, one of the last descendants of the Pandava (fifth century B.C.) His adventures take place mostly in the real cities of that time and the chracterisation is realistic. On the other hand, superhuman `wizard' *(vidyādharasa)* intervene, one of whom, Mānasavega abducts the hero's greatest love, Madanamañcukā. This leads ultimately to a victorious war against the wizards beyond the Himālaya, after Naravāhanadatta has acquired the power of flight from one of them who becomes his friend. More important than this incidental acquisition of wealth and power, however, are the hero's twenty-six conquests of love. The novel moves between the intrigues and struggles of the real world and the realization of wild dreams largely in the realm of 'science fiction' (strange sciences and the construction of 'space machines'). The rasa is thus the 'marvellous' (Daṇḍin) rather than the 'sensitive'.

Aśvaghosa's (first century A.D.) are the earliest epics now available (Pānini's *Jāmavatijaya* is known only from quotations) to show the fully fledged *kāvya* technique: concentration of the matter in about twenty cantos only (about 1,500 quatrains) in many metres; perception of discrete moments through the separate quatrains instead of a continuity of flowing narrative; numerous figures of speech. Each 'moment' may suggest the theme of the whole story, but we are to dwell on its significance before pressing on to know what happens next. Aśvaghoṣa was an earnest Buddhist, so that the ultimate significance he wishes to convey, through the delights of poetry, is the shallowness of the world and the true happiness of renunciation and peace of mind. Yet he appears far from indifferent to the pleasures of the world, describing most realistically just what he hold to be most ephemeral. This ambiguity and tension, which seems to reflect personal experience, inspires all the elaborate art, or 'ornament' of language and meaning, carrying Aśvaghoṣa's philosophy. Two epics are available, the Life of the Buddha *(Buddhacarita)* and the Handsome Nanda *(Saundarananda*, who was most unwilling to become a monk). It is a heavy loss that only fragments are now available of a series of dramas by Aśvaghoṣa, whose powers of characterisation are so well displayed in the epics. The *Śāriputra* and *Rāṣṭrapāla* are again well-known stories of renunciation. A play with a fictitious hero, Somadatta (apparently the son of a merchant), takes us to the milieu of the wealthy amateurs *(nāgarakas)* of the *Kāmasūtra*, with a festival on a hill top and such stock characters as the jester (or 'fool'), rogue, geisha girl (who is the heroine) and maid. Another play had some allegorical characters.

In lyric *kāvya* the classic model is the *Saptaśati*, a Prākrit (Māhārāṣṭri) anthology collected, we are told, by a 'Sātavāhana' emperor (more rarely called 'Hāla', a dialect form), perhaps Pulumāyi II Vāsisthiputra (second century A.D.). This seems to represent folk songs (in a dialect of the peasants, not of the imperial administration), each a single verse in a musical metre. They are miniatures of situations in life, mostly village life on the banks of the Godāvari and in the valleys of the Vindhya. Love is the theme (always, according to the critics, though sometimes hidden) and the singers almost always women. Their joys and sorrows, invitations and complaints, or the comments of gossips, are set in the village with its cattle, buffaloes, ploughing, milling, cooking, weaving, working in rice, sesame, or millet fields, or cotton and hemp gardens. Sometimes the changing seasons and their effects on love form the background. The villages are likely to be poor and affection may either compensate for everything or be severely reprimanded by a more worldly friend. There is plenty of humour, often in the ambiguous language used by the heroines to hide their improper suggestions, Ānandavardhana quoting them for 'revealed' meanings.

Pādalipta's novel *Taraṅgavati*, also in Māhārāstri, seems now to be available only in an abridged paraphrase in the same language by one Yaśas. The action depends on the memory of former lives, particularly of a strange incident in which a hunter accidentally shot one of a pair of ruddy sheldrakes. Killing breeding birds was against the hunters' code, so he remorsefully cremated it, whereupon its mate in despair threw herself into the fire. The pair were reborn in merchants' families in Kauśāmbi. The girl Taraṅgavati suddenly recollects her tragic past on seeing some sheldrakes in a park. Sadly she paints the scenes of her past life on a long scroll, which a maid displays on a balcony for a festival. Her lover happens to pass and is reminded of his own past life. The girl's rich father opposes the match with a mere caravan merchant so the two elope, but are seized by robbers. A young robber free them and Taraṅgavati's father relents when they reach home. After a happy married life they meet a Jaina monk, who tells them he was the young robber, who was the hunter reborn, and had freed them because he remembered his past when the girl told their story. Convinced of the truth of the Jaina teaching about transmigration the two determine to escape it by joining the Jaina ascetic communities.

The Jaina Pādalipta and the Buddhist philosopher (Nāgārjuna are both traditionally connected with the Sātavāhana anthologist. Nāgārjuna wrote an 'epistle' to Sātavāhana and an ethical 'tract *(Ratnāvali)* to the same ruler, as well as 'hymns' (lyric *stotras*) praising the Buddha, representing a flourishing Buddhist tradition in these minor *kāvya* genres. Their most celebrated practitioner was Mātṛceṭa, who wrote an 'Epistle to the Great King Kanika' (Kaniska III?), probably soon after A.D. 176, and some tracts. His greatest works are his hymns, describing the qualities and actions of the Buddha, especially in his former lives as *bodhisattva*, whose self-sacrificing nature is directly opposed to the worldly nature. The style is in appearance simple, unpretentious, but conceals all the art of *kāvya*, especially of originality in expression despite the well-worn subject. The figures are handled with a certain restraint, suggesting the infinite scope of the subject by contrast with the little the poet feels able to say. Mātṛceṭa's reticence implies a detachment remote from Aśvaghoṣa's involvement.

Possibly a contemporary was Śūra, who used a somewhat terse style in tracts but whose masterpiece is the *campū Jātakamālā,* a collection of *bodhisattva* stories (some of them illustrated in Ajantā). The prose is as elegant and fastidious, as compact and elliptical as the verse.

Bhāsa (second century A.D.?), perhaps the greatest Indian dramatist, brings us at last a comprehensive view of the classical theatre. His masterpiece is the 'Dream Vāsavadattā', a full-scale history *(nāṭaka)* in which the heroine sacrifices all her happiness in order to save her husband's (Udayana) kingdom from a powerful enemy. Her courageous action, part of a subtle plan of a minister, bears fruit after great mental suffering, which Bhāsa finely depicts, and she is reunited with Udayana restored to his throne. The 'Consecrations' deals with Rāma's victory over Rāvaṇa, the most interesting character being perhaps the demon king, vainly courting the captive Sitā and then suffering increasing anguish as his armies are defeated and his son killed. The 'Statue' treats the Rāma story more more comprehensively and from the different point of view of Bharata. Forn such *nāṭakas* we discover the aims of classical dramatists, using a familiar story but reinterpreting it and developing new insights into the character. Another presents the young Kṛṣṇa killing Kaṃsa. The 'Five Nights' deals very freely with an episode from the *Mahābhārata* in three acts (belonging, if not to the archaic *samavakāra* type, to that known later as a sallāpa, 'contention'). Further scenes from the great epic are presented in a series of one-act heroic plays *(vyāyogas)* and the death of Duryodhana, or rather his ascent to heaven because he died heroically, in a one-act tragic play *(utsṛṣṭikāṇka)*. 'Yaugandharāyana's Vows' is a 'light play' *(nāṭikā)* on the minister who frees Udayana from captivity. The full-scale 'fictions' *(prakaraṇas) Avimāraka* and *Daridracārudatta* take us to the world of Naravāhanadatta and Somadatta. The merchant Cārudatta is impoverished and consequently almost friendless, then crosses a parasitic scoundrel on the fringes of a corrupt court and narrowly escapes death.

Of Bhāsa's time or a little earlier are two 'satirical monologues' *(bhāṇas)*, by Vararuci and Iśvaradatta. In this type of play the solo actor represents a 'parasite' *(viṭa)*, a professional go-between for temporary relationship. He proceeds about his business through the streets and public places of some metropolis, meeting (in mime) characteristic inhabitants of the geisha quarter. 'Both Go to Meet' *(Ubhayābhisārikā)* thus gives interesting pictures of the follies and vices of Pāṭaliputra, with its cultural life (music and drama), to which the 'Dialogue of the Rogue and the Parasite' adds a discussion on the philosophy of love, the drift of which is that it is an excellent thing to spend money on women, especially if they are beautiful but best of all if they are 'amiable'.

To complete the cross-section of the theatre of Bhāsa's day we have a 'street play' of doubtful date *(Traivikrama*, in dialogue form narrating a story illustrated by a painting) and the one-act comedy *(prahasana)* 'Master-Mistress' *(Bhagavadajjukiya)* by Bodhāyana. The Master, a saintly teacher of yoga, disastrously shows off his powers before a student by projecting his soul into the supposedly dead body of the Mistress (a geisha), whose soul brought back from the Underworld is then lodged in his body. Meanwhile the girl's mother and lover arrive....

Another *nāṭaka* of roughly Bhāsa's period is Dhīrangāga's *Kundamālā* from the apocryphal last book of the *Rāmāyaṇa*, which changes the conclusion to a happy final reunion in accordance with the convention of an auspicious ending.

In this period of reinterpretation of Rāma story the Jaina poet Vimala (c. A.D. 200?) produced an epic *Padmacarita* in Māhārāṣṭrī harmonising with his own religious background. He criticised the *Rāmāyaṇa* for such falsifications as making Rāvaṇa a demon and monster, when he was really a wizard, and presenting other wizards, Rāma's allies, as monkeys when they merely lived in Monkey Island. Rāma, who in Jaina literature is often called Padma, finally attains enlightenment and *nirvāṇa*. This epic marks an important stage in the development of the Jaina version of universal history out of the brief sketches in their *āgama*. Vimala's view is rational and understands events in the light of the Jaina doctrine of moral action, which rules the universe. It is a universe in which everything is alive and assault on life is the greatest evil.

Three plays are attributed to King Śūdraka, supposed to have ruled in the third century. The *Vīṇāvāsavadatta* has the same story as Bhāsa's 'Yaugandharāyana's Vows', but as a full-scale *nāṭaka* and with entirely different scenes: Udayana and Vāsavadattā dominate the stage whereas in Bhāsa's light play they do not appear at all. The 'Toy Cart' *(Mṛcchakṭika)* stands in a peculiar relationship to Bhāsa's *Daridracārudatta*: it is the same play with a new sub-plot, a political revolution which brings fortune to the hero, and with numerous inserted verses elaborating the effects of emotion on the characters. Henceforth all Indian dramas are on the enlarged scale. Śūdraka is the equal of Bhāsa in characterisation and in filling his plays with well-arranged action, whilst putting more of the incidents on stage instead of reporting. His third play is satirical monologue 'Lotus Gift', in which a parasite proceeds through Ujjayinī, describing the rascals he meets, in order to sound out a new mistress for Mūladeva (a historical character subsequently transformed into a legendary prince of thieves).

The anonymous 'Review of the Seasons' (often misattributed to Kālidāsa), a lyric in which the poet describes to his beloved the effects of the six seasons of the Indian year on lovers, is probably of this period.

From the fourth century little survives except famous names and some quotations, which reminds us that the greater part of the old literature of India has been lost. Sarvasena's Māhārāṣṭrī epic 'Victory of Hari', on Kṛṣṇa carrying off the Pārijāta flower from Heaven for Satyabhāmā, defeating Indra, seems to have set a new style, with a stronger focus on the emotions and also longer descriptive digressions.

We get a very good idea of this lost epic from Bhoja's discussions and quotations, to which Kuntaka adds that Sarvasena was, with Kālidāsa, the greatest exponent of the delicate and natural style in *kāvya*. For the emotional content, Sarvasena made much of Satyabhāmā's jealousy of Rukmiṇī.

The dramas of Rāmila and Somila are lost, but Candragomin's 'Joy of the World', a Buddhist play on the *bodhisattva* Maṇicūḍa giving away all his possessions, survives in a Tibetan translation. Of uncertain date are a group of once-famous 'fictions', especially the *Puṣpadūṣitaka* of Brahmayaśas and the *Anaṅgasenāharinandin* of Śuktivāsa. The first is a story of unfair suspicion of the behaviour of the heroine by her father-in-law; the second has its hero in the perilous situation of a rival (in love?) of a prince and falsely accused of theft. These and the anonymous *Taraṅgadatta, Padmāvatīpariṇaya* ('Padmāvati's Marriage', which a rival tries to prevent), and *Prayogābhyudaya* are all known to us from the critics, who by discussing these and many other lost plays completely change the impression of Indian theatre we might have from those available.

The *Pañcatantra* seems to have been written in the fourth century. The author was perhaps the narrator Viśṇuśarman and his country the Vākāṭaka Empire of the south (Deccan). Its popularity was such that new versions were made, with additions from which it has been difficult to recover the original work (Edgerton's reconstruction seems a good approximation). The genre is the 'illustrating novel' *(nidarśanakathā)*, which is satirical and aims to teach by example. Here the subject is 'policy' *(nīti)*, public and private. The frame story is the instruction of three young princes averse to formal education. Within this, five stories present five 'system' *(tantras)* of policy: (1) splitting an alliance (or friendship) which obstructs one's interests, (2) forming an alliance oneself, (3) making war, (4) outwitting a strong but foolish enemy, and (5) a warning on the folly of action without reflection. Four of these are beast fables, which enhances the sharpness of the satire. Some further stories are emboxed, narrated by the characters to illustrate their own discussions of policy.

The other prose literature of this period has suffered badly. The 'Story of Simpletons' is known indirectly from paraphrases. Haricandra, so much admired by Bāṇa, is only a name. Lost novels include the

Ratnaprabhā (Paiśācī, therefore presumably much earlier), *Magadhasenā, Malayavatī*, and *Manovatī* (all named after their heroines). A classical 'biography' was the *Mādhavikā*. The story of Śūdraka, written jointly by Rāmila and Somila, was classed as a novel, therefore apparently fictitious. To widen our view of Sanskrit prose we have inscriptions in *kāvya* style, especially Hariṣeṇa's on Samudra Gupta, and the vast Buddhist religious novel *Gaṇḍavyūha*. A novice *bodhisattva* wanders all over India in search of 'good friends' who guide him. The sometimes formidable prose style harmonises with the view of the universe as infinite, inconceivable, and ambiguous (worldly as usually experienced, beautiful as the *bodhisattva* sees it).

The Gupta Emperor Candra II or 'Vikramāditya', called also Sāhasānka and Harṣa, appears as a poet through quotations and references, his *Gandhamādana* seeming to be an epic. He is more celebrated as a patron, making the poet and critic Mātṛgupta king of Kaśmīra c. A.D. 410. Like his patron, Mātṛgupta is now known only from quotations of his beautiful and powerful verses, but Kuntaka ranks him first among masters of the 'intermediate' style combining 'natural' and 'cultivated' beauty. Mātṛgupta also wrote on dramaturgy, but here too he is known only from quotations. Probably he was a dramatist, but it is a matter of conjecture which anonymous plays discussed later were his (the 'Illusion Madālasā' constructed according to his principles, the 'Joy of Rāma', both with verses in his style?).

Meṇṭha was patronised by both these and is frequently praised later as a great, or the greatest (Padmagupta), poet, perfecting the *vaidarbha* style after Sūra and Sarvasena. His famous epic *Hayagrīvavadha*, on Viṣṇu as the Fish *avatāra* slaying the demon Hayagrīva, is imperfectly known to us from quotations, but an incomplete manuscript exists and perhaps others can be found in Keralā. Meṇṭha's style is truly epic, a forceful narrative but with many touches of humour. The story belongs to the wars of the gods and demons. At the end of the last cycle, when the Earth was overwhelmed by the Flood and Brahmā slept in the universal night, Hayagriva conquered Heaven and carried off the *Veda* from Brahmā's mouth. The rout of Indra and the gods is described with subtle humour and Meṇṭha provoked controversy over his portrayal of Hayagrīva as a noble hero, which, however, reflected greater glory on Viṣṇu who alone could overcome him.

Since Rājaśekhara calls Meṇṭha a reincarnation of Vālmīki, suggesting that he retold the Rāma story, we should search among the *kāvyas* discussed by the critics for a work worthy of such a tribute. By way of conjecture we may draw attention to two remarkable plays which can be reconstructed in outline from the critics. The *Kṛtyārāvaṇa*, 'Rāvaṇa and the Witch', presented the main story from Sītā's abduction to her rescue, in the 'violent' mode of stage business, the *rasa* being the 'furious' but with the 'compassionate' prominent too on account of Rāma's extreme sufferings. 'Rāma Deceived', *Chalitarāma*, shows Rāma misled by surviving enemies, in the apocryphal sequel, into suspecting Sītā's virtue and banishing her. Twin sons are born to her in exile. When they grow up, Lava tries to capture Rāma's sacrificial horse released for a Vedic *aśvamedha*. but is taken prisoner by Lakśmaṇa, Rāma's brother. At court, Lava recognises a golden statue of his mother, her substitute at the rite. Explanations follow, Rāma is convinced that Lava is his own son and discovers that the innocent Sītā is still living. In both plays the *Rāmāyaṇa* is treated with great freedom. The style of the quotations seems consistent with Meṇṭha's, including the humour and the absence of lyricism.

Kālidāsa is associated with 'Vikramāditya; in tradition, but this may refer to Skanda Gupta, who used that title, whilst the poet is also supposed to have met the Vākāṭaka Pravarasena II (c. 410-40). Essentially a lyric poet, he wrote epics and dramas too, taking advantage of the lyric tendency which had always pervaded *kāvya*. He is appreciated for the *vaidarbha* style and especially for 'sweetness', whilst his waywardness sometimes puzzled the critics, sometimes pleased them (Kuntaka found in it the natural play of genius). Kālidāsa's most quoted work is the lyric poem *Meghasandeśa*, 'Cloud Message', in which a distracted lover far from his beloved attempts to send her a message by a passing cloud at the beginning of the rains. The description of the route to be taken affords opportunity for the utmost fancy in that the landmarks are such as would be thought to appeal to a cloud: beautiful rivers who will return his love, high palaces, mountains. The short epic *Kumārasambhava*, 'Origin of Kumāra', includes Indra's humorous plot to make a father of Śiva the gods having been defeated (as usual) by a demon, whom only a son of Śiva can kill. The longer epic *Raghuvaṃśa* is a portrait gallery of the kings of Rāma's line, illustrating the four ends, virtue, wealth, pleasure, and release, pursued by the different rulers. Only in relation to this discussion of ends can we see any thematic unity and development in the poem, which otherwise is a series of detached episodes. At the conclusion the dissolute Agnivaraṇa carries pleasure to a ruinous extreme, but dies leaving his pregnant queen with 'royal fortune' and hope for the future of the dynasty under the guidance of the ministers.

Of Kālidāsa's three plays, the *Mālavikāgnimitra* is dramatically the best and the least lyrical; it is probably the earliest. The story is a love intrigue at the Śuṅga court, the comic *rasa* perhaps predominating. The *Vikramorvaśīya* is a musical play (*toṭaka*, a variety of *nāṭaka*) on the Vedic story of Purūravas and the nymph Urvaśī. The main interest is the character study of Urvaśī, who is purely human. Lyric and *lāsya* elements appear, especially in the pathetic scene where the hero has lost her. The *Abhijñānaśākuntala*. 'Token Śakuntalā', is admired for its lyricism, but its hero does nothing, things happen to him through fate, a curse or divine intervention, his character is a blank. The heroine is better characterised but also the helpless plaything of supernatural powers. Thus there is no real action but only a certain depth of helpless feeling. The story is changed from the more realistic history in the *Mahābhārata* of an ancestor of the Bhāratas. Kālidāsa is a poet of love, of women sharply portrayed, and for Ānandavardhana one of the great exponents of suggestion.

The *Setubandha*, 'Building of the Causeway', by Pravarasena II, is a Māhārāṣṭrī epic on Rāma's invasion of Laṅkā, the main theme being loyalty, especially in the character of Rāma's ally Sugrīva. On the march, Rāma subdues the Ocean God so that his army of monkeys can build a causeway of mountains across to Laṅkā. At the critical moment of the battle, when Rāma is wounded, Sugrīva's heroism saves the day.

'The Kick' is a satirical monologue by ṣyāmilaka (fifth century) set in 'Imperial City', evidently Ujjayinī, with a collection of 'rogues' or parasites at least partly historical and contemporary. The Producer requests informers and hypocrites to leave the theatre, since the play is only for enjoyment. The parasite, Śyāmilaka himself, then convenes the assembly of parasites to try a harlot for the sin of kicking a foolish brāhman. But they find the fault is the brāhman's and prescribe a suitable expiation for him.

Saṃghadāsa's *Vasudevahiṇḍi*, 'Wanderings of Vasudeva', shows the enrichment of Jaina universal history by the incorporation of some of the adventures of Naravāhanadatta from the *Bṛhatkathā*, but narrated of Kṛṣṇa's father Vasudeva instead. Saṃghadāsa knew he was writing fiction in this prose novel in Māhārāṣṭrī, though he illustrates Jaina doctrine by making the adventures the result of action in a former life, but later writers, such as Hemacandra, accepted it all as sober history.

Amaruka perfectly exemplifies the technique of producing rasa by presenting emotional situations, in this case a 'Hundred' (*Śataka*) situations between lovers, each described in miniature in a single verse. Though the form is similar, we are far from the village life of Sātavāhana, for the heroes here are aristocrats or gentry, like the wealthy amateurs of the *Kāmasūtra*. Using long metres, Amaruka concentrates an extraordinary amount of action or talk in each verse, hinting at still more in the past. He writes with tenderness; nothing is higher than love.

Bhāravi's (sixth century) *Kirātārjunīya* is the best epic now available, presenting, as Kuntaka points out, a short episode from the *Mahābhārata* as a complete whole. The narrative style is truly epic and heroic, sweeping vigorously upward from the tense opening scene, the disturbing report of a spy, to the sudden climax when Śiva, the supposed Kirāta fighting Arjuna over a hunting incident, reveals himself and grants the decisive weapons which will enable the Pāṇḍavas to win the Bhārata battle (thus the outcome of the entire *Mahābhārata* is here determined, the story is ended). This rich burden of description customary for an epic is brought in naturally by such scenes as Indra's army of nymphs attacking the ascetic Arjuna in the mountains. The characterisation is brilliant.

Subandhu's movel *Vāsavadattā* is a highly romantic and improbable story treasured by the paṇḍits for the double meanings in almost every sentence.

Viśākhadatta's *Mudrārākṣasa*, 'Signet Rākṣasa', is a play of political intrigue and secret agents, in which the famous minister Cāṇakya (Kauṭalya) destroys the remaining enemies of Candragupta Maurya after the death of Nanda, winning over the best man among them, Nanda's minister Rākṣasa, to the new king's cause. This is one of the rare works in which anything like a 'national' or 'Indian' sentiment is suggested in place of the usual universalistic outlook, most of the enemies being 'barbarians' (*mlecchas*). Only fragments are now available of Viśākhadatta's other plays: the *Devīcandragupta* on Candra

'Vikramāditya' killing the last Śaka, the *Abhisārikāvañcitaka* which is a sequel to Bhāsa's 'Dream Vāsavadattā', and the *Rāghavānanda* bringing out the heroic character of Rāma in the war against Rāvaṇa. All these plays were popular with the old critics and their author was one who excelled at portraying character on the stage.

We may well remember here the rich repertory of the classical theatre in this period by naming a few apparently lost plays important in the discussions of the critics: Nalavijaya in which the loss of Nala's kingdom was reported, not shown, in accordance with a convention; 'Rambhā and Nalakūbara'; *Uṣāharaṇa* on Uṣā and Aniruddha; 'Menakā and Nahuṣa', a *toṭaka* on the union of a king and a nymph; 'Śarmiṣṭha's Marriage' (with Yayāti); 'Joy of the Pāṇḍavas'; *Rāghavābhyudaya*, with Kaikeyi as the root of all Rāma's misfortunes; *Jānakīrāghava* featuring Sītā and deviating greatly from the *Rāmāyaṇa* by bringing Rāvaṇa in at the outset as Rāma's rival for her hand. The last seems the best of these 'histories'. In contrast we have six famous comedies: *Śaśivilāsa, Śaśikalā Kalikeli, Sairandhrikā, Bṛhatsubhadraka* and *Vikaṭanitambā*, all named after their heroes or heroines; the last, 'Broad Buttocks', a learned lady who suffered from her husband's ignorance.

From the Emperor Harṣa (seventh century) we have three plays which have stood the test of time in the theatre, as well as two Buddhist hymns. The *Nāgānanda*, a *bodhisattva* play like Candragomin's, has held the stage down to the present day in Keralā, though the audiences there are not Buddhist. The *rasa* has always been a matter of philosophical controversy and practical interpretation; the excellent commentator Śivarāma concludes that it may be either the calmed or the heroic, besides which all the others are developed too in a harmonious whole. The other two are 'light plays' on invented stories about Udayana, *Ratnāvalī* and *Priyadarśikā*. Harṣa's contemporary, the Pallava King Mahendravarman I, wrote a comedy *Mattavilāsa* satirizing the quarrels among ascetics. The *Veṇīsamhāra* of Nārāyana (in Orissa?) has been accepted as the best play on the Bhārata Battle. Yudhisthira's brother Bhīma is the hero, because he kills Duryodhana and binds up Draupadi's braid of hair (*veṇi*) which she had kept dishevelled until her humiliation was avenged. The play opens with his impatience to fight, whilst Yudhiṣṭhira is still trying for a peaceful settlement.

Bāṇa at Harṣa's court is universally regarded as the greatest master of Sanskrit prose. His style varies according to the content and the genre (biography bold and studied, novel delicate and flowing), but with more of what Kuntaka calls 'cultivated' ('beautiful' through art). The *Harṣacarita* is a biography of the young Harṣa, explaining how he found royal fortune. *Kādambarī* is a psychological novel of the timidities and missed opportunities of youth, leading to tragedy; but no tragedy is final in Indian literature, since transmigration may bring the lovers together is final in Indian literature, since transmigration may bring the lovers together is final in Indian literature, since transmigration may bring the lovers together again. Unluckily Bāṇa died leaving the novel unfinished just before the expected culminating tragedy of Kādambari herself. His son wrote an ending, we do not know how close to his father's intentions, and others also tried their hands at the enigma. Bāna's dramas, of which the best-known was on the Bhārata Battle, seem to be lost, but we have his hymn in praise of the Great Goddess (Caṇdi, Pārvati), full of verbal fireworks such as alliteration. Mayūra, said to be Bāṇa's father-in-law, goes much further in this word play in his hymn to the Sun God.

Of epics in the seventh century we may note first two 'grammatical' poems, in which the narrative is devised in such a way as to provide systematic illustration of Sanskrit-derivations. Bhaṭṭi's *Rāvaṇavadha* thus retells the story of Rāma, often with humorous effect, incorporating as a break four cantos illustrating Bhāmaha's poetics. It proved popular with students and was even translated into Javanese. Bhosa (Bhaumaka, Bhima, Vyoṣa, seem corruptions) in his *Rāvaṇārjunīya* performed the more difficult feat of illustrating the whole of Pāṇini's grammar (except Vedic forms) in the exact order of the original. The story is the defeat of Rāvaṇa by Arjuna Kārtavīrya.

It is possible that the mysterious Bhartṛhari, author of the 'Three Hundred' lyrics on policy, the sensitive, and renunciation, was Bhaṭṭi (=Bhartṛ) Bhartṛhari is the philosopher, bitter and ironical; his vacillation between love and detachment sometimes baffled critics seeking to determine the *rasa*.

Dharmakīrti, the Buddhist philosopher, may be compared with Bhartṛhari, though with a different individual turn, in his lyrics of despair at seeing how anything good excites only envy in others, beauty likewise being wasted.

Māgha's epic 'Slaying of Śiśupāla' is outwardly regular, but in content he is essentially a lyric poet, so that half the poem is like an anthology of descriptive verses, much appreciated by critics, relating to places the hero happened to pass on his expedition. The story is Kṛṣṇa's killing of Śiśupāla at Yudhiṣṭhira's *rājasūya* consecration, but changing the original narrative in the *Mahābhārata* completely to create more *rasa*, as Kuntaka points out.

Daṇḍin, the critic, was also famous, says Rājaśekhara, for two other works, an epic telling two stories simultaneously (those of Rāma and Yudhiṣṭhira) and the novel *Avantisundarī*. The poetic *tour de force* seems lost; of the novel we have 400 pages supplemented by a summary, but the conclusion is still missing. Deliberately confounding history and fiction, or biography and novel, according to his own critical doctrine, Daṇḍin sets his imaginary story of Rājahaṃsa and his two sons against a detailed panorama of Purāṇic history. The latter having in part the form of prophecy by ancient sages, Daṇḍin uses the humorous device of having King Rpuñjaya of Magadha (sixth century B.C.) read his own history, with dismay at learning he is to be the last of his line. The King takes evasive action, retiring to a forest and consulting a sage, who enables him to survive more than a millennium until all the prophesied dynasties of Magadha have petered out. Rpuñjaya then returns and consecrates his son Rājahaṃsa, but he is defeated by the King of Avanti and driven into hiding in the forest. Here his sons Haṃsavāhana and Rājavāhana, reincarnations of Kṛṣṇa's sons Pradyumna and Sāmba, are born, and the elder is mysteriously abducted by a wild goose. Rājavāhana grows up to restore the family fortune by conquering the world. The critical point in his career is his clandestine marriage with Avantisundarī, daughter of his father's enemy, which almost proves fatal to him and further embroils him with the wizard Vīraśekhara, son of Mānasavega of the *Bṛhatkathā*, who was about to abduct her for himself. Rājavāhana is taken captive and carried along with the Avanti army, to be released in a battle which follows and reunited with the Avanti army, to be released in a battle which follows and reunited with seven boyhood friends who have meanwhile made their fortunes. The favourite episode of this reunion, each telling his own adventures, has been circulated separately under the misleading title 'Ten Boys' (or 'Ten Princes'). The continuation beyond this is missing, but it is clear that the story will culminate with the conquest of the wizards, rescue of Avantisundari, and reunion with Haṃsavāhana (who is perhaps Narvāhanadatta temporarily ejected from his empire). Daṇḍin is fond of fantastic incidents and coincidences, explained by his philosophy of fatalism, but in contrast he has many episodes of extreme realism demonstrating the attainment of power and wealth through unscrupulous cunning. His outlook is completely amoral.

Kumāradāsa from Ceylon may have studied with Daṇḍin in Kāñcī. His epic *Jānakīharaṇa* retells the *Rāmāyana* from the incarnation of Viṣṇu as Rāma, preceded by the curse on his father which is supposed to have caused his exile, to the victory over Rāvana. The style is more epic than Māgha and the narrative rapid and with much briefer descriptions; there is much play of sounds.

Mātrarāja is one of the master of Kuntaka's 'intermediate' style. His *Tāpasavatsarāja* is a play on the same story as Bhāsa's 'Dream Vāsavadattā', but with Udayana as the central character instead of Vāsavadattā. The *Udāttarāghava*, 'Exalted Rāghavas' (Rāma and Bharata), like Bhāsa's 'Statue', starts with Rāma's interrupted consecration and exile and ends with the triumphant reunion of the two brothers. Mātrarāja made serious changes in the story in order to enhance the characters morally, thereby provoking controversy. The Emperor Yaśovarman (eighth century) objected to such changes, in the Prologue of his own Rāma play *Rāmābhyudaya*. This, though not now available, is extensively known as a classic of dramatic construction much discussed and quoted by the old critics. Adhering closely to the *Rāmāyaṇa*, Yaśovarman produces unity of action by starting only with Rāma's first clash with the demons, in exile. The action and characterisation are powerful (e.g. Rāvaṇa's anger).

Bhavabhūti, the favourite poet and dramatist of some connoisseurs, from Mahārāṣṭra settled at Yaśovarman's court in Kānyakubja. His *Mālatīmādhava* is a 'fiction' of the triumph of love over obstacles, especially over political convenience. A king proposes to have the daughter of one of his ministers offered to a court favourite, as part of a political alliance. The girl loves another and the lovers resist the plan, aided by sympathetic Buddhist nuns in the role of go-betweens. In an unsuccessful attempt at elopement the hero shows him mettle, attracts popular support, and thus so impresses the king that he changes his plans, preferring to have a brave young man under his patronage. The *Uttararāmacarita* takes up the apocryphal last book of the *Rāmāyana,* the grievous renewed exile of Sītā. Public opinion held her unfit to be queen after being the prisoner of Rāvaṇa. Here Bhavabhūti brings out most fully the pathos of human experience, bitter yet touched by the sweetness of association with happy moment in the past, the contrast intensifying both the pain and the sweetness. The minds of sublime heroes are as hard, as diamonds yet as soft as flowers, says Bhavabhūti, since Rāma has unflinchingly done his public duty whilst privately suffering mental agony. A second Rāma 'history', which is incomplete as now available, the *Mahāviracarita*, unified the action by introducing Rāvana at the beginning as Rāma's rival (cf. The *Jānakirāghava*, in which, however, Sitā is the central character instead of Rāma). Disappointed when Rāma wins Sitā, it is Rāvaṇa who brings about the intrigue and Rāma's exile, placing Sitā within his reach. Bhavbhūti's plays are in the best dramatic tradition of conflict and passion, but on a scale giving the fullest scope to lyrics evoking the feeling of his characters, in relation to society and even more to nature. His lyrics are perhaps unequalled in expressiveness and in the beauty of their sound.

Vākapatrāja, also at Yaśovarman's court, wrote an enigmatic epic in Māhārāṣṭri, 'Slaying of the Gauda', on his king. The expected history of the victory over a king of Magadha (= Gauda) is merely alluded to and the body of the narrative describes a pleasure excursion, rather than a military expedition, to the four quarters of India. The nostalgic atmosphere and bitter verses on good and evil, on the vanity of the present age when success is reserved for mediocrity and jealously withheld from excellence, suggest that Yaśovarman had already met his tragic end in battle with the King of Kaśmīra. The ephemeral military victories of a generous poet-emperor, dear to the assembly to whom Vākpatirāja reads his epic, are superseded by a more durable poetic conquest.

The eighth century is rich in extant novels. Kutūhala's *Lilāvatī*, sometimes bracketed with Bāṇa's *Kādambari* as typical novels, is unlike it in being in Prākrit (Māhārāṣṭri) and in verse. The critics found verse acceptable for Prākrit novels (including Apabhraṃśa and in due course Hindi), the form being otherwise unaffected. Kutūhala like Daṇḍin blends history and fiction, for his hero is Sātavāhana and is guided by Nāgārjuna, but marries a princess from Ceylon after an adventure in the 'Underworld' (Pātāla) and other fanciful episodes; in fact he claims to have invented the story in order to amuse his wife.

Haribhadra's immense Samarāditya, in Māhārāṣṭri prose, is a Jaina 'virtue' (*dharma*) novel, being written from the standpoint of ethics instead of pleasure or worldly success. It is also an 'entire' (*sakala*) novel, in that it follows the heroes' experiences through a series of lives, from the origin of a subconscious disposition (the 'cause', *nidāna*) which torments them until its secret is revealed to them. Samarāditya in a former life was negligent towards an intended guest, an ascetic; the latter misunderstood this as deliberate injury and conceived an inveterate hatred, pursuing and injuring his imagined enemy through nine lives. Thus in one they are husband and wife and the wife repeatedly tries to kill her husband through this irrational hatred. The *Dhūrtākhyāna*, 'Rogues' History', is an 'illustrating novel' satirising Brahmanism and especially Purānic history and mythology. A group of rogues temporarily immobilised by the rains pass the time by holding a contest in telling lies about themselves, the loser to stand dinner for the party. Each lie must be confirmed as credible by adducing a parallel from the Purānas. In the end a female rogue confounds the others with a tale to the effect that they are all her runaway slaves. Haribhadra makes it clear that his aim in debunking myths is not sectarian but rationalist (*yuktimant*): his satire is directed at the growth of fantasy which has concealed the truth hidden in all the Indian religions.

Haribhadra's pupil Uddyotana wrote another long Māhārāṣṭrī 'entire novel', in *campū* form, illustrating the driving force of five passions, anger, pride, deceit, greed, and delusion, in five souls through several lives. He calls it a 'mixed' novel, depicting pleasure and success as well as the dominant virtue theme. It does indeed contain interesting episodes such as meeting a group of alchemists in the mountains smelting metals and trying to obtain gold.

Dāmodaragupta's illustrating novel' *Kuṭṭanīmata*, 'Theory of the Bawd', is in verse though in Sanskrit. The heroine goes to a marvellously ugly old bawd for instruction in making money from wealthy citizens and receives it with stories illustrating the science of harlotry and such pitfalls as falling in love and trouble with fathers. The reader of this satire, its author claims, will never be deceived by parasites, hetairas, rogues, and bawds.

Murāri, 'disregarding Bhavabhūti', again dramatised the main Rāma story. His *Anargharāghava* includes so many lyrics, admittedly beautiful but often hardly relevant, as to make his drama too tenuous.

Yogeśvara in the Pāla Empire of Magadha is known through anthologies for his vivid descriptions of the hard but usually cheerful life of the villages.

In the ninth century Abhinanda retold part of the Rāma story as a Sanskrit epic, beginning about the same point as Pravarasena. He begins in a simple style not unlike Vālmīki's, but with numerous figures, and elaborates the speeches in a leisurely manner. This *Rāmacarita* keeps close to the original and is very long, though its description are strictly subordinate to the narrative. Abhinanda's sweet, melodious language, imagery, and occasional theological reflections made him a favourite of some critics. He also wrote dramas, among which the heroic play *Bhīmaparākrama* on an episode from the *Mahābhārata* is available.

Ratnākara's *Haravijaya* brought almost equal from the critics, though it is an epic opposite to Abhinanda's in every way except great length. There was little to narrate, for Śiva's victory over the demon Andhaka is a very simple story, so the epic is instead filled with descriptions, exceeding even Māgha in these and in linguistic difficulty. The description of Śiva's *tāndava* dance is an appropriate and attractive opening, establishing a transcendental setting.

Śivasvāmin's epic *Kapphiṇābhyudaya* returns to the scale, and partly the style, of Māgha, whilst the poet claims to follow Meṇṭha and his style varies greatly according to the topic. The story is from Buddhist legend: a war in which the Buddha intervenes as peacemaker and sends the invader home to rule justly. Buddhaghoṣa's *Padyacūdāmaṇi* on the life of the Buddha is an expression of devotion rather than an epic.

Apabhraṃśa epic, its conventions established by Caturmukha whose works have not yet been found, comes into its own with two examples by Svayambhū, the *Padmacarita* on Rāma and the *Ariśṭanemicarita* on the twenty-second jina and the Jaina version of the events of the *Mahābhārata* with the life of Kṛṣṇa. Svayambhū takes his narratives from earlier Jaina works; he is praised for the beauty of his language and figurative expressions and is remarkable for his tolerant and syncretistic outlook.

Śaktibhadra's *Āścaryacūdāmaṇi* has proved one of the most popular plays, partly because it makes so much of the transformations of the demons, particularly Rāvaṇa and his sister, going beyond Mātrarāja, who already had several such disguises. The play begins with Rāma's encounter with Rāvaṇa's sister disguised and Sitā's abduction by the disguised Rāvaṇa, and ends with Rāma's triumph.

The transformation are counteracted (but too late) by a magic ring and the magic crest jewel which gives the play its title.

The philosopher Jayanta wrote a play on the religious situation in Kaśmira, the *Āgamaḍambara*, 'Pomp of Scriptures'. His aim is to show the superior knowledge and humanity of the brāhmans and satirise the Buddhists, Jainas, Lokāyatikas, and Kāpālikas. Though some unworthy sects should be proscribed, the better schools share the high moral purpose of the Vedic tradition and among these there should be toleration; their scriptures are different entrances to the same house.

King Kulaśekhara (c. A.D. 900) wrote two plays, which have remained popular, to inaugurate new techniques of production on the Keralā stage, claiming to apply Ānandavardhana's doctrine of 'revealed' meaning. It is supposed that all the reforms of the Keralā actors stem from him, including the repetition of the speeches in gesture language and the extemporised 'Tamil' (now Malayālam) patter of the 'fool', equivocally making fun of present-day personalities along with other characters in the play, but this seems unlikely. The *Subhadrādhanañjaya* has the story of Arjuna eloping with Kṛṣṇa's sister, after numerous misunderstandings and the opposition of Kṛṣṇa's brother. The Tapatīsaṃvaraṇa is the love of Saṃvaraṇa, one of the Bhārata emperors, and the daughter of the Sun God. Kulaśekhara's novel *Āścaryamañjari*, praised by Rājaśekhara, seems to be lost. A popular heroic play *Kalyānasaugandhika*, on Bhima fetching the Saugandhika Flower for Draupadi but being challenged by his unknown brother Hanumant on the way, was written by Nilakaṇṭha, perhaps at Kulaśekhara's court. Vāsudeva there composed a series of rhymed epics in Sanskrit, on Yudhiṣṭhira, Kṛṣṇa, Śiva, and Nala. Though a regular feature of Apabhraṃśa and modern Indo-Aryan poetry, rhyme in Sanskrit is a special effect like alliteration or punning. Vāsudeva's rhymes are complicated, but seem natural and effortless, which explains the widespread appreciation of his works. Līlāśuka probably at Kulaśekhara's court wrote the very popular lyric *Kṛṇṣakarṇāmṛta,* on Kṛṣṇa as the sexually precocious infant loved by all women, but interpreted as symbolising God attracting all souls, thus an early example of Vaiṣṇava devotional Kāvya. Another classic rhyming poem, partly double-meaning also, is Nītivarman's Kīcakavadha on Bhīma slaying Kīcaka, of unknown date. Dhanañjaya's Dvisandhāna (c. A.D. 800) is the earliest double-meaning epic available, simultaneously narrating the Rāmāyaṇa and Mahābhārata.

Rājaśekhara was a junior contemporary of Kulaśekhara. Though primarily a dramatist, he is appreciated rather for the innumerable brilliant lyric verses scattered through his works, being perhaps the most popular poet with the anthologists. His epic *Haravilāsa* seems to be lost. His *Bālarāmāyana* is perhaps the longest play ever written exceeding even Murāri's on the same subject, and he even remarks that it is designed to be read, expecting that it would not often be performed. Yet, unlike Murāri, Rājaśekhara has some very effective scenes, such as the confrontation of Rāvaṇa and Sitā in Act I on the occasion of Sitā's *svayaṃvara* ('self-choice' wedding). Of a similar play on the *Mahābhārata* we have only the first two acts. A 'light play' *Viddhaśālabhañiikā* is a comedy of palace intrigue, as is the *Karpūramañjaeī*, a saṭṭaka or light play in Māharāṣṭrī. The vivid expressions which charmed the anthologists bring a strong sense of Rājaśekhara's lively personality to the reader. This is perhaps strongest of all in his critical work *Kāvyamīmāmsā*, where he sets up in pseudo-pedantic style as the model professional writer and legislates a life of palatial comfort, but strenuous well-organised work, for authors.

Kṣemīśvara (tenth century) follows Råjaśekhara with two plays on stories not new to the theatre but not available to us in earlier dramas. The *Naiṣadhānanda* on Nala is particularly effective, with its opening scene of the hero stòpped by Indra, then his exiling and the doubly portrayed incident of Nala's separation from Damayantī, presented by both of them in turn. The *Caṇḍakauśika* on Hariścandra opens ominously but with touches of irony through the presence of the 'fool' and the queen's groundless suspicion of her husband's night vigil; after this the compassionate and horrific *rasas* are developed to the utmost in the slave market and cemetery scenes. This play has the atmosphere of a Buddhist *bodhisattva* drama such as Candragomin's, presented in Brāhmanical terms. In both plays Kṣemīśvara is faithful to his *itihāsa* sources. The style is simple and the action relatively rapid; unlike Rājaśekhara's, these are primarily plays for the stage and not for readers and anthologists. It is remarkable that both deal with utter disaster, the loss of kingdoms followed by terrible trials but eventual restoration, and possible that the stories were chosen as comment on contemporary events (Mahīpāla's struggles).

Bhallaṭa's (*fl.* 880-900) collection of *anyāpadeśas*, 'citations of something else', is the classic in a lyric form much appreciated later, which criticises social abuses through the imagery of natural phenomena. His target is the worthless and crooked people who successfully push their way into positions of authority and wealth.

In Siddha's great allegorical novel of transmigration, *Upamitibhavaprapañcā* (A.D. 906), 'release' is the only escape from the tyranny of King Action and Queen Time. Jainism is thus shown as a subversive political movement. The hero struggles upwards from life to life, this being an 'entire' novel, against evil passions. Whereas Haribhadra, his model, studied senseless evil in human relationships, Siddha is concerned with internal struggles.

Dhanapāla's *Tilakamañjari* (c. 970), though formally similar, is an interesting contrast to Bāna's *Kādambari*. Since the author completed it, it offers a model of construction of a novel, beginning about the middle and bringing in other segments of the story in the wrong order narrated by characters, maintaining suspense to the end. Though the author was a Jaina, this is purely a 'pleasure' novel like those of Guṇāḍhya and Bāṇa. The more than ninety characters are quite different from Bāṇa's: youth is less diffident and tragic, especially in the person of the impetuous Malayasundari, and the heroes are resourceful, though scrupulous (unlike Daṇḍin's).

A different Dhanapāla about the same time wrote the novel *Bhaviṣyadatta* in Apabhraṃśa verse, a story of merchant life and sea voyages in which a second wife tries to destroy her stepson.

The *campū* now seems to increase in popularity. Trivikrama's *Nala* (c. 915) is renowned as a marvellous exercise in double meanings; his simpler *Madālasā* is neglected. Somadeva's *Yaśastilaka* (959) on the Jaina legend of Yaśodhara, a king poisoned by his unfaithful wife, and his subsequent rebirths, resembles an 'entire novel'. His didactic intentions are evident throughout.

Puṣpadanta's *Mahāpurāṇa* is generally acclaimed as the best Apabhraṃśa epic. A modest and disillusioned wanderer who finally accepted patronage with reluctance, his poetry is deeply felt and his wit pungent. The subject is the vast universal history of the Jainas, dominated by the 'sixty-three great men' (including Rāma, Rāvaṇa, Kṛṣṇa, and the *jinas*). A short *Yaśodharacarita* retells the legend just mentioned. The *Nāgakumāracarita* might be classed as a verse novel, or rather a romance, of an infant prince who falls down a well and is adopted by a dragon, but the story is a traditional one of one of the twenty-four Kāmadevas, the most handsome men.

Three eleventh-century epics are based on contemporary history. Padmagupta's *Navasāhasāṅkacarita* on a Parmāra king of Avanti (Mālava) romanticises his marriage with a Karṇāṭaka princess into a war with 'demons' and union with a 'dragon' girl after descending into the underworld. But the Paramāra Rājputs themselves are of supernatural origin and their poet relates the creation of their ancestor in Vasiṣtha's sacrificial fire. Regardless of the history, this epic has been enjoyed by critics for its descriptions and other poetic qualities. The same is true of Bilhaṇa's *Vikramāṅkadevacarita* on a Cālukya emperor, which is close to actual facts yet has been more admired as a purely literary classic. Bilhaṇa also wrote a 'light play' on another patron and the beautiful elegy *Caurapañcāśikā*, supposedly autobiographical, of a liaison with a princess which almost cost him his life. Atula's *Mūṣakavaṃśa* is the history of a dynasty in north Keralā from its legendary origin in the time of Paraśurāma. Though very useful as history, this epic too has been preserved for its poetry.

Lakṣmīdhara's *Cakrapāṇivijaya* is an epic on the traditional story of Kṛṣṇa's defeat of the demon Bāṇa, son of Bali, after the clandestine marriage of his grandson Aniruddha with Bāṇa's daughter Uṣā. There are no long descriptive digressions here, the story of love and war itself giving plenty of scope for the poet's powers. Mahāsena's epic *Pradyumnacarita* gives a Jaina version of the story of Aniruddha's father. Kanakāmara's Apabhraṃsa epic *Karakaṇḍacarita* narrates an old legend of a 'saint' recognised by both Jainas and Buddhists. Jaina epics in several languages, mostly on one or other of the twenty-four *jinas*, are too numerous from the tenth century onwards to be discussed here, despite the literary value of many of them.

Soḍḍhala's *Udayasundarī* (c. 1025) is a Sanskrit *campū* novel more romantic and less realistic than most, with metamorphoses and adventures in the underworld and little characterisation, but beautifully and imaginatively written. The critic King Bhoja's *Śṛṅgāramañjari* is an entertaining 'illustrating novel' on the various types of love. These are shown in cautionary tales instructing a geisha on which kinds of lover to accept or avoid, and the heroines generally have a bad time. Bhoja's simple and elegant campū version of the *Rāmāyaṇa* has been much more widely appreciated in recent centuries. Vādībhasimha's *Gadyacintāmaṇi* is one of the rare prose 'biographies' extant, but on the old Jaina legend of Jīvandhara. This legend owes much to the *Bṛhatakthā* and the work is almost a novel. It is noteworthy for its fine prose style, perhaps second only to Bāṇa's. A more regular biography is Someśvarsa's *Vikramāṅkābhyudaya*, on his father who was also Bilhana's subject.

Some anonymous popular collections of short stories, of unknown date and in multiple recensions, may be noted here. The *Śukasaptati* has as theme faithless wives and crafty harlots. The *Vetālapañacaviṃśatī* and *Siṃhāsanadvātriṃśika* both concern the legendary Vikramāditya in most versions but originally it seems Sātavāhana was the hero (with Nāgārjuna). In the first, the king has to answer riddles with which the stories end, in the second the stories are about him. We may add that Somadeva II (c. 1050) used a sketch of the *Bṛhatkathā* as a frame for a huge collection of stories skillfully narrated, the *Kathāsaritsāgara*. The romance of Mādhavānala and Kāmakandalā is a popular tale of illicit love, ending happily through the intervention of the chivalrous Vikramāditya. The *Malayasundrī* likewise exists in several paraphrases, but the original is attributed to Keśin (seventh century B.C.). In fact it is a romance of magic and a wicked stepmother, a fairy story not likely to be earlier than the ninth century A.D.

Kṣemendra's illustrating novels are bitter satires on corrupt bureaucracy and successful deceit and vice. The *Kalāvilāsa* introduces Mūladeva ('Whose God is Capital') in his School of Theft, instructing a student in the science of deception and the various professions through which greed is satisfied: bureaucracy, harlotry, itinerant music and acting, jewellery, medicine, astrology, drug peddling, trade, begging, imposture, etc. Under bureaucracy the different types of arrogance are treated. These are further displayed as weaknesses in the *Darpadalana*. The *Narmamālā* satirises the private lives of the bureaucrats and their wives. The *Deśopadeśa* displays scoundrels and cheats, including the miser, parasite, and undisciplined students. The *Samayamātṛkā* is the life of the bawd Kankālī, who outlives her many husbands.

Kṣemendra's plays seem to be lost, but *Probodhacandrodaya*, a very different allegorical play on Vedānta by his contemporary Kṛṣnamiśra, has been a model for similar plays advocating various schools of thought.

The best twelfth-century epic is Harṣa's *Naiṣadhacarita* on Nala. The sensitive *rasa* predominates, with much of the comic also. The author was a philosopher and displays his learning, but the descriptive effusions are relevant to the story and the style full of charm. The scale is grand and Harṣa did not finish the work. Sukumāra's *Kṛṣṇavilāsa*, on the young Kṛṣṇa up to his carrying off the Pārijāta, in very simple style, is the most popular epic in Keralā. Maṅkha's *Śrikaṇṭhacarita* on Śiva burning the three citadels of the demons is among the most beautiful epics, particularly for its descriptions of mountain scenery by the Kāśmīrī author, but its action is brief. Jayānaka's *Pṛthvīrājavijaya* prematurely celebrated the ill-fated Cāhamāna king. Kalhaṇa's *Rājataraṅginī*, a detailed *vaṃśāvalīs* or history of Kaśmira, under the influence of the *Mahābhārata* aim to produce the calmed *rasa* through the complation of futile ambitions (the *vaṃśāvalīs* continue the history of the *Purāṇas* and are rarely literary).

The Jaina theatre flourished with eleven plays by the critic Rāmacandra, on Nala, Rāma, Kṛṣṇa, Hariścandra, etc., and three fictions. Rāmabhadra and Hastimalla dramatised Jaina legends. Heroic plays are now numerous, by Vijayapāla, Prahlādanadeva, Kāñcana, and Vatsarāja as well as Rāmacandra. The same Vatsarāja (c. 1200) wrote examples of the three types of archaic play on the gods and demons, a comedy, and a satirical monologue; his gods and demons are as humorous as his bogus ascetic and gambler. Śaṅkhadhara's *Laṭakamelaka* is a two-act comedy in which a ninety-nine-year-old bawd finds herself a husband among a crowd of charlatans. Jayadeva's *Gitagovinda*, a *rāgakāvya* drama in songs linked by narrative, is a most popular classic which has often been imitated. Its Sanskrit lyrics use the metres of vernacular Apabhraṃśa to express Rādhā's love for Kṛṣṇa.

The Jaina novel continued to flourish (relatively few non-Jaina novels have been preserved, though many titles are known from the critics). Dhaneśvara's *Surasundari*, in Māhārāṣṭrī verse, is a regular novel in the manner of the *Tilakamañjarī*, except that at the end the hero and heroine leave the world and attain enlightenment. Sādhāraṇa's *Vilāsavatī* is in Apabhraṃśa and Mahendrasūri's *Narmadāsundarī* is a *dharma* novel in Māhārāṣṭrī verse and prose.

The Trukish conquests of more than half India between 900 and 1300 were perhaps the most destructive in human history. As Muslims, the conquerors aimed not only to destroy all other religions but also to abolish secular culture. Their burning of libraries explains the large gaps in our knowledge of earlier literature. Our view now depends mainly on what has been preserved in the far south, in Keralā, supplemented by some Jaina libraries which miraculously escaped and by such outlying collections as those of Nepal. Though the Indian tradition was thus cut off over wide areas, it developed vigorously where Indian rule continued, including Rājasthān, Orissā, etc., as well as the south. In fact about 90 per cent of the extant Sanskrit literature, even, belongs to the period since A.D. 1200 and was written the regions remaining under Indian rule. If we now devote little space to it, compared with the classics above, that should not be regarded as an adverse judgement (we reject the prejudiced opinion about 'decadence') but as due partly to lack of space and partly to the general neglect and lack of printed editions. What follows is a small selection among the noteworthy kāvyas.

Amaracandra's *Bālabhārata* has been popular in Rājasthān as distilling the essence of the whole *Mahābhārata* in a kāvya epic. The author belonged to the literary circle of the minister Vastupāla of Gujarāt in the thirteenth century, from which more than ten epics and six dramas survive to show the work of such a group. Among these, the works of Someśvara and Bālacandra are outstanding and the play 'Crushing of the Arrogance of the Amīr' by Jayasiṃha is remarkable as presenting the contemporary history of Vastupāla's victory over the Turks. In this age of perpetual Turkish wars there is a strong turn towards heroic themes. In Orissā, Jayadeva's *Prasannarāghava*, though widely studied for its difficulty and word music, is a variation on Murāri's Rāma play. Sakalavidyācakravartin's *Gadyakarnāmṛta* is a biography of a Hoysala emperor of Karṇāṭaka. The lyrics of Utprekṣāvallabha and Lakṣmīdāsa are admired. Of dramas in the south, we may note Kavivallabha's fiction and Ravivarman's *Pradyumnābhyudaya*.

Among many interesting playwrights in the fourteenth century are: Pratāparudra, for plays on Yayāti and on Uṣā; Narasimha who made a well-constructed drama out of the novel *Kādambarī*; Pūrṇasarasvati who staged a delightful fable of a wild goose marrying a lotus amid dangers from an elephant, a thundercloud, and a storm; Sukumāra for a Rāma play; and Jyotirīśvara in whose comedy two 'ascetics' quarrel over a woman and call in a brāhman arbitrator who decides to keep her for himself. A satirical monologue popular in Kerala since the region of Rāmavarman seems inappropriately entitled *Viṭanidrā* in one manuscript and is therefore nameless as well as anonymous. The intrigue is quite different from earlier plays of the type. Agastya's epic *Bālabhārata* has been more popular in the south than Amaracandra's in the north. It is perhaps superior in narrative power, whilst shorter and more independent. Agastya, a great master of Sanskrit expression, wrote also a prose *Kṛṣṇacarita* based on the *Bhāgavata Purāna*, in a sweet and flowing style and producing the atmosphere of a novel rather than a biography. The *Purāṇa* source was a relatively modern one, itself almost a *Kāvya*, which replaced the *Harivaṃśa* supplement to the *Mahābhārata* and became extraordinarily popular as the Kṛṣṇa cult spread. Among other *Kāvyas* based on it, the *campū* of the 'New' Kālidāsa (date uncertain) is very famous. Vidyācakravartin's fine but rather alliterative epic *Rukminīkalyāna* follows the same source. In this century the three rival systems of Vedānta blossomed in the shelter of Vijayanagara with poetic as well as philosophical champions. The Advaitin Vidyāraṇya wrote an epic on the founder of his school, the Dvaitin Nārāyaṇa one on his and many other poetic works. Other Dvaitins wrote epics on different episodes of the Kṛṣṇa cycle. The Viśiṣṭādvaitin Venkatanātha perhaps deserves his greater literary fame than any of these with his epic *Yādavābhyudaya* on the birth and rise of Kṛṣṇa, a lyric poem and an allegorical play. More interesting and original than any of these is the Princess Gangās epic *Madhurāvijaya* on her husband's victory over the Turks in south India, with circumstantial descriptions such as the horrors of the Turkish atrocities in the places they had occupied. It was not new for a woman to write a major *Kāvya*, for the critics mention several in earlier centuries, such as ṣilā who emulated Bāṇa as a novelist, but nothing seems to survive except the mysterious Vijayā's play *Kaumudimahotsava* of uncertain date. Dāmodara's epic *Śivavilāsa* on the marriage of Rāmavarman of Keralā is interesting for social history. Kṛṣṇānanda took the Nala story and wrote an epic contrasting with Harsa's in being short, complete, following easily in *vaidarbha* style, and free from digressions. Ahobala's *Virūpākṣavasantotsava* is a most entertaining *campū* describing the crowds at a popular festival. Guṇasamṛddhi's *Añjanāsundarī* continues the series of Jaina *dharma* novels.

The greatest fifteenth-century writer was probably Diṇḍima (Kavisārvabhauma), praised by later authors, but his works, including an epic *Rāmābhyudaya* and a comedy, are not yet printed. Kāmāksī, apparently his daughter-in-law, modestly praises him in her own 'New' Rāmābhyudaya, called 'exquisite' by a modern critic. Other members of the Diṇḍima family wrote historical epics on the Vijayanagara emperors. The circle of the Eighteen and a Half in Keralā is famous and marks a peak of activity in the theatre and in poetry (Uddaṇḍa, Dāmodarabhaṭṭa, etc.) Gopāla's comic *campū* describes the eleventh *avatāra* of Visnu—as a mango. Śaṅkara's epic *Kṛṣṇavijaya* with its delightful word music is second only to Sukumāra's in popularity in Keralā. In Rājasthān Nayacandra's tragic historical epic *Hammīra* on Cāhamāna king introduced a new spirit into heroic poetry. In Orissā and Āndhra a historical *campū* by Vāsudevaratha and biography by Vāmana are more traditional in outlook. Ananta's Bhārata is recognised as one of the best *campūs*, mainly for its elaborate style. The tradition of the drama in Mithilā was continued by Vidyāpati, using a mixture of Sanskrit and Maithili (instead of Prākrit). His modernising ideas appear also in his Sanskrit illustrating novel *Puruṣaparīksā*, introducing recent heroes in place of Purānic ones.

The 'classical' literature in fact everywhere developed in the closest interaction with the 'modern', i.e. with the vernacular. In the north it is arbitrary to draw a line between 'Hindi' (Braj, Rājaṣthānī, Maithilī, etc.) and Apabhramṣa, for they are the same language, using the same genres and metres. Tulsīdās's epic has the same form as Puṣpadanta's. In the south, Sanskrit and Dravidian writers share ideas. The Oriyā *Mahābhārata, Rāmāyaṇa*, and *Bhāgavata*, assimilating antiquity into the life of the fifteenth and sixteenth centuries, influenced the Sanskrit epics of Divākara, Mārkaṇḍeya, and Jīvadeva. The last also wrote plays and belongs to the Vaiśṇava movement of the sixteenth century, for which Rūpa produced his theory of devotional drama on Kṛṣṇa and plays exemplifying it. Many such plays were written and performed in Orissā, then circulated elsewhere, and popular forms such as the *rāgakāvya* and one-act *goṣṭhī* (e.g. Jayadeva's *Vaiṣṇavāmṛta*) were revived for the purpose. The Keralā variety of Vaiṣṇavism is expressed in *Nārāyaṇa's* lyric Nārāyaṇīya on the whole life of Kṛṣṇa, probably the finest devotional poem in Sanskrit. This Nārāyaṇa is among the greatest and most prolific Sanskrit writers of recent centuries. He wrote a long series of campūs on Purānic and Vedic themes for performance as *kūttu* monologues by comic actors. The Emperor Kṛṣṇadevarāya of Vijayanagara wrote of Kṛṣṇa play. Queen Tirumalā's *Varadāmbikāpariṇaya* is a beautiful biographical campū of her husband Acyutarāya, concluding remarkably with his marriage to another queen and consecration of the latter's son as heir apparent. Equal in style and much richer in content is the long biography *Vyāsayogicarita* of a contemporary logician by Somanātha.

In the seventeenth century Jagannātha, moving between Āndhra, Assam, and the Mughal Empire, reflects the brief flickering of Indian culture within that Empire in the wake of Akbar. His Sanskrit lyrics are popular with the paṇḍits. Jagadīṣvara's *Hāsyārṇava* is a comedy satirising King River of Bad Policy and his depraved administration and probably aimed at the Mughal government after it had reversed Akbar's policy in 1632. The Keralā king Mānaveda, after his *Pūrvabhārata campū* which complements Ananta's and is even more difficult, achieved a unique success with his play *Kṛṣṇagīti* which today is still performed nightly at Guruvayur (with one night a week rest). In form it is a *rāgakāvya* and the prototype of *kathakali*, but with songs in Sanskrit. It covers the entire life of Kṛṣṇa, following especially Śankara's epic. The great upsurge of religion in this period was partly balanced by an output of satirical monologues and comedies too numerous to list and presenting every conceivable subject. A more elaborate satire is Veṅkaṭādhvarin's *campū Viśvagunādarśa*, a dialogue between an optimist and a pessimist; it contains one of the earliest references to the British (at Madras). Bracketed with this among the best *campūs* is Nīlakaṇṭha's *Nilakaṇṭhavijaya*, on the churning of the ocean by the gods and demons and how Śiva got his blue throat, which is full of humour. Among his many other works the satire *Kalividambana* is familiar to studies for its verses on the evils of the present age. Among dramas we may note Mahādeva's play on Rāma, a tangle of spying, suspicion, and impersonation as the demons try to deceive him. With the rise of the Marāthās we have Paramānanda's epic *Sūryavaṃśa* on Śāha, Śivājī, and Śambhu. Classical literature flourished at all the Marāṭha courts. In Orissā among epic poems Govindamiśra's 'Origin of Pradyumna' and Gaṅgādhara's historical *Kośalānanda* are noteworthy.

Rāmapāṇivāda with a wide variety of works in Sanskrit and Māhārāṣṭrī is the greatest eighteenth-century writer. An epic on Rāma seems his most admired work; a play on the same hero shows the ultimate stage of unification of the elements of the legend, from the killing of Tāṭakā. Two street plays, dialogues between a king and his fool, and the two-act comedy *Madanaketucarita* are more immediately entertaining. A' campū and two Māhārāṣṭrī poems belong to the Kṛṣṇa cycle. Rāmpāṇivāda is an elaborate stylist on the models of Bāṇa and Rājaśekhara. Ghanaśyāma is an innovator in the theatre with plays in new forms instead of the traditional act arrangement. The

Navagrahacarita is war among the planets; the *Damaruka* a series of satirical and philosophical dialogues. The *Ānandasundarī* is a regular Māhārāṣṭrī *saṭṭaka*, introducing a telescope in a naval battle. The theatre of this period is extremely rich, including plays on contemporary events. Veṅkayāmātya wrote plays of all the ten types described in the *Nāṭyaśāstra*. Durgeśvara's *Dharmoddharaṇa* is an allegorical play on the restoration of religion and learning under the Marāṭhas, at Vārāṇasi, Ujjayinī, etc. Rājasthān and Orissā naturally shared in the Indian revival (Kṛṣṇakavi, Candraśekhara, etc.) which is marked in Vārāṇasī by the brief career of the scholar-novelist Viśveśvara.

Under the British, the Indian tradition was submerged by the imposition of English as medium of administration and education, except in the 'Native States' such as Travancore and Cochin. The modern vernaculars under this domination party copied European models and developed a hybrid literature which is neither European nor Indian. With political independence the cultural scene has hardly changed as yet and the unity of India is threatened by the centrifugal force of the vernaculars. Vernacular writers often seek European orbits, considered 'modern', lacking the national character and relationship among themselves which only the common Indian tradition could give them. Sanskrit is the only truly national language India has ever had, linking all region and all classes with the immortal springs of Indian thought. If it disappears, with its cultural heritage, India will never be a nation and will surely break up into a series of European-type states. The decision still lies in the future; meanwhile the semi-underground classical tradition conserves its vigour and the twentieth century has produced several hundred Sanskrit plays, whilst the theatre of Bhāsa is being revived in Keralā. India's cultural unity may yet be saved and through it her political unity.

A.K. Warder

LECTURE I

ARYAN COLONISATION OF SOUTHERN INDIA AND CEYLON

I propose to open my first series of lectures as Carmichael Professor with the history of the pre-Maurya period, i.e., of the period extending from about 650 to 325 B.C. It is true that we do not know much about the political history of this period; but political history cannot be the whole history of any country. Again it is the administrative, social, religious and ethnological history which is of much greater importance and far transcends political history in point of human interest and edification. And, for the construction of this history for the period we have selected, we have sufficient materials. We have works of the Sūtra period relating both the Law and Grammar. We have thus the Dharmaśāstras of Baudhāyana, Gautama, Āpastamba and so forth, and the *Aṣṭādhyāyī* of Pānini and Kātyāyana's supplementary aphorisms or *Vārttikas* on it. Further, it was prior to the rise of the Mauryas that the Buddha lived and preached. And there is a general consensus of opinion among scholars that all the earlier works of the Buddhist Pali cannon were put together in the period to which we are confining ourselves.[a] Let us, therefore, utilise these materials and try to see how India was socially, religiously and even politically from 650 to 325 B.C.

The principal characteristic of this period is the completion of the colonisation of Southern India and Ceylon by the Aryans, and this forms the subject of today's lecture. It is worthy of note that the southern half of India was called Dakṣiṇāpatha which means 'Road to the South'. Already in a Vedic hymn,[1] although it is one of the latest, we meet with an expression *dakṣiṇā padā,* meaning 'with southward foot', and used with reference to a man who is expelled to the south. This cannot of course denote the *Dakṣināpatha* or Southern India as we understand it, but rather the country lying beyond the region then inhabited by the Aryans. It was in the Brāhmaṇa period, however, that they for the first time seem to have crossed the Vindhya range which separates the southern from the northern half of India. In the *Aitareya Brāhmaṇa,*[2] e.g., a prince named Bhīma is designated *Vaidarbha,* 'prince of Vidarbha'. This shows that the Aryans had come down below the Vindhyas and settled in Vidarbha or western Berars immediately to the south of this mountain range. The same Brāhmana[3] represents the sage Visvāmitra to have adopted Śunaḥsepa as his son and named him Devarāta, much to the annoyance of fifty of fifty of his sons who in consequence were cursed by their father to 'live on the borders' of the province then occupied by the Aryans. The descendants of these sons of Visvāmitra, the Brāhmaṇa further tells us, formed the greater bulk of the Dasyus and were variously known as Andhras, Puṇdras, Śabaras, Pulindas and Mūtibas[3]. Of these the Andhras, Pulindas and Śabaras at any rate are known from the *Mahābhārata and Rāmāyṇa*

[a][This is not strictly correct.—D.C.S.]

and the Purāṇas to have been tribes of Southern India; and though the exact provinces inhabitated by them in the time of the *Aitareya Brāhmaṇa* cannot be definitely settled, it cannot for a moment be doubted that they lived to the south of the Vindhyas[b] and that the Aryans had already come in contact with these Non-aryan peoples.

Let us now see what we learn from Pāṇini, the founder of the most renowned School of Grammar and who lived about 500 B.C.[c] In his *Sītras* or grammatical aphorisms, he shows an extensive knowledge of the ancient geography of India. Most of the countries, places and rivers mentioned by him are, of course, to be found in the Punjab and Afghanistan. Belonging to India farther south, he mentions Kaccha (iv.2. 133) Avanti (IV. 1. 176), Kosala (IV. 1. 171) and Kalinga (IV. 1. 170). But he makes no mention of any province to the south of the Narmadā except that of Aśmaka (IV. 1. 173).[d] One of the oldest works of Pāli Buddhist literature, the *Suttanipāta*[4] speaks of a Brāhmana *guru* called Bāvarin as having left the Kosala country and settled near a village on the Godhāvari (Godāvari) in the Assaka (Aśmaka) territory in the Dakkhināpatha (Dakṣiṇāpatha). The story tells us that Bāvarin sent his sixteen pupils to pay their homage to the Buddha and confer with him. The route by which they proceeded northwards is also described.[5] First, they went to Patiṭṭhāna of the Muḷaka[6] country, then to Māhissatī, to Ujjenī, Gonaddha,[7] Vedisa and Vanasahvaya; to Kosambi, Sāketa and Sāvatthi (capital of the Kosala country); to Setavya, Kapilavatthu and Kusināra; to Pāvā, Vesālī (capital of Magadha),[e] and finally to the Pāsāṇaka Cetiya where the Buddha then was. The description of this route is very important in more ways than one. In the first place, it will be seen that Bāvarin's settlement was much to the south of Patiṭṭhāna, i.e. Paiṭhaṇ in the Nizam's territory,[f] because Patiṭṭhāna was the principal town of the Muḷaka province, to the South of which was the Aśmaka country where Bāvarin then was. Secondly, it is worthy of note that Bāvarin's disciples went to North

[b] [The Puṇḍras, later found in North Bengal, do not appear to have lived near the Andhras.—D.C.S.]

[c] [Pāṇini is now often assigned to the 5th century B.C.—D.C.S.]

[d] It is not improbable that these Aśmakas lived in the north-western part of the Indian sub-continent. Cf. the Assacenians located by the Greeks in the Swat valley.—D.C.S.]

[e] [Vesāli (Vaiśālī) was the capital of Magadha for sometime during Siśunaga's reign. In the age of the Buddha, Magadha had its capital at Rājagṛha.—D.C.S.]

[f] [Now in the Aurangabad District of Maharashtra.—D.C.S.]

India straight through the Vindhyas. This disproves the theory of some scholars who hold that the Aryans were afraid of crossing the Vindhyas and went southwards to the Deccan by an easterly detour round the mountain range.[8] After leaving Patiṭṭhāna or Paithan, we find the party reaching Māhissatī, i.e. Māhiṣmatī, which has been correctly identified with Māndhātā on the Narmadā on the borders of the Indore State.[9] Evidently, Bāvarin's pupils must have passed to Māhiṣmati, i.e., to the other side of the Vindhyas through the Vidarbha country.

Let us now turn to Pāṇini and the School of Grammar that he founded. We have seen that Aśmaka is the only country in the Deccan which he mentions. The case, however, is different with Kātyāyana who wrote aphorisms called *Vārtika* to explain and supplement Pāṇini and who has been assigned to the middle of the 4th century B.C. Now, to a Pāṇinian *Sūtra: Janapada-sabdāt kṣatriyād = an* (IV. I. 168), Kātyāyana adds the *Vārtika: Pāṇḍor—ḍyan,* from which we obtain the form Pāṇḍya,[10] If this *Vārttika* had not been made, we should have had the form not *Pāṇḍya* but *Pāṇḍava.* Again we have a *Sūtra* of Pāṇini: *Kambojāl—luk* (IV. 1. 175) which lays down that the word Kamboja denotes not only the Kamboja country or the Kamboja tribe, but also the Kamboja king. But then there are other words which are exactly like *Kamboja* in this respect, but which Pāṇini has not mentioned. Kātyāyana is, therefore, compelled to supplement the above *Sūtra* with the *Vārtitka: Kamboj-ādibhyo lug-vacanam Coḍ-ādy-artham.* This means that like *Kamboja* the words *Coḍa, Kaḍera* and *Kerala* denote each not only the country and the tribe, but also the king. It will thus be seen that Coḍa and Kerala, which are obviously countries situated in Southern India, were known to Kātyāyana but not to Pāṇini. Of course, no sane scholar who has studied the *Aṣṭādhyāyī* will be so bold as to assert that Pāṇini was a careless or ignorant grammarian. But we have not one word, but at least three words, *viz., Pāṇḍya, Coḍa* and *Kerala,* the formation of which has not been explained by Pāṇini, and any accurate and thorough going grammarian would have done it if they had been known to him. The only legitimate conclusion that can, therefore, be drawn is that the names of these southern countries were not known to Pāṇini, or in other words, were not known to the Aryans in the seventh century B.C., but were known to them shortly before the middle of the fourth century B.C. when Kātyāyana lived. As regards Ceylon or Tamraparṇī as it was called in ancient days, it was certainly known to the Aryans long before the rise of the Maurya power. It has been mentioned not only by Aśoka as Taṁbapaṇi in his Rock Edict XIII, but also as Taprobane by

Megasthenes[11] who, as most of you are aware, was the ambassador sent by Seleucus Nicator of Syria to the Court of Candragupta, founder of the Maurya dynasty and grandfather of Aśoka. Contemporaneously with Megasthenes lived Kauṭilya, who in his *Arthaśāstra*[12] speaks of pearls being found among other places in the Tāmraparṇī river, in Pāṇḍya-kavāṭaka, and near the Mahendra mountain—all situated on the extremely of the Southern Peninsula.

Now, the name of one of these southern kingdoms was Coda, which was called Coṛa in Tamil and Coḷa in Telugu.[g] The people also were called by the same name. I cannot resist the temptation of saying that it is from this Coḷa people that the Sanskrit word *cora* meaning 'a thief' has been derived. An exactly analogous instance we have in the word *Dasyu* or *Dāsa,* which originally denoted the Dahae people of the Caspian Steppes,[13] but which even in the Vedic period acquried a derogatory sense and soon after signified 'a robber'. If Dasyu thus originally was the name of a Nonaryan tribe and used in the sense of 'a robber', it is perfectly intelligible that the name of another Non-aryan people, *viz.,* the Coṛas, was similarly employed to express a similar meaning. And this seems to have been the case, because the Vedic terms for a thief are *taskara, tāyu, stena* and *paripanthin,* but never *cora,* this word being for the first time found in the *Taittirīya Āraṇyakaṭ*[14] which is a late work. This conclusion is strengthened by the fact that, in Latin and Greek also, there is no word, signifying 'a thief', which corresponds to *cora* in sound.

The case, however, was different in regard to the name of the other people, *viz.,* Pāṇḍya. Kātyāyana, we have seen, derives it from *Pāṇḍu.* This shows that the Pāṇḍyas were an Aryan tribe, and not an alien tribe like the Colas or Coṛas. Now, a Greek writer called Pliny tells us a tradition about these Pāṇḍyas, on the authority of Magasthenes, that they were descended from Pandaea, the only daughter of the Indian Hercules, *i.e.,* of Kṛṣṇa. She went away from the country of the Saurarenas whose principal towns were Methora or Mathura and Cleisobora or Kṛṣṇapura, and was assigned by her father just 'that portion of India which lies southward and extends to the sea'.[15] It is thus clear that the Pāṇḍyas were connected with the north and were an Aryan race. The account given by Megasthenes, however, like many traditions of this nature, is to be regarded as a combination of both truth and fiction. In the first place no authority from any epic

[g] [This does not seem to be accurate.—D.C.S.]

or Purāṇa is forthcoming to show that Kṛṣṇa had a daughter and of the name of Pāṇḍyā. Secondly, though Mathuruā is connected with the infancy of Kṛṣṇa, he lived as a ruler, not at Mathura but at Dvārakā from where alone he could send his daughter. These are, therefore, the elements of fiction that got mixed up with the immigration of the Pāṇḍyas. What appears to be the truth is that there was a tribe called Pāṇḍu round about Mathurā, and that when a section of them went southwards and were settled there, they were called Pāṇḍya. This is clear, I think, from Kātyāyana's *Vārttika: Pāṇḍor = ḍyaṇ,* which means that the suffix *ya* was to be attached not to Pāṇḍu, the name of the father of the Pāṇḍavas, but to Pāṇḍu, which was the name of a Kṣatriya tribe as well as of a country. Evidently Pāndya denotes the descendants of the Pāṇḍu tribe, and must have been so called when they migrated southwards and established themselves there.[16] Nay, we have got evidence to show that there was a tribe called Pāṇḍu. Ptolemy, who wrote the geography of India about 150 A.D., speaks not only of the kingdom of Pandion or Pāṇḍya, but also of the country of the Pandoouoi in the Punjab.[17] These Pandoouoi can be no other than the Pāṇḍu people. Again, Varāhamihira, the celebrated astronomer, who flourished about the middle of the 6th century A.D., makes mention of a tribe called Pāṇḍu and places them in Madhyadesa.[18] There can, therefore be no doubt about the existence of a people called Pāṇḍu. And as according to Varāhamihira they were somewhere in Madhyadesa, it is quite possible that, in the time of Megasthenes, they were settled round about Mathurā. Megasthenes' statement that the Pāṇḍyas of the south were connected with the Jamuna and Mathurā seems to be founded on fact, because the Greek writers, Pliny and Ptolemy, tell us that the capital of the Pāṇḍyas in the south was Modoura,[19] i.e., Madura, the principal town of the district of the same name in the Madras Presidency. The fact that the Pāṇḍyas of the south called their capital Madhurā clearly shows that they came from the north from some country whose capital was Mathurā and thus gives remarkable confirmation to what Magasthenes has told us. This is quite in accordance with the practice of the colonists naming the younger towns or provinces after the older.[h]

---

[h] [Like *Pāṇḍava,* the word *Pāṇḍu* may also mean 'the scion of Pāṇḍu'. It is to be noted that early Greek writers place king Porus (i.e. Puru or Paurava) in the region where Ptolemy locates the Pāṇḍu people and, in the *Mahābhārata,* Pāṇḍu is a descendant of Puru. Moreover, there is an early Jain tradition regarding the foundation of Pāṇḍu-Mathurā by the five Pāṇḍava brothers (Mehta and Chandra, *Prakrit Proper Names,* Vol. I, p. 424). The present name of 'Madras Presidency' is 'Tamilnadu',—D.C.S.]

We thus see that an Aryan tribe called Pandu went southwards, and occupied the southernmost part of the peninsula, where they were known as Pāṇḍya and their capital as Madhurā or Mathurā. But the story of the migrations of this enterprising Aryan tribe does not end here. We have to note that there is a third Mathura in Ceylon, and also a fourth Madura in the Eastern Archipelago.[20] The natural conclusion is that the Pāṇḍyas did not rest satisfied with occupying the extreme southern part of the Peninsula, but went farther southward and colonised Ceylon also. For, as just stated, the Pāṇḍyas no doubt appear to have come from Mathurā, the capital of the Śaurasena country as told by Megasthenes, because this alone can explain why they gave the name Mathurā to the capital of their new kingdom situated at the south end of India. And the fact that we have another Mathura in Ceylon shows that the Pāṇḍyas alone could go there and have a third capital of this name. Besides, as the Pāṇḍyas occupied the southern extremity of India, it was they who could naturally be expected to go and settle themselves in Ceylon. But they seem to have gone there, not from the Madura but from the Tinnevelly District.[i] I have told you that the ancient name of Ceylon was Tāmraparṇī, but we have to remember that Tāmraparṇī was the name of a river also.[21] This doubtless is the present river Tāmraparṇī in the Tinnevelly District. Scholars have no doubt tacitly admitted that there was a connection somehow between this river and Ceylon; but this connection can be rendered intelligible only on the supposition that the Tinnevelly District was called Tāmraparṇī after the river, just as Sindhu or Sind was named after the river Sindhu or Indus. In that case, it is intelligible that when the Pāṇḍyas went to Ceylon, they named it Tāmraparṇī after the country they had left. Again, coming as they did from the Tinnevelly District, they would naturally land in the north-western part of the Island. And it is quite in keeping with this supposition that we find the ancient civilised and populous district of Ceylon, the so called Kalah, located not in the south, east or noth-east, but in the north-west part of the Island.[22]

Let us now see how the Aryan colonisation of Southern India must have been accomplished. We know that when the Aryans migrated in ancient times from Afghanistan and the Punjab do the different parts of Northern India, they did so under the leadership of Kṣatriya tribes, and hence their new settlements were called after the names of those

---

[i] [Now called Madurai and Tirunelveli.—D.C.S.]

tribes. A curious legend in this connection is worth quoting from the *Satapatha Brāhmaṇa* from which it would appear that, when the Aryans pushed forward to the east of the Sarasvatī, they were led by Māthava the Videgha, and high priest.[23] They went at first as far east as the Sadānīrā which formed the boundary between Kosala and Videha and which therefore corresponds to the Little Gandak of the present day.[24] For some time they did not venture to cross this river. They did, however, cross it, and, at the time when the *Satapatha Brāhmaṇa* was composed, were settled to the east of it in a province called Videha no doubt after the name of the tribe to which the king Māthava belonged. Nay, we have Pāṇini's authority to that effect; thus, according to him, *Pancālānām nivāso janapadaḥ Pāncālaḥ,* i.e., the word *Pāncālaḥ* denotes the country or kingdom which the Kṣatriya tribe called Pancāla occupied. What happened in North India must have happened in South India also. I have already referred to the tribe called Pāṇḍu who were settled in the southernmost part of India and after whom it was callled Pāṇdya. This was certainly a Kṣatriya tribe. Again, we have a passage in Kauṭilya's *Arthasāstra, viz., Dāṇdakyo nāma Bhojaḥ kāmāt Brāhmaṇakanyām=abhimanyamānas=sa-bandhu-rāṣtro vinanāsa* (a Bhoja known as Dāṇḍakya or king of Daṇḍakā, making a lascivious attempt on a Brāhmaṇa girl, perished along with his relations and kingdom).[25] Bhoja was, of course, the name of a Kṣatriya tribe, as we know from the *Mahabharata* and *Harivaṁśa.*[26] And a prince of this tribe is here said to have been a ruler of Daṇḍakā, which is another name for Mahārāṣtra',[27] As all the incidents which Kauṭilya mentions along with that of Dāṇdakya Bhoja took place long before his time and as he himself was, we know, the prime minister of Candragupta, founder of the Maurya dynasty, and consequently lived at the close of the fourth century B.C., it appears that the Bhojas must have taken possession of Mahārāṣṭra, at least in the fifth century B.C., if not earlier. I have already told you that the Buddhist work *Suttnipāta* speaks of Patiṭṭhāna or Paiṭhaṇ in the Nizam's Dominions.[j] But there was an older Patiṭṭhāna or Pratiṣṭhāna on the confluence of the Ganges and the Jamuna, which was the capital of Aila Pururavas.[29] The practice of naming the younger town after the older one is universal, and is well known even in the colonies of European nations. I have already quoted an inṣtance from India, *viz.,* that of Mathurā. And Pratiṣṭhāna is but another instance. It thus seems that, on the bank of the Godāvarī,

[j] [Now in Maharashtra—D.C.S.]

we had a colony from the country, of which the older Pratiṣṭhana was the capital, and it is probable that we have here a colony of the Aila tribe.[29] Even as last as the third century A.D., we find North Indian Aryan tribes or families going southwards and settling themselves somewhere in Southern India. A Buddhist *stūpa* has been discovered at Jagayyapeta in the Kistna District, Madras.[k] We have got here at least three inscriptions of this period, which refer themselves to the reign of king Māthariputra Śri Virapuruṣadatta of the Ikṣvāku family.[30] This indicates that the Kistna and adjoining Districts were held in the third century A.D. by the Ikṣvākus[31] who certainly must have come from the north. We know that Rāma, the hero of the *Rāmāyaṇa,* belonged to the Ikṣvāku race. So did the Buddha, the founder of Buddhism. The Ikṣvākus are also mentioned in the Purāṇas as a historical royal dynasty ruling in North India. The Ikṣvākus of the Kistna District must, therefore, have come from the north.

It is true that the Aryan civilisation was thus to a certain extent spread over Southern India through conquest. But this cannot be the whole cause. Causes of a pacific and more important nature must also have operated. We are so much accustomed to hear about the enterprising and proselytising spirit of the Buddhist and Jain monks that we are apt to think that Brāhmaṇism had never shown any missionary zeal. Is this, however, a fact? Did not the Brāhmaṇas or at any rate any of the hymn-composing families put forth any missionary effort and help in the dissemination of Aryan culture? I cannot help thinking that the ancient Ṛṣis were not mere passive inert thinkers, but were active though not aggressive propagators of their faith. Tradition, narrated in the *Mahābhārata* and *Rāmāyaṇa,* says that it was the Brāhmaṇa sage Agastya who first crossed the Vindhya range and led the way to the Aryan immigration.[32] When Rāma began his southward march and was at Pancavaṭī, Agastya was already to the south of the Vindhyas and was staying in a hermitage about two *yojanas* from it. This is not all. We find him ever more penetrating farther and farther into the hitherto unknown south, and civilising the Dravidians. Nay, this is admitted by the Tamil people themselves. They make Agastya the founder of their language and literature and call him by way of eminence the *Tamiṛmuni* or Tamilian sage. They still point to a mountain in the Tinnevelly District, which is commonly

[k] [Now Krishna District, Andhra Pradesh.—D.C.S.]

called by the English Agastier, *i.e.* Agastya's hill, 'Agastya being supposed to have finally tired thither from the world after civilising the Dravidians'.[33] I am not unaware that these are legends. It is however, a mistake to suppose that legends teach us nothing historical. It may very well be doubted whether Agastya, as he figures in these legends, is a historical personality. But a man is certainly lacking the historical sense if he cannot read in these legends the historical truth that Ṛṣis took a most prominent but unobtrusive part in the Aryan colonisation and the diffusion of Aryan culture. The old Ṛṣis of India, I think, were as enthusiastic and enterprising in this respect as the Buddhist and Jain missionaries, and were often migrating with their host of pupils to distant countries. I shall take only one instance, I hope you remember the Brāhmana *guru* Bāvarin, whom I mentioned earlier. His story appears in the *Suttanipāta.* He is described therein as perfect in the three Vedas. He had sixteen disciples all Brāhmaṇas, and each one of them again had his host of pupils. They all bore matted hair and sacred skins, and are styled Ṛṣis. With these pupils of his and the pupils pupils' Bāvarin was settled on the bank of the Godāvarī in the Aśmaka territory where he performed a sacrifice. He was thus settled on the confines of Dakṣināpatha, as it was then known if not beyond. And yet we are told that originally he was at Srāvasti, capital of the Kosala country. He and his pupils had thus traversed at least 600 miles before they came and were settled on the Godāvarī. It will thus be seen that the Ṛṣis were in the habit of moving in large numbers and to long distances, and making their settlements where they performed sacrifices. This is exactly in keeping with what we gather from the *Rāmāyaṇa.* To the south of the Vindhya, we learn, there were many Brāhmaṇa anchorites who lived in hermitages at different places and performed their sacrifices before Rāma penetrated Daṇḍakāraṇya and commenced his career of conquest. There was an aboriginal tribe called Rāksasa who disturbed the sacrifices and devoured the hermits and thus placed themselves in hostile opposition to the Brāhmaṇical institutions. On the other hand, under the designation of Vānara, we have another class of aborigines who allied themselves with the Brāhmaṇas and embraced their form of religious worship. Even among the Rākṣasas, we have an exception in Vibhiṣaṇa, brother of Rāvana, who is said to be *na tu Rākṣasa-ceṣtitaḥ.*[34] 'nọt behaving himself like a Rākṣasa'. This was the state of things in Southern India when Rāma came there. It clearly shows that the Ṛṣis were always to the forefront in the work of colonising Southern India and introducing Aryan civilisation there. Amongst them, Agastya was the only Ṛiṣi who fought the Rākṣasas and killed them. The other Ṛisis, like true missionaries, never resorted to the practice of realisation, though they believed, rightly or wrongly, that they had the power of ridding themselves of their enemy. One of them distinctly says to Rāma:

Kāmaṁ tapaḥ-prabhāveṇa śaktā hantuṁ nīśācarān/
cir-ārjitaṁ na c=ecchāmas=tapaḥ khaṇḍayituṁ vayam//

"It is true that by the power of our austerties we could at will slay these goblins; but we are unwilling to nullify [the merit of] our austerities."[35]

And it was simply because, through genuine missionary spirit, the Ṛṣis refused to practise retaliation that Rāma, like a true Kṣatriya, intervened and waged war with the Rākṣasas. This noble spirit of the ancient Ṛṣis, manifested in their mixing with the aborigines and civilising them, is not seen from the *Rāmāyaṇa* only. It may also be seen from the story of the fifty of Viśvāmitra's sons, mentioned in the *Aitareya Brāhmaṇa* and referred to at the beginning of this lecture. They strongly disapproved of his adoption of Śunaḥśepa, and were for that reason cursed by Viśvāmitra to live on the borders of the Aryan settlements. And their progeny, we are told, were the Andhras, Puṇḍras, Śabaras and so forth. If we read the legend aright, it clearly indicates that even the scions of such an illustrious hymn composing family as that of Viśvāmitra migrated southward boldly, and what is more, married and mixed freely with the aborigines, with the object of diffusing Aryan culture amongst them.

But by what routes did the Aryans penetrate South India? This question we have now to consider. The main route, I think, is the reverse of the one by which Bāvarin's pupils went to Magadha from Aśmaka. This was described by me earlier. The Aryan route thus seems to have lain through the Avanti country, the southernmost town of which was Māhissatī or Māndhātā on the Narmadā, from where the Aryans crossed the Vindhyas and penetrated Southern India. They began by colonising Vidarbha from which they proceeded southwards first to the Muḷaka territory with its principal town Patiṭṭhāna or Paiṭhaṇ and from there to the Aśmaka country. By what route farther southward they immigrated is not clear: but the find-spots of Aśoka's inscriptions perhaps afford a clue. One copy of his Minor Rock Edicts has been found at Maski in the Lingsugur Taluk of the Raichur District, Nizam's Dominions,[36] and three more father southward in the Chitaldrug District of the Mysore State.[37] A few Jain cave inscriptions have come to light also in the Madura District[38] and appear to belong to the second century B.C. and possibly earlier. As Aśoka's edicts and these cave inscriptions are in Pāli,[l] these certainly were the districts colonised by the Aryans. The Aryans thus seem to have gone south from the Aśmaka territory through the modern Raichur and Chitaldrug Districts, from where they must have gone to the Madura District which was originally in the Pāṇḍya kingdom. This seems to agree with the tradition of their immigration preserved among the Tamil Brāhmaṇas. These Brāhmaṇas have a section called Bṛhaccaraṇa which means the Great Immigration, and must refer to a large southward movement.[39] They are subdivided into Mazhnāḍu and Molagu. The Mazhnāḍu sub-section is further divided into Kandra-māṇikkam, Maṅgudi and Sathia-maṅgalam, etc., all villages along the Western Ghats—showing that, in their southward movement, they clung to the highlands and peopled the skirts of the present province of Mysore[m] and the Coimbatore and Madura Districts—a conclusion which agrees with that just drawn from the find-spots of Aśokan edicts and the cave inscriptions in Southern India.

Another route by which the Aryans seem to have gone to South India was by the sea. They appear to have sailed from the Indus to Kaccha, and from there by the sea-coast to Surāṣṭra or Kathiawar, from Kathiawar to Bharukaccha or modern Broach, and from Bharukaccha to Suppāraka r Sopārā in the Thānā District of the Bombay Presidency.[n] Baudhāyana, the author of a Dharmaśāstra,[o] quotes a verse from the Bhāllavin School of Law, which tells us that the inhabitants of Sindhu, Sauvīra and Surāṣṭra, like those of the Deccan, were of mixed origin. This shows that the Aryans had begun colonising those parts. Towards the end of the period we have selected, they seem to have advanced as far south as Sopārā. But as already stated, they must have gone by the sea-route, because it is quite clear that no mention is traceable of any inland countries or towns between the sea-costs and the Deccan.[40]

---

[l] [It is better to call it Prakrit.—D.C.S.]

[m] [I.e. the original Mysore State which now form the southern part of the present state of Mysore or Karnataka.—D.C.S.]

[n] [Now Maharastra State.—D.C.S.]

[o] [Better—Dharmasūtra.—D.C.S.]

Now, wherever in India and Ceylon the Aryans penetrated, they introduced not only their civilisation, i.e. their religion, culture and social organisation, but also imposed their language on the aborigines. It is scarcely necessary for me to expatiate on the former point, for it is an indisputable fact that the Hindu civilisation that we see everywhere in India or Ceylon is essentially Aryan. You know about it as much and as well as I do. This point, therefore, calls for no remarks. In regard to the Aryan language, however, I cannot do better than quote the following opinion of George Grierson, an eminent linguist. "When an Aryan tongue", says he, "comes into contact with an uncivilised aboriginal one, it is invariably the latter which goes to the wall. The Aryans does not attempt to speak it, and the necessities of intercourse compelled the aborigines to use a broken 'pigeon' form of the language of a superior civilisation. As generations pass, this mixed jargon more and more approximates to its model, and in process of time, the old aboriginal language is forgotten and dies a natural death."[41] I completely endorse this view of George Grierson except in one respect. This exception, you will at once see, is the Dravidian languages which are at present spoken in Southern India. It is, indeed, strange how the Aryan language failed to supplant the Dravidian speech in this part of India, though it most successfully did in Northern India where I have no doubt the Dravidian tongue prevailed before the advent of the Aryans. This will be seen from the fact that 'Brahui, the language of the mountaineers in the Khanship of Kelat in Beluchistan, contains not only some Dravidian words, but a considerable infusion of distinctively Dravidian forms and idioms'.[42] The discovery of this Dravidian element in a language spoken beyond the Indus tends to show that the Dravidians like the Aryans, the Scythians and so forth, must have entered India by the North-Western route. It is also a well-known fact, accepted by all scholars, that there are many Sanskrit words which are really Dravidian, and kittel, in his Kannada-English Dictionary, gives a long list of them. But in compiling this list he seems to have drawn exclusively upon Classical Sanskrit which was never a *bhāṣā* or spoken language. At least one Dravidian word, however, is known from the Vedic literature, which is admitted to be composed in the language actually spoken by the people. The word I mean is *maṭacī* which occurs in the *Chāndogya Upaniṣad* (1.10.1) in the passage *Maṭacī-hateṣu Kuruṣu āṭikyā saha jāyayā Uṣastir-ha Cākrāyana ibhya-grāme pradrāṇaka uvāsa.* Here evidently the devastation of the crops in the Kuru country by *maṭacī* is spoken of. All the commentators except one have wrongly taken *maṭacī* to mean 'hailstones'; but one commentator, who is an exception, rightly gives *rakta-varṇaḥ kṣudra-pakṣi-viseṣaḥ* as an alternative equivalent.[43] This shows that these 'red-coloured winged creatures' can be no other than locusts, and that it is they which laid waste the fields of the Kuru country as they do to the present day in every part of India. it is interesting to note that this explanation of the commentator is confirmed by the fact that *maṭacī* is a Sanskritised form of the well-known Canarese word *miḍice* which is explained by Kittel's Dictionary as 'a grasshopper, a locust' and which is, used in this sense to this day in the Dharwar District of the Bombay Presidency.[44] Scholars are unanimous on the point that the *Chāndogya Upaniṣad* is one of the earliest of the Upaniṣads. Nobody doubts that this Upaniṣad was put together in the North of India, especially in the Punjab, and that the Sanskrit language in which it is composed represents the current speech of the day. And yet we find in it a term which is a genuinely Dravidian word. I have no doubt that more such will be forthcoming from the Vedic literature if scholars of the Dravidian languages undertake this task. And this will confirm the conclusion that the Dravidian tongue was prevalent in North India before the Aryans came and occupied it. The same conclusion is forced upon us by an examination of the vernaculars of North India. Take Bengali, for instance; the words *Khokā* and *Khuki* which mean 'boy' and 'girl' in Bengali are nothing but the Oraon *Kokā* and *Kokī*. The Bengali *telo,* 'head',[p] is the Telugu *tā-lā* and Tamil *tā-lai*. *Notā,* 'tongue', is Tamil *nālu*. The plural suffix *gul* is used in Tamil to denote 'many'. *Guli* and *gulā* are used for the same purpose in Bengali. Instances can be multiplied;[45] but those given are enough, to show that even the vernacular Bengali, which bristles with Sanskrit and derivating words, is indebted to Dravidian languages for a pretty large portion of its vocabulary and structural peculiarities. What is strange is that Dravidian words have been traced also in Hindi speech. Even the commonest Hindi words *jhagdā, āṭā* and so forth have been traced to Dravidian vocables.[46] No reasonable doubt can therefore be entertain as to the Dravidian speech once being spoken in North India.

We thus see that the Dravidian tongue was once spoken in North India, but was superseded by the Aryan, when the Aryans penetrated and established themselves there. It, therefore, becomes extremely

[p] [Sanskrit *tolu*; *brahmatālu*; also cf. *tala* in *karatala*, etc. Better Telugu tala, Tamil *talai* and *gal*..—D.C.S.]

curious how, in Southern India, the Aryan speech was not able to supplant the Dravidian. But here a question arises. Is it s fact that even in that part of the country no Aryan tongue was ever known or spoken by the aborigines after the Aryans came and were settled here? I take my stand on epigraphic records as they alone can afford irrefragible evidence on the subject. Let us first take the province whose vernacular at present is Telugu. The earliest inscriptions found here are those of Aśoka. Evidently I mean the version of his Fourteen Rock Edicts engraved at Jaugaḍa in the Ganjam District, the extreme north-east part of the Madras Presidency.[q] But I am afraid I cannot lay much stress upon it, because though Telugu is no doubt spoken in this district, Oriya is not unknown here, sat any rate in the northern portion of it. And it is a well-known fact that, in a province where the ranges of any two languages or dialects meet, the boundary which divides one from the other is never permanently fixed, but is always changing. I shall not, therefore, refer here to the Fourteen Rock Edicts discovered in the Ganjam District, but shall come down a little southwards and select that district where none but a Dravidian language is spoken—I mean the Kistna Distract. Here no less than three Buddhist *stūpas* have been discovered, along with a number of inscriptions. The earliest of these is that at Bhaṭṭprolu, the next is the celebrated one at Amarāvatī, and the third is that at Jagayyapeṭa. The inscriptions connected with these monuments are short donative, records, specifying each the name and social status of the donor along with the nature of his gift. An examination of these records shows that people of various classes and statuses participated in this series of religious benefactions. We will here leave aside the big folk, such as those who belonged to the warrior or merchant class, and who, it might be contended, were the Aryan conquerors. We will also leave aside the monks and nuns, because their original social status is never mentioned in Buddhist inspirational records. We have thus left for our consideration the people who are called *herañika* or goldsmiths, and, above all, the *commakāras* or leather-workers. These at any rate cannot be reasonably supposed to form part of the Aryan people who were settled in the Kistna District, and yet we find that their names are clearly Aryan, showing that they imbibed the Aryan civilisation even to the extent of adopting their

[q] [The Ganjam District is now in Orissa. The Erragudi and Rajula mandagiri edicts of Aśoka were later discovered in the Karnul District of the Telugu-speaking Andhra Pradesh. 'Kistna' is now 'Krishna'.—D.C.S.]

names. Thus, we have a goldsmith of the name of Sidhatha or Siddārtha, two leather-workers (father and son) of the names of Vidhiha or Vṛddhika and Nāga.[47] All these unmistakably are Aryan names; but this string of names does not stop here. We have yet to make mention of another individual who is named Kanha or Kṛṣṇa. This too is an Aryan name; but the individual, it is worthy of note, calls himself Damila,[48] which is exactly the same as *Tamil* or Sanskrit *Dravida.* And, in fact, this is the earliest word so far found signifying the Dravidian race. We thus see that as a result of the Aryan settlement in the Kistna District, the local people were so steeped in Aryan civilisation that they went even to the length of taking Aryan proper names to themselves. But could they understand or speak the Aryan tongue? Do the inscriptions found in the Kistna District throw any light on this point? Yes, they do, because the language of these records is Pāli,[49] and Pāli, we know, is an Aryan speech. This clearly proves that an Aryan tongue was spoken in the Kistna District from at least 150 B.C. to 200 A.D.—the period to which the inscriptions belong. I am aware it is possible to argue that this Aryan language was spoken only by the Aryans who were settled there, and no necessarily by the people in general, and, above all, the lower classes. This argument is not convincing because it is inconceivable that earlier Buddhism, whose one aim was to be in direct touch with the masses, and which must have obtained almost all its converts of this district from all sorts and conditions of the indigenous people including the lowest classes, could adopt an Aryan tongue unless it was at least as well known to and actually spoken by the people in general as their home tongue. This inference is confirmed by the fact that three copies of what are called Aśoka's Minor Rock Edicts have been found in the Chitaldrug District of the Mysore State,[50] i.e. in the very heart of what is now the Canarese-speaking[r] province. One of the edicts enumerates the different virtues that constitute what Aśoka meant by *dhaṁma,* and the other exhorts all people especially those of low position to put forth strenuous endeavour after the highest life. All the inscriptions of Aśoka, especially these Edicts, had a very practical object in view. They were intended to be understood and pondered over by people of all classes, and as the language of these epigraphic records is Pāli, the conclusion is irresistible that, though perhaps it was not the home tongue, it could

[r] [Better—Kannaḍa-speaking. Prakrit may have been understood only by a section of the people in these areas. —D.C.S.]

be spoken, at least well understood, by all people including the lower classes. but this is not all. We have got incontestable evidence that up to the 4th century A.D., Pāli was also the official language of the kings even in those provinces where Dravidian languages are now supreme. At least one stone inscription and five copper-plate charters have been found in these provinces, ranging from the second to the fourth or fifth century A.D. The stone inscription was found at Maḷavaḷḷi in the Shimoga District, Myore State.[51] It registers some grant to the god Maḷapaḷi by Viṇhukaḍa Cuṭukalānaṁda[52] Sātakarṇi of the Kadamba dynasty[53] who calls himself king of Vaijayanti, and records the renewal of the same grant by his son. Vaijayanti, we know, is Banavāsī in the North Kanara District, Bombay Presidency. At Banavāsī, too, we have found an inscription of the queen of this king. Both Banavāsī and Maḷavaḷḷi are situated in the Canarese-speaking country, and yet we find that the official language here it Pāli. The same conclusion is proved with reference to the Tamil-speaking country by the five copper-plate grants referred to above. Of these five, three belong to the Pallava dynasty reigning at Kāncipura, one to a king called Jayavarman, and one to Vijayadevavarman.[54] The very fact that every one of these is a title-deed and has been drawn up in Pāli shows that this Aryan language must have been known to officials of even the lowest rank and also to literate and even semi-literate people. One of the three Pallava charters, e.g., issues instructions, for the maintenance of the grant therein registered, not only to the *rājakumāra* or royal princes, *senāpati* or generals, and so forth, but also to the free-holders of various villages (*gāmāgāmabhojaka*), guards (*ārakhādhikata*) and even cowheards (*go-vallava*) who were employed in the king's service. The princes[55] and generals may perhaps be presumed to be of the Aryan stock and consequently speaking an Aryan tongue; but the free-holders of the various villages, guards and cowherds, at any rate, must be supposed to be of Nonaryan race. And when instructions are issued to them by a charter couched in Pāli, the conclusion is inevitable that this Aryan tongue, at least up to the fourth century A.D., was spoken and understood by all classes of people in a country of which the capital was Kāncipura and which was and is now a centre of the Tamil language and literature.[s]

[s] [The argument is weak and the conclusion wrong. The Aryan court language in the South must have enjoyed the position of Persian in Mughul times and English in the British days and was intelligible only to the educated few.—D.C.S.]

Just now I have many a time remarked that Pāli might not have been the home tongue of the people, but was well understood by them. Perhaps some of you would like to know what I exactly mean by this. I shall explain myself by giving an instance. We know that there are many Canarese-speaking districts which were conquered and held by the Marāthās. Some of them still belong to the Marāthā Chiefs. If you go to any one of these districts, you will find that, although the indigenous people speak Canarese at home and among themselves, Marāṭhi is understood by many of them and even by some of the lower classes. This is the result of the Marāṭhā domination extending over only two centuries, and has happened notwithstanding the fact that the Canarese people have their own art and literature. As the inscriptions referred to above show, the Aryans had established themselves in Southern India for at least seven centuries. It is, therefore, no wonder that the Aryan tongue could be spoken, at any rate well understood, by the original Dravidians even to the lowest classes, as is clearly evidenced, I think, at least by the inscriptions of Aśoka and those connected with the Buddhist *stūpas.*[I] We must not, however, lose slight of the fact that the Aryan language for some reason or other had not become the home tongue of these Dravidians. Evidence in support of this conclusions, curiously enough, is forthcoming from an extraneous and unforeseen quarter. A papyrus of the second century A.D. was discovered in 1903 at Oxyrhynchus in Egypt, containing a Greek farce by an unknown author.[58] The farce is concerned with a Greek lady named Charition, who has been stranded on the coast of a country bordering the Indian Ocean. The king of this country addresses his retinue as 'Chiefs of the Indians'. In some places, the same king and his countrymen use their own language especially when Charition has wine served to them to make them drunk. Many stray words have been traced; but so far only two sentences have been read, and these leave no doubt whatever as to their language having been Canarese. One of the sentences referred to is *bere konca madhu pātrokke hākī*, which means 'having poured a little wine into the cup separately'. The other sentence is *pānaṁ ber etti kaṭṭi madhuvaṁ ber ettuvenu,* which means 'having taken up the cup separately and having covered [it], I shall take wine separately'. From the fact that the Indian language employed

[I] [It is impossible to believe that the Aryan language was intelligible in the South in early times more than Sanskrit is understood there today. Of course only a few have knowledge of Sanskrit.—D.C.S.]

in the papyrus is Canarese, it follows that the scene of Charition's adventures is one of the numerous small ports on the western coast of India between Karwar and Mangalore and that Canarese was at least imperfectly understood in that part of Egypt where the farce was composed and acted, for if the Greek audience in Egypt did not understand even a bit of Canarese, the scene of the drinking bout would be denuded of all its humour and would be entirely out of place. These were commercial relations of an intimate nature between Egypt and the west coast of India in the early centuries of the Christian era, and it is not strange if some people of Egypt understood Canarese.[u] To come to our point, the papyrus clearly shows that, in the second century A.D., Canarese was spoken in Southern India even by princes, who most probably were Dravidian by extraction. The Canarese, however, which they spoke, was not pure Canarese, but was strongly tinctured with Aryan words. I have quoted two Canarese sentences from the Greek farce, and you will have seen that they contain the words *pātra* (cup), *pāna* (drink) and *madhu* (wine), which are genuine Aryan vocables as they are to be found in the Vedas. The very fact that even in respect of ordinary affairs relating to drinking we find them using, not words of their home language as well would naturally expect them to do, but words from Aryan vocabulary, indicates what hold the Aryan speech had on their tongue.

Nevertheless it must be confessed that even seven centuries of Aryan domination in South India was not enough for the eradication of the Dravidian languages. it would be exceedingly interesting to investigate the circumstances which precluded the Aryan tongue here from supplanting the aboriginal one. Such an inquiry, I am afraid, is irrelevant here. And I, therefore, leave it to the Dravidian scholars to tackle this most interesting, but also most bewildering, problem.[57]

Though the causes that led to the preservation and survival of the Dravidian languages are not known at present, this much is certain, as I have shown above, that up till 400 A.D. at any rate, an Aryan tongue was spoken and known to the people in general[v] just in those provinces where the Dravidian languages are now the only vernaculars.

---

[u] [It is difficult to believe that the audience of a Greek farce played in Egypt understood Kannaḍa. If the language of the two sentences is Kannaḍa, they must have been meant to be an unintelligible jargon.—D.C.S.]

[v] [It was merely the court language understood by some people.—D.C.S.]

If such was the case, we can easily understand why is Ceylon to the present day we have an Indo-Aryan vernacular. For we have seen that the tide of the Aryan colonisation did not stop till it reached Ceylon. Naturally, therefore, not only the Aryan civilisation, but also the Aryan speech was implanted from South India into this country, where, whoever, as in North India, it succeeded in completely superseding the tongue originally spoken there. This satisfactorily answers, I think, the question about the origin Pāli in which the Buddhist scriptures of Ceylon have been written. The Island was converted to Buddhism about the middle of the third century B.C. by the preaching of Mahinda, a son of the great Buddhist emperor Aśoka. Naturally, therefore, the scriptures, which Mahinda brought with him from his father's capital, must have been in Māgadhi, the dialect of the Magadha country. As a matter of fact, however, the language of these scriptures, as we have them now, is anything but Māgadhi, though, of course, a few Māgadhisms are here and there traceable. This discrepancy has been variously explained by scholars. Kern holds that Pāli was never spoken and was an artificial language altogether—a view which no scholar endorses at present.[w] Oldenberg boldly rejects the Sinhalese tradition that Mahinda brought the sacred texts to Ceylon. He compares the Pāli language to that of the cave inscriptions in Maharashtra and of the epigraph of king Khāravela in the Hāthigumphā in Orissa, i.e. old Kalinga,[x] says that they are essentially the same dialect and comes to the conclusion that the Tipitaka was brought to the Island from the peninsula of South India, from either Maharashtra or Kaliṅga, with the natural spread of Buddhism southwards.[58] I am afraid, I cannot agree with Oldenberg in his first conclusion. On the contrary, I agree with Rhyas Davids that the Sinhalese tradition that Buddhism was introduced into Ceylon by Mahinda is well-founded and must be accepted as true. On the other hand, Oldenberg has, I think correctly pointed out that Pāli of the Buddhist scriptures is widely divergent from Māgadhī, but is essentially the same as the dialect of the old inscriptions found in Maharashtra or Kaliṅga. The truth of the matter is that the Aryans, who colonised Maharashtra and Kaliṅga,[59] spoke practically the same dialect, as is evidenced by inscriptions, and that when they went still farther southwards and occupied Ceylon, they naturally introduced their own dialect there, as is also evidenced by

---

[w] [Pāli was a literary language like Sanskrit.—D.C.S.]

[x] [Kaliṅga was part of the coastal areas of Orissa and Andhra Pradesh—D.C.S.]

the inscriptions discovered in the Island. I have told you before that the Aryan colonisation of Ceylon was complete long prior to the advent of the Mauryas, and we must, therefore, suppose that this dialect was already being spoken when Mahinda came and introduced Buddhism. Now, we have a passage in the *Cullavagga*[60] of the *Vinayapilaka,* in which Buddha distinctly ordains that his word was to be conveyed by different Bhikṣus in their different dialects. The Māgadhī of the sacred texts brought by Mahinda must thus have been replaced by Pāli, the dialect of Ceylon, and we can perfectly understand how in this gradual replacement a few Māgadhisms of the original may here and there have escaped the weeding-out, especially as Māgadhī and Pāli were not two divergent language, but only two dialects of one and the same language.

REFERENCES

1. *Ṛgveda,* X. 61. 8.
2. VII. 34. 9.
3. VII. 17-18; also *Sśāṅkhayana Śrauta Sūtra,* xx. 26.[The *Śāṅkhāyana Śr. S.* gives the last name as Mūcīpa or Mūvipa—D.C.S.]
4. Vs. 976-77. [The *Suttanipāta* is probably not earlier than the 3rd century B.C.—D.C.S.]
5. *Ibid.,* Vs. 1011-13.
6. In the text of the *Suttanipāta* edited by V. Fausboell, the reading *Aḷaka* is adopted (Vs. 977 and 1011), and the variant Muḷaka is noticed in the foot-notes. There can, however, be no doubt that *Muḷaka* is the correct reading. We know of no country of the name Aḷaka. Muḷaka, on the other hand, is well known. Thus in the celeberated Nasik cave inscription of Vāsiṣṭhīputra Puḷumāvi, the Muḷaka country has been associated with Asaka (Aśmaka), exactly as it has been done in the *Suttanipāta* (*Ep. Ind.,* Vol. VIII, p. 60). The same country seems to have been mentioned as Maulika by Varāhamihira in his *Bṛhatsaṁhitā* (XIV. 8).
7. Considering that the Godāvarī has been called Godhāvarī in the *Suttanipāta,* Gonaddha can very well be taken to stand for Gonadda-Gonarda, the place from which Patanjali, author of the *Mahābhāṣya,* hailed, R.G. Bhandarkar has shown on the authority of the *Mahābhāṣya* that Sāketa was situated on the road from Gonarda to Pāṭaliputra (*Ind, Ant.,* Vol. II, p. 70). This is exactly in accordance with what the *Suttanipāta* says, for Sāketa, according to the route taken by Bāvarin's pupils, was on the way from Gonaddha to the Magadha country. The native place of Patanjali was, therefore in Central India somewhere between Ujjain and Besnagar near Bhilsa. [For Gonarda, see Sircar,

Stud. Geog. Anc. Med. Ind., 2nd ed., pp. 264 ff. 'Bhilsa' has now been changed to 'Vidisha'. Read *Setavyā* and *Kusinārā.*—D.C.S.]

8. See, e.g., *Early History of the Dekkan* (2nd ed.), p. 9.

9. *JRAS,* 1910, pp. 445-56. [Accordiing to some, it is modern Maheshwar in the East Nimar Dist., Madhya Pradesh.—D.C.S.]

10. I am not yet in a position to determine finally whether this is a *Vārttika* of Kātyāyana or a supplement of Patanjali. R.G. Bhandarkar in his *Early History of the Dekkan* (pp. 7-8, note 3) adopts the former view, whereas the text of Patanjalī's *Mahābhāṣya,* as edited by Kielhorn in the Bombay Sanskrit Series, inclines one to the latter view. Even if this last proves ultimately to be the correct view, this in no way vitiates my main conclusion, because, as the Pāṇḍyas are referred to both by Megasthenes in his *Indika* and by Aśoka in his Rock Edicts, their immigration to and settlement in South India were compete long before the rise of the Maurya power.

11. *Ind. Ant.,* Vol. VI, p. 129.

12. Ed. Shama Sastry, p. 75. For the river Tāmraparṇi, see further in the sequel. See also Aśoka's Rock Edict II. Kauṭliya's Pāṇḍya-Kavāṭaka seems to be the same as Pāṇḍya-vāṭka or Pāṇḍya-vāṭabhava of the *Bṛhatsaṁhitā* (80.2 and 6). Mahendra here seems to be the most southerly spur of the Travancore Hills (*JRAS,* 1894, p. 262). [The *Rāmāyaṇa,* IV. 41, mentions the Tāmraparṇi river, then the *yuktaṁ Kavāṭaṁ Paṇḍyānām* and then Mt. Mahedra. See Sircar; *Cosm. Geog. E. Ind. Lit.* p. 62. Aśoka's RE II and XIII mention the same Tāmraparṇī.—D.C.S.]

13. Hillebrandt, *Vedische Mythologie,* Vol. I, p. 95; E. Kuhn's *Zeitschrift,* Vol. 28, p. 214.

14. X. 65. [Cf. *caura=cora* in Pāṇini, V. 2:113; *also eur in 111.1.25.—D.C.S.]*

15. *Ind. Ant.,* Vol. VI, pp. 249-50, 344.

16. We also meet with similar *taddhita* forms in later history. Thus we have instances of early tribes being called Calukya, Kadamba and so fourth, whose descendants later on came to be called Cālukya, Kādamba and so on. [This s not strictly accurate.—D.C.S.]

17. *Ind. Ant.,* Vol. XIII, pp. 331, 349.

18. *Bṛhatsamhitā,* XIV.3.

19. *Ind. Ant.,* Vol. XIII, p. 268.

20. Caldwell, *Comp. Grammar of the Dravidian Languages,* Intro, p. 16,

21. *Mahābhārata,* III. 88. 15: That the Pāṇḍyas held the Madura District is quite certain, because it was the territory immediately round about

Madhurā, their capital. That they held also the Tinnevelly Distirct is clear from what Ptolemy and the author of the *Periplus* tell us about the Pāṇḍya kingdom (*Ind. Ant.*, Vol. XIII, p. 331). Northwards their rule seems to have extended as far as the highlands in the neighbourhood of the Coimbatore gap. Its western boundary was formed by the southern range of the Ghats. That the Aryans had occupied the Tinnevelly District at this time is evident from the fact that we have here not only the sacred river Tāmraparṇi, but also the sacred place Agastya-tirtha—both mentioned in the *Mahābhārata*.

22. *Journ. Ceylon Br. R.A. Soc.*, Vol. VII, pp. 57 ff.

23. *SBE,* Vol. XII, pp. xIi ff., 104 ff.

24. *JRAS,* 1907, p. 644.

25. *Kauṭilīya Arthaśāstra* [Bibliotheca Sanskrita, No. 37), p. 11.

26. *Mahābhārata,* 1. 85, 34; II. 14. 6; VI. 9. 40; *Harivaṁśa,* 1895, 8816, 12838.

27. R.G. Bhandarkar, *Early History of the Dekkan,* p. 4.

28. Wilson, *Viṣṇu Purāṇa,* III, 237; *Vikramorvaśīya* (BSPS ed.), p. 41. It is believed to be the present Jhusi opposite the Allahabad fort.

29. In the *Mahābhārata* are mentioned both the Aila-vaṁśa (I. 94. 65) and the Aila-vaṁśyas (II. 14.4). The Ailas are mentioned also in the Purāṇas.

30. Lüders, *List of Brāhmī Inscriptions, etc.,* Nos. 1202-04. [We have now many more inscriptions of several kings of this family.—D.C.S.]

31. It is not at all unlikely that Māṭharīputra Śrī-Vīrapuruṣadatta was a prince of Dakṣina-Kosala which, in the the third century A.D., may have extended as far as the east coast. We know that Uttara-Kosala, with its capital of Sāketa or Ayodhyā, was ruled over by the Ikṣvākus, and it seems that when the Ikṣvākus spread themselves southwards, their new province also was called Kosala, *dakṣina* being applied to it to distinguish it from their original territory which therefore became Uttara-Kosala. [Dakṣina-] Kosala was certainly well-known in the fourth century A.D., as it is mentioned in the Allahabad pillar inscription of Samudragupta and included in Daksiṇāpatha. [South Kosala was known to the Rāmāyaṇa tradition (cf. Sircar, *Stud. Geog. Anc. Med. Ind.*, 2nd ed., p. 270). Cf. also the name of 'Kausalyā', wife of a Kosala king of the Ikṣvāku race. She does not appear to have been born in the Ikṣvāku clan.—D.C.S.]

32. *Mahābhārata,* III. 104; *Rāmāyaṇa,* III. 11.85.

33. Caldwell, *op. cit.,* Intro., pp. 101, 119.

34. *Rāmāyaṇa,* III. 17, 22.

35. *Ibid.,* III. 10, 13-14.

36. *Hyderabad Archaeological Series,* No. 1, p. 1. [It is now in the Mysore or Karnataka State. The monograph was rewritten by Sircar and published by the Government of Andhra Pradesh, Hyderabad, in 1958. For Māhiṣmatī, cf. above, p. 5, note 9.—D.C.S.]

37. *Ep. Carn.,* Vol. XI, Inro., p. 2.

38. *Annual Report on Epigraphy* for the year ending 31st March, 1912, p. 57. [The inscriptions may not be so early.—D.C.S.]

39. *Ind. Ant.,* 1912, pp. 231-32.

40. It will be stated further on in the text that no less than three Buddhist *ṣtūpas* have been found in the Kistna District with quite a number of Pāli inscriptions showing that the Aryans had colonised that part. The question arises from where did the Aryans go there. They must have gone either from Kaliṅga or Aśmaka, most probably from the latter. See note 59 below. [For 'Kistna', better read 'Krishna', and for 'Pāli', better '*Prakrit'*,—D.C.S.]

41. *Imperal Gazetteer of India,* Vol. I, pp. 351-52.

42. Caldwell, *Comp. Gram of the Dravidian Languages,* Intro, pp. 43-44.

43. *JRAS,* 1911, p. 510.

44. *Ind. Ant.,* 1913, p. 235. [Now Mysore or Karnataka State. For 'Canarese', better read 'Kannaḍa'.—D.C.S.]

45. For a detailed consideration of this subject, see B.C. Mazumdar, *Bāngālabhāṣāy Drāviḍī Upādāna,* in *Vaṅgīya Sahitya Pariṣat Patrikā,* Vo. XX, Part. I.

46. *Ind. Ant.,* 1916, p. 6.

47. *Arch. Surv. S. Ind,* Vol. I, pp. 91, 102-03.

48. *Ibid.,* p. 104.

49. I use this term in the sense in which it has been taken by Francke in his *Pāli and Sanskrit.* Perhaps this should have been styled 'monumental Pāli' to distinguish it from 'literary Pāli', i.e. the Pāli of the Buddhist scriptures. ['Prakrit' is the better than 'Pāli'. In the period in question, coins bear legend in Prakrit. The silver coins of the Sātavāhanas exhibit a kind of Dravidianised Prakrit. See Sircar, *Stud. Ind. Coins,* pp. 107 ff.—D.C.S.]

50. *Ep. Carn.,* Vol. XI, Intro., pp. 1 ff. ['Chitaldrug' is 'Chitradurga'.—D.C.S.]

51. Lüders, *List of Brāhmi Inscriptions,* No. 1195:96.

52. I had occasion to examine coins of two princes of this dynasty found in the North Kanara District, Bombay. Their names on them are clearly Cuṭukalānaṁda and Mulānaṁda (*Prog. Rep.,* W. Circ., 1911-12, p. 5, para. 18). Rapson is inclined to take Cuṭu and Muḍa (Muṇḍa) as dynastic

names (*Catalogue of the Coins of the Andhra Dynasty, etc.*, Intro., pp. Lxxxiv-Lxxxvi). In my opinion, the whole Cuṭaka(ku)lānaṁda and Mulānaṁda are proper names of individual epithets, for to me it is inconceivable how they could mention their dynastic names only on the coins and not individual names or epithets at all. [The coins give the names Cuṭukaḍānaṁda and Muḍānaṁda and the first of them is found in inscriptions as Cuṭukulānaṁda. We have now additional evidence in support of Bhadarkar that it was a personal and not dynastic name. See Sircar, *Stud. Ind Coins,* p. 131. The North Kanara District is now in the Mysore or Karnatkaa State.—D.C.S.]

53. Rapson has conclusively shown that Viṇhukaḍa Cuṭukalānṁda and Śivaskandavarman of the Maḷavaḷḷi inscriptions were related to each other as father and son (*ibid.*, pp. liv-lv). But then it is worthy of note that the latter has been called king of the Kadambas in one of these records. It thus appears that both father and son belonged to the Kadamba dynasty—a coclusion which thoroughly agrees with the fact that their title *Vaijayantipuraraja, Mānavya-sagotta* and *Hāritiputta* are exactly those of the Kadambas known to us from their copper-plate charters (*Bombay Gazetter,* Vol. I. Part II, p. 287). For comments on these views, see Sircar. *Suc. Sāt. L. Dec.*, pp. 220ff. Śivaskandavarman was the son of Cuṭukulānanda's daughter.—D.C.S.]

54. Lüders' List, Nos. 1200, 1205, 1327, 1328 and 1194, [Better-Vijaya-Devavarman.—D.C.S.]

55. Personally I think most of the princes in Southern India were of Dravidian blood as is clearly evidenced by their names such as Pulumāvi, Viḷivāyakura, Kaḷalāya, Cuṭukala and so forth.

56. *JRAS,* 1904, p. 399 ff.

57. Let me say here that the exact question to be answered is why the Dravidian language was supplanted by the Aryan language in North India, but not in South India, although Aryan civilisation had apparently permeated South India as much as North India.

58. *Vinayapiṭaka,* Vol. I, Intro., pp. liv-lv.

59. Personally I think, the Aryans went to Kaliṇga not by the eastern, but by the southern route. it is worthy of note that while the Pāli Buddhist canon knowns Aṅga and Magadha and Assaka (Aśmaka) and Kaliṅga, it does not know Vaṅga, Puṇḍra and Suhma—exactly the countries intervening between Aṅga and Kaliṅga, through which they would certainly have passed and where they certainly would have been settled if they had gone to Kaliṅga by the eastern route. There is, therefore, nothing strange in the dialect of Kaliṅga being the same as that of Maharashtra or the Pāli.

60. V. 33. I.

Conclusion

This Volume covers the period of Indian History from A.D. 320, when the Gupta Empire was founded, to about A.D. 740, when Yaśovarman of Kanauj died. Rightly called the '*Classical Age*' of India, this period saw a springtime efflorescence in all spheres of life. The creative urge of the time has contributed both character and richness to the evolution of the national mind in every succeeding century.

Empires rise, decline and fall; communities and nations integrate or disintegrate; the latter either develop a collective mind, outlook and will, or lose one or the other only to lose them all eventually. In the one case they evolve an articulate personality; in the other they cast it off and disappear.

The integration and disintegration of human aggregates form the basic patterns of history as viewed through continuous time, To study them, however, they must be viewed in sections, as in this volume. If such a study is to have any meaning, the volume and direction of the flowing stream must be constantly borne in mind.

"It is not enough to conserve, record and understand what has happened: it is necessary also to assess the nature and direction of the momentous forces working through the life of India in order to appreciate the fulfilment which they seek."

Throughout the history of India, the process of integration comprises two simultaneous movements: one owes its origin to Aryan Culture and operates by virtue of the momentum which the values of that culture possess; the other works itself upward from the way of life of the Early Dravidian and other non-Aryan cultures in the country into the framework of the Aryan Culture modifying its form and content, though not the fundamentals, weaving a harmonious pattern continuously. The first movement provides vitality and synthesis; the second contributes vigour and variety. But it is the harmonious adjustment of both that gives to India, age after age, her strength, tenacity and sense of mission.

The adjustment made against the background of racial fusion is symbolised by the sacredness accorded both to the *Nigama,* the Vedic tradition, and there *Āgama,* the Dravidian tradition; by the equal ritualistic importance of the Vedic *homa* and the Dravidian *pūjā;* to the inseverable Godhood of the Aryan Vishṇu and the non-Aryan Śiva. It must never be forgotten that Vyāsa, the founder and prophet of *Ārya-dharma,* and Śri Kṛishṇa, the World Teacher, whose message is its fundamental scripture, are both sons by high-browed Aryans of non-Aryan mothers.

Vedic culture, the culture of the Vedic Aryans, brought an increasing number of people within its fold as it spread through the country. Sweeping changes were made in the religious, social and cultural outlook and institutions of each successive age. But the vitality of the central ideas and fundamental values was never so lost as to bring about complete disintegration. In some periods, however, the two movements produced adjustments at many, if not all, levels; the vitality was converted into irresistible vigour; full nourishment was drawn from the soil of race memory and tradition. At such times a great Age, like the Age of the Guptas, would dawn in India. On the other hand, when the two movements failed either by external or internal maladjustments to support each other, conflict between the two became inevitable; growth ceased to be vigorous; disintegration began as in the beginning of the eleventh century, when the raids of Mahmūd of Ghaznī overwhelmed parts of north India, the Age of Expansion ended, the Age of Resistance began.

The evolution of India, during the period of the Magdhan supremacy, dealt with in the Second Volume of this series, began with the dawn of history in India in the seventh century before Christ. But long before this, Indians, who had adopted the Aryan way of life, had developed common way of life; and their sense of unity preserved by tradition and activated by race-memory, recaptured in each generation, was expressed through common action. By vitalising the fundamental values of their culture, they had created vigorous adjustments necessitated by the conditions of each age. During this process, the best elements in the society had, from the earliest times, developed a ruling purpose—the fulfilment of *Rita* or *Dharma*—which gave them the capacity to will themselves into a well-defined and vigorous social organism.

The Magadhan Period closed with the invation of the Yueh-chis. Disintegration followed in northern and western India and was accentuated by the break up of the Kushāṇa Empire which they had founded. The process of integration was also hindered by Buddhism which was not organically rooted in race memory and race tradition, and stood, in many respects, in antagonism to them. But it was an expansive movement and naturally attracted foreigners; in India, it stimulated the national mind and culture by impact rather than by inspiration. The Śuṅgas and the Sātavāhana conquerors however drew strength from its roots.

The third century after Christ is still shrouded in obscurity. But, according to the *Bhāgavata-purāṇa,* northern India was undergoing a period of disintegration. Nāgas ruled in Champāvatī and Mathurā; Ābhīras ruled in Saurāshṭra and Avantī; in the region of Ābu and Mālava the rulers were devoid of culture 'like unto the *mlechchha*'. In Sindh, on the banks of the Chandrabhāgā, in the land of Kunti in Kāshmir, the Śūdras, Vrātyas and the *mlechchhas* ruled. These rulers, the author says, lacked the power of the Spirit, disregarded *Dharma* and Truth, and were 'contemptible and irascible'—*phalgudāḥ tīvramanyavaḥ*. His only hope lay in the new rulers, Viśvasphaṇi in Magadha and Vindhyaśakti, a Brāhmaṇa, ruling on the banks of the Narmadā.

But there is little doubt, that by the beginning of the fourth century, the forces of disintegration had lost their momentum. In Southern India the old forces were being given new forms and directions.

In spite of unselttled conditions, India was free from foreign attentions. The race memory looked back with pride on those times when *chakravartī-samrāṭs,* or universal emperors like Māndhātā and Bharata held sway over the whole world. The notion of a universal emperor, supported by a universal church, so popular in mediaeval Europe, was basically different from this concept. The *chakravartī* was the political and military counterpart of *Dharma;* like Mahāvarāha—the great Boar—he was the saviour of *Dharma;*and the supporter of the fundamental law of the *Dharma-śāstra;* like Paraśurāma, he was the repressor of the lawlessness of kings, *rājyochchhettā*. He was able to conquer the world but only as the *chakravartī* of Ārayāvarta

The popular conception was expressed by *Vāyu-purāna* thus: "The *chakravartīs* are born in each age as the essence of Vishnu. They have lived in ages past and will come again in the future. In all the three ages—past, present and future even in the *Tretā* age other *chakravartīs* have been and will be born.

"Strength, *Dharma,* happiness and wealth, these wondrous blessings shall characterise these rulers. They will enjoy wealth, plenty *Dharma,* ambition, fame and victory in undisturbed harmony.

"They will excel the Ṛishis in their power to achieve results, by their lordliness, by providing plenty and by discipline. And they will excel the gods, demons and men by their strength and self-discipline."

The conception of Āryāvarta, the sacred land of the Āryas, was a living one; for it was impregnated with an abiding veneration for the fathers who had lived and died so that it might live, great and eternal.

The *Vishṇu-purāṇa* expressed the eternal hope of the Indian heart: "Even the gods sing thus: 'Blessed are the men who live in the land of Bharata, which is like unto the high road to Heaven and to Liberation; for they are higher than gods themselves."

In India the concept of *Dharma* was primarily related to Āryāvarta. Bhāratavarsha, *Karmabhūmi,* was the land of *Dharma,* and it stretched from the oceans to the Himālayas. In the popular mind, however, the boundaries of Āryāvarta extended far beyond those defined by the early *Dharma-śāstras*. Āryāvarta was the region where Āryas flourished and where the *mlechchhas* if they overran it, could not abide for long. It was Āryāvarta, without any frontier, geographical or political. Medhātithi, a great commentator on Manu, was to give expression to this idea some centuries later: "A king of meritorious conduct could conquer even the land of the *mlechchhas,* establish *chāturvarnya* there, assign to the *mlechchhas* a position occupied by the *chanḍālas* in Āryāvarta and render that land as fit for sacrifice as Āryāvarta itself."

In the beginning of the fourth century, the powerful Pallava king Śivaskanda-varman in southern India celebrated the *aśvamedha.* About A.D. 320, Chandragupta I, the founder of the Gupta Empire, revived the *chakravartī* ideal in northern India. His marriage with Kumāradevi, the Lichchhavi princess, probably resulted in the union of her principality with Magadha and launched him on a career of wide conquests. Fortunately for him, there was no other rival for imperial supremacy in northern India at the time and no foreign invader threatened the country from the north-west.

Placed between A.D. 335-380, Samudra-gupta, the next emperor, laid the foundation of an irresistible military machine which probably included a navy. With his large standing army he wiped out the feeble kings and effete republics of the Gangetic basin. The territory from Hardwar to the borders of Assam was consolidated into a compact homeland which he directly administered under system which, with suitable modifications, was soon adopted in many parts of the country and persisted in some form even up to the British period. Samudragupta's sacred horse, followed by his army, extracted tribute from the kings ruling in most parts of the country and served to bring about friendly relations with the Shāhānushāhi kings of the north-west. He reached the zenith of his power when he performed the *aśvamedha* sacrifice and gave munificent donations.

Politically, this was the age of integration in India. After more than three hundred years of fragmentation and foreign domination, northern India was again united under the vigorous rule of a powerful monarch of versatile talents. A brilliant general, a farsighted statesman, a man of culture and a patron of the arts and letters, he became the symbol and architect of a mighty creative urge among the people which, while drawing vitality from tradition and race memory, took on a new shape and power.

Samudragupta was succeeded by his no less brilliant son, Chandragupta II, known as Vikramāditya, acclaimed as the greatest of the Gupta Emperors. In his reign which is placed between A.D 376 and 414, the last vestige of foreign rule disappeared from the land and the direct sway of Pāṭaliputra extended from the Bay of Bengal to the Arabian Sea. The country to the south of the Narmadā was dominated by two friendly powers—the Vākāṭakas and the Pallavas—who shared the Gupta emperors' enthusiasm for strengthening *Dharma.* The dominions of the descendants of Vākāṭaka Vindhya śakti extended from

Bundelkhand to Hyderābād. A daughter of Chandragupta II was married to one of them, and she ruled as regent for thirteen years; and till the dynasty disappeared, the Vākāṭakas continued in subordinate alliance with the Guptas. The Pallavas, who held unquestioned sway in the south, maintained friendly relations with the Guptas, ever when they were not subject to their hegemony.

Under the leadership of Chandragupta II, the Gupta eagles flew over parts of Balkh across the Hindukush. Peace, plently and power, associated with an all-pervading moral sense, were, in his reign, integrated with an intellectual and cultural efflorescence, and to the mind of the succeeding generations, it symbolised the fulfilment of the highest national aspirations.

Even in A.D. 1944, India, then under foreign rule, spontaneously held the second millennial celebrations of the reign of a Vikramāditya around whom the glorious memory of the great Gupta Emperor had created a halo. It was a unique tribute of posterity to this great Vikramāditya who, in the Collective Unconscious of India, symbolised the highest aspirations of national greatness.

Chandragupta was succeeded by his son, Kumāragupta (A.D. 415 to 455) and, later, by his grandson, Skandagupta (A.D. 455 to 467) who inflicted a defeat on the invading Hūṇas. Both of them stabilised what their predecessors had acquired and consolidated. These one hundred and fifty years of Gupta rule can rightly be called the Golden Prime of India.

The Gupta emperors upheld *Dharma* in all its aspects and, in consequence, its content was enriched and its scope enlarged. An overarching law of life, though it existed from Vedic times, it received under them the form which in the main it still retains. They drew their inspiration from it, and in so doing carried the people with them. Historical continuity and conscious-unity were preserved by a faith in the Vedas as the source of all knowledge and inspiration. Within the framework of this faith, myths, traditions and rituals, language and literature, the canons of conduct, ideals and modes of life, became integrating agencies. Through the *Purāṇas,* which sang of sacred legends, of rivers, mountains, cities, of royal houses, and of semi-divine heroes and sages, the past remained a glorious heritage to inspire the future with fresh vigour.

In this age, the most powerful integrating force was the *Dharma-śāstras*. They provided the basis of Aryan society and the mode of social adjustment; prescribed laws of inheritance and of civil and criminal justice; and laid down rules to govern all major situations from birth to death. Of them all, *Manusmṛiti* was held in the highest sanctity throughout the country, not only in the north but in South India as well. The Tamil kings upheld its authority; one of the oldest classics of Tamil literature bears the clear impress of its great influence.

Theoretically, according to the *Dharma-śāstras*, the social structure envisaged a four-fold of social groups, *chāturvarṇya;* in fact, it was a hierarchy of such groups ranged according to the standard of culture attained by each, with intervening groups to accommodate products of racial fusion. The Brāhmaṇas stood at its head as devoted to learning, culture and self-discipline. The hierarchy was cultural, not a racial one. Outsiders were allowed to enter and benefit by it, but not so fast to destroy the social equilibrium. Opportunity was thus given to those who were aliens to Indian culture to rise in the scale of life, but never so rapidly as to endanger the stability of the existing social order.

The bed-rock of social organisation inherited from the Vedic Aryans was the patriarchal family. The father was its head; the mother, its mistress; all members of the family including the helpless had a secure asylum in it. As a corollary, the devotion of wife to her husband and to the family was imperative. Her position has never been more beautifully described than in Kanva's advice to Śakuntalā in Kālidāsa's play:—

> "Wait on thy betters; act the part of darling friend unto ev'ry fellow bride
>
> Tho' by thy husband treated ill, in wrathfulness do not rend awry thy face;
>
> Be vastly courteous unto them that on thee wait, in thy fortunes take no pride
>
> thus turn to housewives, women young, while those perverse
> are the bane of all the race."

(*Abhijnāna-Sākuntalam* iv, 8)

Castes mixed in marriage with comparative freedom; *anuloma* marriages were very common; the *pratiloma* marriages were by no means rare.

The *Dharma-sāstras* were not enforced at the point of the sword. Even the backward and the immigrant classes dropped their group customs and usages, and cheerfully adopted the social system prescribed by them. Thus, Aryanisation of India was not achieved by the fiats of rulers or mass coercion by superior classes, but by the willing acceptance by all those realised that the dynamics of the *Dharma-sāstra* provided, for the age, the best conditions for social, spiritual and cultural uplift.

Sanskrit, a living language, elastic in structure and rich in expression, possessing a rich, varied and beautiful literary achievement, was the living embodiment of the *Dharma* and a powerful integrating force. Inscriptions began to be written in Sanskrit, even in the far South. A new thought or a new literary masterpiece in the language attracted the attention of all the intellectual centres. For instance the works of Kālidāsa, a contemporary of Chandragupta II Vikramāditya, became the models of literary beauty throughout the country within a few years of his death.

Under the Gupta emperors, the *Mahābhārata* acquired a unique position as an integrating psychological force. It immortalised the proud and joyous manhood of *Bhāratavarsha,* and provided a common source of inspiration in courts, schools and in society as a whole.

The cultural uprising was based upon the central idea underlying *Dharma* from early time. It predicated an unalterable faith in human endeavour, self-restraint (*saṃyama*) and self-discipline (*tapas*). Emphasis was laid on individual experience and *becoming* rather than on belief and the scriptural word; it was reached only when a man could shed his limitations and become divine in this life. Running through a diversity of religious beliefs and social outlook, it also laid an emphasis on the observance of the great vows—*mahāvratas*—of non-violence, truth, non-stealing, continence and non-possession as essential steps in progress. All conduct, in order to be worthy of respect, had to be harmonised and regulated by ethical and spiritual values calculated to help the fulfilment of this ideal.

The four Gupta emperors,—omitting, of course, the ignoble Rāmagupta,—in maintaining the ideals of a *chakravartī,* made the state at one and the same time, powerful, stable, dynamic and happy. The age saw the speculative thought among others of Vasubandhu and the Nāyanmārs; the perfect lyric and drama of Kālidāsa; the astronomical discoveries of Varāhamihira; the iron pillar of Delhi; the beginnings of the structural temples; the beauty of the early Ajaṇṭā frescoes; the rise of Vaishṇavism and Saivism; the completion of the *Mahābhārata* and the composition of *Vāyu* and the *Matsya-Purāṇas*. The empire was not merely based on conquests or administrative efficiency; its greatness lay in its integral outlook. Its strength was based as much on military-strength as on internal order and economic plenty; the sap of its vitality was drawn from the roots of ancient tradition and race memory which they maintained, re-interpreted and replenised. The upsurge of the Kshatriya hierarchs of Madhyadesa and Magadha, loyally pledged to stability, constituted the steel-frame of the imperial structure. Nor was the splendour of the empire an isolated phenomenon surrounding the individuality of the rulers. The people, having discovered in their traditional way of life something noble and splendid, only saw it reflected in the greatness of their rulers. The Vākātakas and the Pallavas the far south, the two other dominant powers in the country closely allied with the Guptas, joined in availing themselves of the agency of the Brāhmaṇas, the missionaries and instruments of *Dharma,* by lavish generosity.

The Gupta emperors became the symbols of a tremendous national upsurge. Life was never happier, our culture never more creative than during the Golden Prime of India.

In the middle of the fourth century of the Christian era, something resembling a volcanic eruption took place in the history of the human race. The Hūṇas, like a veritable stream of lava, issued from their homeland on the northern shores of the Caspian Sea and spread over Europe and Asia. Homeless and lawless, they rode their horses awake and asleep. Their fierce yells spread terror wherever they were heard. They engaged all the civilised peoples of the world in fearful cataclysmic wars; and, wherever they could, they killed, destroyed, burnt and devastated with demoniac ruthlessness. In Europe, Attila the Hun brought about the downfall of even the powerful Roman Empire.

About A.D. 455, the Hūṇas began to enter India. Emperor Skandagupta drove them back by a supreme effort. Twelve years later, he died. The outposts of the empire, already weak, could offer no further resistance. The barbarian hordes, after passing through Persia and destroying the Kushāṇa rulers of the north-west, began to pour into India.

A war of succession appears to have followed the death of Skandagupta, weakening the empire in the hour of its danger. Next in order of succession, five emperors including Narasiṁhagupta Bālāditya, between A.D. 500 and 570, held precarious sway over parts of the empire, which in spite of its decadence was still a name to conjure with. Many parts of the empire outside the bounds of the compact core of the empire became independent. In Saurāshṭra, a province of the empire, the Maitraka general practically threw off his allegiance on the death of Skandagupta.

By A.D. 512, the Hūṇas under Toramāṇa, overran north India up to Eran in the Saugar district of Madhya Pradesh. Toramāṇa's son, Mihirakula, a veritable terror, spread fire and carnage from the Punjāb to Gwālior and by A.D. 525 became the master of a vast territory.

Northern Indian soon recovered from the shock of the barbarian impact and resisted Mihirakula. The records which have survived are much too vague and fragmentary to indicate the nature and extent of this war of liberation. But the names of two great liberators have come down to us.

Yaśodharman Vishṇuvardhana, who was possibly an ex-feudatory of the Empire, fought the Hūṇas grimly. His swift victories arrested the progress of Mihirakula, and enforced allegiance. Mālwā, which included central parts of what is modern Gujarāt, once a province of the Empire, when liberated, formed part of the domains of Yaśodharman, and his conquests are described as having covered the territory form the Himālayas to the Ganjām district.

Mihirakula met with no less heavy reverses in his eastern campaigns. The challenge was taken up by Īśāna-varman Maukhari, a quasi-independent feudatory ruling over Madhyadeśa represented by modern Uttar Pradesh. He barred the progress of the Hūṇas to the east and in the course of several encounters inflicted a shattering defeat upon them.

Emperor Narasiṁhagupta Bālāditya, the ruler of the Eastern Empire, dealt a final blow to the Hūṇa and sent him reeling back to his dominions on the North-West Fronter only to find, according to

Hiuen Tsang, that his throne Mihirakula then fell back on Kāshmir which he captured, and died soon after.

Yaśodharman Vishṇuvardhana blazed a meteroric brilliance and vanished into darkness. In A.D. 533, Mālwā was being ruled by the Governor of Īśāna-varman, the Maukhari conqueror. Two years later, Kumāragupta III, son of Narasiṁhagupta Bālāditya, re-established the imperial sway in Mālwā and declared himself 'Lord of the three seas'. But the empire decayed rapidly, and though Gupta sovereignty was recognised by the Maitrakas till about A.D. 550, and acknowledged in Kalinga even as late as A.D. 569, it is clear that the emperor had become a *roi fainéant*.

Īśāna-varman, the great liberator, possibly overthrew the descendants of Yaśodharman, conquered the Śūlikas of Āndhra, and on the death of Kumāragupta III emerged as the unchallenged master of Madhyadeśa and Mālwā. He kept the Gauḍas at bay and established himself at Kanauj which, thereafter, was the imperial capital of north India for close upon five centuries. Śarva-varman (A.D. 576-580), the successor of Īśāna-varman, maintained the supremacy of his dynasty.

The Hūṇas disappeared as they came. The Gupta Empire, grown very weak, was dissolved; the virile Maukharis emerged victorious. But with their rise began a new phase in Indian History. Kanauj emerged as the symbol of a new order.

The Golden Prime of India became a thing of the past; the military superiority of Magadha disappeared. Out of the welter emerged a set of new dynasties: the Maukharis of Kanauj, the Pushpabhūtis of Thāneswar, the Maitrakas of Valabhī and the Chālukyas of Bādāmi. The Pallavas of Kanchī alone among the old dynasties continued to flourish. In the warrior clans of what is now Rājasthan, living in the region of Mount Ābū and descended from Brāhmaṇa ancestors, emerged from obscurity as a closely knit hierarchy with the Pratīhāras at their head.

Due to the exaggerated eulogies of his biographer, Bāṇa, and the enthusiastic Hiuen Tsang, Śrī Harsha has been given more than his share of importance. No doubt he preserved the unity of Madhyadeś, but he suffered a serious defeat at the hands of Pulakeśin II, of Bādāmi and had to make terms with the Maitrakas of Valabhī. The territories he conquered were neither as extensive as the empire of the Guptas who preceded him, nor that of the Pratīhāras who followed him; nor did he leave behind an empire.

We learn from the Chinese pilgrim that Śrī Harsha not only followed Buddhism but also had a marked antipathy to the Brāhmanical religion. But the seals, which refer to his elder brother as Buddhist, describe him as a devoted Śaiva.

Śrī Harsha, unlike the Guptas, was not able to release a new integrating impulse. The Emperor, with a large army, had conquered far and wide, staged spectacular festivals, made generous gifts; his character stood high. But he left no hierarchs and no successors; on his death the fabric he had erected, fell to pieces. The causes which led to this sudden collapse of Kanauj may be found not only in the circumstances that brought him to supremacy, but also in his personal character. The old Kshatriya houses in Madhyadeśa, who had supported the Gupta Empire, were exhausted or hostile; Śrī Harsha could infuse no new hope or strength in them. Kanauj and Thāneswar, though friendly states, were rivals. When Kanauj was faced with extinction at the hands of Śaśāṅka, Śrī Harsha was called in as a matter of military urgency to a joint rulership over both states. But his hold over the two states was personal; the hierarchs of both kingdoms possibly hated each other. Śrī Harsha failed, where Chandragupta I the founder of the Gupta Empire, had succeeded so well; he was unable to create a common hierarchy which could carry forward his work.

At the height of his career Śrī Harsha was an ardent Buddhist. In all probability, he held himself aloof from his ministers, and the leaders of society, superior and self-righteous. He could not restore the life-blood of the old social organisation, for he could not identify himself with its urges, nor could he revive the *chakravartī* tradition. The secret of establishing a military power founded on traditional strength, was not his; nor did the mass of the people feel that the conquests of Śrī Harsha were their own triumph. The internationalism, for which Buddhism stood, negatived the building up of a compact unity rooted in the land. He could conquer; he could not build. The way of the Guptas was, therefore, barred to him.

The empire he had won simply disappeared. After Śrī Harsha, his daughter's son, Dharasena IV, the ruler of the comparatively small kingdom of Valabhi, assumed the pretentious title of an emperor. Within fifty years of Śrī Harsha's death, Yaśovarman, a powerful ruler and the patron of Bhavabhūti, restored Kanauj to its glory—but for a while.

But the strength and vigour of India, between A.D. 550 and 750, was found in the South. While the Maukharis were founding an empire which had its seat at Kanauj, Pulakeśin I, of the Chālukya family (A.D. 550), had already founded a kingdom in the Bijāpur district of Bombay with its capital at Vātāpī, modern Bādāmi. About the end of the sixth century, his son, Kīrtivarman, embarked on wars against the kings who ruled to the north of the Godāvarī.

Pulakeśin II, who had already subdued the Pallavas of Kānchi, repelled the invasion of Śrī Harsha in c.A.D. 620 and adopted the style "Lord of the three Mahārāshṭras containing 999 villages". He annexed Vengī, modern Godāvarī district, and appointed his brother Vishṇuvardhana as its governor on the east coast. Four years later, Vishṇuvardhana became virtually independent and founded the dynasty of the Eastern Chālukyas. Pulakeśin with his warriors and elephants which 'marched to victory while intoxicated' founded the empire of Dakshiṇāpatha. After a rule of about two centuries during which the Chālukyas provided the greatest stabilising influence in the country, they were replaced by the Rāshṭrakūṭas.

The great Pallava king, Mahendra-varman I (A.D. 600-630) at one time defeated even Pulakeśin II and captured his capital. Though the Chālukyas avenged this defeat soon after, the Pallavas remained the most powerful kings in the far south.

Throughout the period of over four hundreds years from A.D. 320 to 750, India was administered by well-organised governments. The political interest during this time is primarily confined to the history of northern India. This was due mostly to the power and extent of the Gupta Empire. But the contribution of the Chālukyas and the Pallava kings in stabilising the country and fostering the integrating forces should not be underestimated.

Conditions in the north and the west zones of India, from and inclusive of Afghānistān (then a Hindu territory) up to the Varmadā, were thrown into confusion. Within a few years of the death of Mihirakula, however, a new and vigorous impulse is also visible; an ulse to revive *Dharma,* to relate it to the new life, to fashion values to new conditions, not only in the affected zones, but in other parts of India as well, and particularly in the south. The foundations of life, shaped during the Gupta period, remained unshaken in a large part of the country; its pattern, however, soon underwent a change.

Some aspects of this new impulse, the home of which was in the south, can be easily traced. The *Purāṇas,* some of which were redacted or newly written in the Gupta times, were the popular gospels of the new impulse. They did not serve merely a religious purpose. They revived the glories of the distant past; they invested new places in the country with stimulating sanctity, weaving the unity of Bhāratavarsha; they also re-interpreted old values in the light of new conditions, giving them a new vigour.

Śaivism, a popular cult long before the rise of the Gupta Empire, became a very vigorous integrating movement. The worship of Śiva as Paśupati is as old as Mohenjo-daro. The new cult, which Śaṅkarāchārya called Lakuleśa Pāśupata had spread over the country, and was the most influential protagonist of *Dharma* and the formidable opponent of Buddhism and Jainism.

In spite of the Gupta Emperors being devoted to Vishṇu, the worship of Śiva was more popular. Mihirakula, the Hūṇa king, like some early Kushāṇa kings, was a devotee of Śiva; and so were most of the members of Śrī Harsha's family; and so were the Maitrakas of Valabhī and most of the rulers of the South, including the Vākāṭakas. Mahendra-varman, the great ruler of the Pallava dynasty, became a convert to Śaivism, and built magnificent temples in his kingdom. Kānchī became a great centre of the faith and his successors identified themselves with the renaissance associated with Śaivism. Many Śaiva Nāyanmārs who flourished during this period pressed even Vedānta into the service of Śaivism. Māṇikkavāchakar's *Tiruvāchakam* became the highest Śaiva scripture in the Tamil language.

The Gupta Emperors were very catholic in their religious outlook; Buddhism was not only tolerated, but like other religions, lavishly supported. The lay Buddhists were an integral part of society regulated by the canons of the *Dharma-śāstras.* Therefore, when Śaivism and Vaishṇavism became powerful integrating forces, Buddhism which at best was a protestant movement, never an integrating force, began to lose its hold over the masses. Its content progressively approximated to Hinduism. Its spiritual nihilism, when exposed to the Bhakti movements, tried to approximate to the latter at least in its external aspects, and finally came to be absorbed in the wide fold of Hindusim; and later when Buddha was accepted as the *avatāra* of Vishṇu, no trace of its separate existence as a rival was left. As a cult, however, it continued for a few more centuries.

After A.D. 500 the Bhakti cults gave to the religious movements the emotional content, which, for centuries, remained of immense significance in Indian life; it helped to form enduring values which gave strength to the Age of Resistance after the cataclysmic diasater which the Turks brought in their wake. The Ālvārs of Tamil Nad were simple-hearted *bhaktas;* they loved and wooed their gods and expressed their feeling with a directness hardly surpassed in emotional content and ardent faith in the religious literature of the world.

Sanskrit continued to be the language of religion and ritual; of state-craft, learning and science; of the law texts which regulated social conduct; and of literature, thought, poetry and drama. It was the national medium of intercourse. The Sanskrit speaking world was one, all-Indian. It was with its aid that in the next century Śankarācharya, a Brāhmaṇa from Malabār, in all too short a life, was to organise religious institutions, dominate the speculative thought of the country, and inaugurate a sweeping religious and intellectual movement throughout the country.

The *Mahābhārata*, the *Rāmāyaṇa* and the *Purāṇas* continued to be the source of countrywide unity. The Puranic literature remained simple and direct; its growth as an influence could be measured by the evolution of the literature from the meagre recitals of *Matsya* and *Vāyu-Purāṇas* to the richly magnificent *Bhāgavata,* again a contribution of the south. The *Kathā* became the most powerful educative and integrating force. The Paurāṇikas were the missionaries of the new age; an agency of social uplift which brought an ever-expanding circle of adherents into the fold of Aryan culture.

In North India, the dialects, which the higher classes spoke, were not far removed from Sanskrit. But in the South the Dravidian languages continued to develop on their own lines, no doubt influenced and enriched by Sanskrit. Elements in the population speaking dialects, not of Indo-Aryan origin, also began to find a place among the higher classes in large numbers. Cultural influences were therefore spread not only through Sanskrit, but percolated to the masses through the medium of the growing dialects which acknowledged the supremacy of Sanskrit and became subsidiary forces of integration.

Chāturvarṇya was called upon to bear a severe strain due to the need of absorbing foreigners and of Aryanising non-Aryans who were given a place in it. A change therefore came over it altering the structure of society. *Varṇāśrama* took the shape—though not yet distinct—of an organisation of interdependent castes, not a fourfold social order. Society thus lost the freshness of outlook which the *dvijas* of India, as a class fundamentally one, had imparted to it. The history of the following centuries shows how, as the social structure grew inelastic, the political sanction of a *chakravarti* was denied to cultural and social solidarity, and the people ceased to have an expansive outlook.

The leading role as a highly trained and purposive agency in integration was played by Brāhmaṇas: men of learning and teachers; literary men and religious preceptors; 'svāmins' who specialised in the sacrificial lore; the Pāśupatāchāryas who, feared and respected by the people, wielded vast influence over kings and founded temples and monasteries, all of which became the centres of the new socio-religious movement of power. *Smārta* Brāhmaṇas were not only interpreters, commentators and lawyers, but also expounders of *Dharma*. The influence of the Brāhmaṇas was felt throughout the country. They slowly reclaimed and raised millions of backward people. Under their inspiration, communities were uplifted and the cultural and spiritual elevation of the individual secured.

During this period, the system of education did not change appreciably from what it was in the preceding age. Universities like Nālandā, great centres of learning, came into existence.

The Āryāvarta consciousness, as stated before, had three aspects; Āryāvarta was the land of *Dharma* in which no *mlechchha* could abide; *chāturvarṇya,* the social basis, was its eternal law; the *chakravartī* was to maintain both. The sentiment that no *mlechchha* could abide in India was deeprooted and active; equally active was the belief that *Dharma* prevailed in Bhāratavarsha. The *chakravartī* idea, however, clearly lost its meaning; *Dharma* could not, and therefore need not, be linked with the duty of maintaining the whole country within its fold. Wars of conquests lost their spiritual significance; they were not, as in the earlier periods, an expression of a people and a culture on the move; they were undertaken only for dynastic ends or, more often, to curb the aggressive intentions of neighbouring kings. People and culture were one; the *Smṛiti* law was the universal *Dharma;* but *chāturvarṇya* became a social pattern in its own right. Āryāvarta consciousness, in consequence, receded into race memory.

The Kshatriya community was no longer a compact military caste of Madhyadeśa dominated by a single cultural tradition. It came to be infiltrated by the foreign, aboriginal and other non-Aryan groups, not yet acclimatised to *Dharma*. Inter-marriages between the Brāhmaṇas and the Kshatriyas became rare; the Kshatriyas busied themselves with wars and saw no justification for undergoing any rigorous intellectual training.

The segregation of *dvija* castes into water-tight compartments and difficulty of social fusion, therefore, became distintegrating factors.

An empire could only be built on the shoulders of a hierarchy. Such a well-knit hierarchy had helped to found the Gupta Empire in the days of the early emperors; it had been interested in maintaining the authority of the emperor, howsoever weak or helpless, against ambitious neighbours or recalcitrant feudatories in the interest of cammon purpose which they shared with the masses. The change in the social structure created conditions in which such a hierarchy, homogeneous in culture and looking forward with faith to the political unity of Āryāvarta, could not be brought into existence.

In spite of the conventional encomiums contained in the inscriptions, conquerors were continuously emerging from obscurity who cared more for dynastic power than for *Dharma*.

After the Guptas, conquest on a large scale became increasingly difficult. The army, from ancient times, was divided into four sections: The elephants, the cavalry, the infantry and the chariots. During the period under review, as attested by *Harsha-charita* and as recorded by Hiuen Tsang, chariots were sparingly used in warfare. A king rode to war mostly on an elephant; and a king bent on conquest had to maintain a large number of elephants. Cavalry was used largely, but the horses were generally maintained by the feudal chiefs who brought them to the battlefield for use, just as they did their own footmen. Usually, the army consisted of Kshatriya feudal chiefs who had their own estates, their regional attachments and their code of honour prescribed by the *śāstras* and the traditions. In the hands of powerful leaders, they could be heroes, but not mercenaries.

They were generally rewarded by grants of land, and their leaders were mostly connected with the ruling dynasty by blood. The petty king, even in war, was no more than "the head of inter-related overlordships." Unless, therefore, a conqueror had sufficient means to have an effective elephant force and a paid army of his own, he had in practice to depend on his feudal chiefs and could scarcely aspire to be a *chakravarti*.

According to an old tradition inherited from the era of small kingdoms, it was not open to a conqueror to overthrow the ruling dynasty of another territory and annex it to his own. He had therefore to find a loyal chieftain who could command the loyalty of the important Kshatriya families of the conquered territory. The Kshatriyas slowly became rooted in their own region. The successful merger of conquered territory necessarily implied the uprooting of the local chiefs and their replacement by the feudal chiefs of the conqueror and his dynasty. This involved the re-distribution of fiefs in the conquered territory among the feudal chiefs of the conqueror ready to be transplanted to a new and uncongenial soil; and, the capacity in the conqueror to support his newly planted chiefs as his instrument of power without weakening his own military efficiency. These factors appear, during the period under review, to have worked against the political consolidation of states.

Many conquerors tried to disregard these factors; most of them failed. Samudragupta succeeded because he ruthlessly extirpated the small states of Northern India and could rely upon the military classes of Madhyadesa. With the fall of the Gupta Empire, North India split into smaller units. With the humane traditions of India, attempts at extirpating a regional hierarchy could scarcely be made except by ruthless conquerors; in consequence, the regional attachment of the Kshatriyas increased; and with their patrons, the Brāhmaṇas who depended on them also developed regional loyalties. The kingdoms became smaller, and small-state-mindedness became a part of the national mind.

The only exception, in the period under review, was the emerge once of the Pratīhāra, the Chāhamāna and the Chālukya clans, closely allied in marriage and tradition; the Paramāras and the other warrior clans of Gurjaradeśa were either off-shoots of these three branches or were absorbed in the hierarchy in course of time. That was why the Pratīhāras were able to found an empire.

In this climate large scale wars resulting in large scale displacement of population were out of the question. Groups tended to be rooted in the region.

The third community, that of the Vaiśyas—at least in north India—belonged to the same class as Brāhmaṇas and Kshatriyas; Śrī Harsha himself was a Vaiśya; his daughter, however, married Dhruvasena II, styled Bālāditya, the Kshatriya king of Valabhī. But they were a dynamic element in the social organisation. Between the members of the community *inter se* there was more equality of cultural attainments. Foreign trade and the needs of commerce brought them into close contact with common people, both Indian and non-Indian. Naturally, therefore, they were less fastidious in taste and outlook. In many parts of the country, Buddhism and Jainism, with their sympathy for the masses, had a greater appeal for them.

The fourth community, the Śūdras, were not a race of lower men, but what may be termed 'the rest'. They were the redeemable of *Dharma* and formed an essential part of society, not looked down upon but only needing attention. Marriages between Śūdras and the members of 'other classes' were common. Bāṇa, the Brāhmaṇa friend of Emperor Śrī Harsha, had himself a brother born of a Śūdra step-mother.

A vital movement in the social organisation of the country enabled one little connubial group, which did not originally form part of the Aryanised society, while undergoing the necessary cultural discipline, to rise from a lower to a higher status, to the Aryanised class. The movement of groups from one order of castes was not difficult. Intermarriage led to a free admixture of blood and prevented an impassable cleavage of cultural ideas. Only when a lower group attained the status of a higher caste, as was common, it became difficult for the group or the family to attain the high standard of culture demanded of a Brāhamaṇa or a Kshatriya execpt after some generations.

The administrative machinery, introduced by the Guptas in consonance with the *Dharma-śāstras* and adopted in the advanced parts of the whole country, continued to function. During the succeeding centuries, the administration did not depart very much from the canons laid down during the Gupta times which, with some changes, and mostly in rural areas, continues in some form even now.

For all practical purposes, administration continued to be in the hands of the same class of people and was regulated by age-old tradition and generally accepted canons of social conduct. Its efficiency continued to be enforced, less by official pressure than by the enlightened opinion of respectable members of the community, who were guided by the leading Brāhmaṇas and Kshatriyas of the locality.

About the end of the period under review, the Arabs appeared on the Indian scene, but for the first time in their meteoric rise the progress of the 'world conquerors' was arrested. The naval raids against Thana, Broach and Debal were repulsed. The attempts to reach India through the Khyber Pass, then guarded by the Hindu states of Kābul and Zābul, failed. Though some sort of Arab suzerainty was established with difficulty for a brief period (A.D. 700-714), for the next century and a half, Kābul and Zābul maintained their autonomy practically unimpaired.

The Arabs also tried to enter India through the Bolan Pass, but the strong Jats of Kikān or Kikānān, though often defeated, never yieded, and that Pass remained sealed to the invaders.

The Arabs then attempted to advance through the Makran coast. Their army was equipped on a lavish scale; troops were requisitioned even from distant Syria. Sindh had just emerged from civil wars; Dāhar, the ruler, had probably gained control over southern Sindh only a few years before the invasion. Very little resistance was offered to the Arab fleet carrying military equipment. Nehrun and Siwistān, the two main strongholds of southern Sindh, opened their gates to the invaders. The unpatriotic character of the Buddhists, the general superstition of a section of the people, and the want of loyalty towards the family of royal usurpers, left the issue in no doubt. Sindh was conquered in A.D. 712.

The conquest of Sindh was not the outcome of the military superiority of the Arabs; in fact, this was their first and the last achievement on Indian soil. After this conquest whenever they came in conflict with powerful Indian States, their spell of victory was broken. About A.D. 725 one Arab army, sent to invade north India, met a disatrous setback at the hands of Nāgabhaṭa I of the Imperial Pratāihāra line; another, which had entered Lāṭa (South Gujarāt), was destroyed by Pulakeśin Avanijanāśraya in a battle which took place near Navsāri. In spite of unremitting pressure, exerted for over two centuries, the Arabs were only left with the two petty states of Mansura and Multān in the ninth and tenth centuries. When compared with their dazzling victories over the contemporary states in the Middle-East, in Europe and over Persia, this insignificant result obtained in India was a tribute to the superior military strength and political organisation of the Indians.

Appendix

MAIN EVENTS AND DATES

462 B.C.-236 A.D.	Magadha Sovereignty and Satavahana Imperialism.
320-750	Gupta Empire and Harshavardhana.
750-1000	Gurjara-Pratihara, Rastrakuta, Pala Empire of Bengal and Cholas of Tanjore.
800-1000	Paramar Empire of Malwa.
1000-1026	Raids of Mahmud of Ghazni.
1026-1300	Chalukya of South, raids of Md. Ghori.
1300-1525	Turkish Power and Sultanate of Delhi.
1526-1707	Mughal Supremacy.
1707-1818	Maratha Supremacy.
1818-1947	British Supremacy
1947-onwards	Independent India after partition.
10	Huemo Kadphises I, the Kushana Chief, invaded India and established his authority in North-Western India.
45	At the death of Kadphises I at the age of eighty, his son Wimakadphises or Kodphises II succeeded him.
52	Apostle St. Thomas' Mission (Thomas Dadymus) arrived in India by the North-Western route. He was the first person to preach Christianity in India. He established a small church at Mylapur in Madras, known as St. Thomas Church, where he was buried. (See 68 & 1510).
67	Kashyapa Matanga is the recorded first Indian scholar to visit China. He settled down at Lo Yang by the Lo river.

68 Ten thousand Jewish refugees with their families emigrated from Jerusalem to the Malabar coast, after the destruction of the second Temple of Jerusalem. (See 744 and 1567).

St. Thomas was killed at Mylapur in Madras. (See 52)

69 Hala, the seventeenth Satavahana King, ascended the throne. Prakrit literature flourished under his patronage.

78 Kaniska ascended the Kushan throne, who extended his authority to Punjab and Uttar Pradesh. He introduced 'Saka' era, probably to commemorate his coronation. His relationship to the previous monarchs Khadphises I or II is not known. (Also see 111 & 1957).

100 Kaniska, with his religious preceptor Parswa, summoned a Buddhist council on the lines of that of Pataliputra.

111 Kushana King Kaniska was suffocated to death with his quilt at the instance of his minister Mathara and other chiefs, since Kaniska was considered too ambitious and greedy to rule the world. Huviska succeeded Kaniska as the Kushana ruler. (See 78 & 1957).

126 Vilivayakura II Gautamiputra, the Satavahana ruler, expelled the Saka invaders from North-Western Deccan.

138 An Indian embassy was sent to Roman Emperor Antonius Pius. (See 21 B.C.)

145 Rudradaman, the Saka king, attacked his son-in-law Pulumayi II of Satavahana dynasty, and grabbed a large portion of his territory.

155 Pandya army of South India invaded Ceylon and captured the capital Anuradhapura.

180 Kushana ruler Huviska died and was succeeded by Vasudeva during whose regime the Kushana empire started to break up. (See 226).

200 Chinese monk Chang Yang Sung visited Nicobar Island, which supposedly got its name from the monk's writings 'Lo Jen Quo' or Land of Naked, and 'Nalo Chen Quo' or Land of Cocoanut. (See 209)

209 Chinese monk Chang Yang Sung arrived at Andaman Island. (See 200)

226 Kushana ruler Vasudeva died and Kushana power collapsed. (See 180)

236 Satavahana dynasty virtually extinguished; although a branch line, the Chutus, continued to rule around Vanavasi, a city

in South Maharashtra. Abhiras (foreigners) succeeded Satavahanas and ruled for 67 years. Isvarasena was perhaps the founder of his shortlived dynasty called 'Kalchuri'.

305 Ghatotkacha, father of Chandragupta I, established himself as a feudal ruler in Pataliputra. (See 319).

319 Chandragupta I succeeded his father Ghatotkacha in Pataliputra on February 26 and established Gupta dynasty. The epoch making Gupta era began. (See 305).

345 Thomas Cana, a merchant from Syria, came to Travancore and founded a Christian colony there.

353 Pope Julius I declared that December 25 was to be observed as the date of birth of Jesus Christ and is so observed in India as well. Earlier different countries fixed different dates such as January 6, February 2, March 25, April 19, May 20 and November 17. None seems to know the correct date.

360 Meghavarna, King of Ceylon, who earlier concluded a treaty of alliance in 52, sent as embassy to Samudragupta's Court in Pataliputra, for the permission to erect a monastery in Bodh Gaya where people could live in comfort. The embassy included one of the brothers of King Meghavarna.

399 Fa-Hsian of China visited India by land route to collect Buddhist manuscripts, texts etc. He left India in 414 by sea route and died in the same year.

401 Buddhsit inscriptions of Udaygiri was made.

412 Buddhist inscriptions of Sanchi were made.

431 Gunavarman, the Crown Prince of Kashmir who converted the Japanese to Buddhism, died in Nanking of China.

432 Buddhist inscriptions of Mathura were made.

455 Skandagupta was the last renowned Gupta ruler of Pataliputra. After his death in 480 Gupta empire declined, but lasted for about a century thereafter.

The first whtle Hun attack under Chu-Khan (Konkha) on Gupta empire was repulsed.

457 The famous Jain temple of Girnar in Gujarat with nearly 4,000 steps was built.

465 The Huns under Toramana entered India. (See 500).

470 Nayan Pal conquered Kanauj slaying its monarch Ajaipal. The race was since then named as Kanauj Rathore. Jaichand was the last monarch of Kanauj. (See 1193)

473 Kesari family obtained the throne of Orissa and held it till 1131.

476 Aryabhatta, the astronomer and mathematician, was born in Kusumapura (Pataliputra). He is supposed to be the inventor of Algebra, and the author of Aryashtaka and Dasagitika. (See 1975).

495 Ballabhi dynasty was established in Gujarat by Senapati Bhattarka, who defeated a foreign tribe called Maitraka, probably of Iranian origin.

500 The Hun leader Toramana established himself in the Central India as a Maharaja. (See 465).

505 Barahamihir, the astronomer, was born. (d. 587).

510 The Hun leader Toramana was defeated and perhaps died in the battle with Bhanu Gupta of Gupta dynasty of Pataliputra. Toramana was succeeded by his son Mihirkula, who made Sialkot of Punjab his capital. Mihirkula was branded as a blood-thirsty tyrant. (See 528 & 542).

522 Bhaskara I, the great Indian mathematician, was born.

524 Nasirban, King of Persia, attacked Gujarat. The Rajput King lost and fled. His queen gave birth to a child in a cave and he was named Grahaditya or Gaho, who was the 135th ancestor of the Ranas of Udaipur. (See 713, 735 and Surya Race).

528 The combined forces of Isana Varman (Yashodharman), Maukhari King of Malwa and Narasimhagupta Baladitya, King of Magadha, defeated the Hun leader Mihirkula, who retired to Kashmir and captured the throne there. Huns thereafter never seriously threatened India. (See 510 & 542).

542 The Hun Chief Mihirkula died in Kashmir. (See 510 & 528).

587 Astronomer Barahamihir died. (b. 505).

598 Brahmagupta, the astronomer, was born. He, developed the usage of 'Shunya' or zero. He was the author of Brahmasphuta-Siddhanta.

600 Mahendravarman I established Pallava dyansty in Kanchipuram, which lasted till 894.

605 After the death of Prabhakarvardhana, King of Thaneswar, his son Rajyavardhana II became the King. But he was treacherously killed the next year by Sasanka, King of Gaur (Bengal).

Grahavarman, Maukheri King of Kanauj and husband of Harshavardhana's sister Rajyashree, was defeated and killed by the King of Malwa. (See 606).

606 Prabhakarvardhana's younger son Harshavardhana took the thrones of Thaneswar and Kanauj at the age of about seventeen years as prince Siladitya. His formal coronation was delayed till 612. (See 605, d. 647).

609 Chalukya Prince Pulakesin II came of age. But his uncle Mangalesha, the Regent for the young prince, refused to hand over the kingdom. Pulakesin II by his own prowess waged war on Mangalesha, killed him in battle and declared himself the King. He was the ablest monarch of the dynasty.

Aihole inscriptions were made during the rule of Chalukya (Badami) King Pulakesin II.

612 Harshavardhana's formal coronation took place in October and he took the title 'Rajaputra'. (See 606).

Harshavardhana held a religious conference in Prayag.

620 Bana wrote 'Harsha-Charita'.

622 The Muslim year 'Hijri' began and is now followed by the Muslims everywhere.

625 Pulakesin II sent an embassy to Persian court of Khusru II.

629 Hiuen Tsang (b. 600) came to India alone by land route. The traveller-pilgrim sojourned in different parts of India and left India in 645 and died in China in 664.

636 The first recorded Arab expedition in India took place by a naval enterprise under Uthman-ath-Thakafi, Governor of Bahrain. It plundered the West Coast of India, during the rule of Caliph Omar bin Khattab, perhaps without his knowledge.

637 Sasanka, King of Gaur (Bengal), died. It ushered in a political turmoil in Bengal. Anarchy continued until Gopala was made the King of Bengal in 750 by the people themselves.

641 Harshavardhana despatched a Brahmin envoy to Tai Tsung, the second Tang Emperor of China. (See 643).

642 Chalukya King Pulakesin II of Maharashtra was utterly defeated by Narasimhavarman I, the Pallava King of Kanchipuram, perhaps with the assistance of King of Ceylon.

643 Harshavardhana launched a campaign against Gunjam, which was his last military campaign.

644 Harshavardhana organised 'Kumbh Mela' at Prayag near Allahabad which was perhaps the sixth one.

645 Hiuen Tsang left India. (See 629).

647 Harshavardhana died, (See 606).

Tai Sung sent an envoy named Wang Hiuen Tse to Harshavardhana's court. Harshavardhana died before his arrival. Arjuna, an ex-minister of Harshavardhana, usurped his throne. He attacked Tse who escaped to Tibet. (See 648 & 657).

648 Strong-Tsan Gampo, King of Tibet, sent an army with Wang Hiuen Tse, which attacked and captured Trihut of Bihar. Arjuna (See 647) was caught and taken to Tibet. Trihut was under Tibet's rule till 703. (See 657).

657 Wang Hiuen Tse again came to India through Nepal and visited sacred spots like Vaisali, Bodh Gaya etc. He returned home through Afghanistan and Pamir. (See 647 & 648).

662 Munjala, the astronomer, wrote Laghumanasa Ganakatarangini.

672 Chinese pilgrim I-Tsing reached India. He took up his residence in Nalanda monastery in 675 and returned to China in 695.

710 A small Arab trading vessel from Basra arrived at the mouth of the Indus and was promptly seized by the local Hindu authorities. (See 712).

712 Arabs attacked and captured Sind under the command of Muhammad Bin Quasim. Debal fell in April. Muhammad defeated and killed Dahir, the Hindu King, at Rawar on June 20. He then took the capital Alor in the same month. The widow queen and other women burnt themselves to death to escape dishonour. All males of the age of 17 years and above who refused to embrace Islam were killed. But the Arabs lost control in 779. Thereafter Sind continued as a small independent Muslim State. (See 710).

713 Bappa of Guhila (Gehlote) dynasty of Mewar was born. He belonged to the Surya (Solar) race and theoretically was the 142nd generation from Brahma. (See 735 & 764).

Arabs captured Multan.

724 Lalitaditya I Muktapida of Naga or Karataka dynasty, the most famous of all Kashmir rules and the builder of renowned Martanda temple, succeeded to the throne of Kashmir.

731 King Yashovarmana of Kanauj sent an embassy to the Emperor of China for his assistance against Yashovarmana's enemies. (See 740).

735 Bappa's son Guhila captured Chittorgarh throne from Manmori belonging to Parmar dynasty. He established the Guhila dynasty of Mewar. (See 713 & 764).

736 Dhillika, the first city of Delhi, was founded by Anangpal Tuar, the Tomara prince. Tomaras (Tuars) ruled in the Haryana region and they belonged to one of the 36 celebrated Rajput tribes. Tomara rule of Delhi ended in 1151 when Visala Deva, one of the Chauhans of Ajmer, captured Delhi.

740 King Yashovarmana of Kanauj was defeated and slain by Lalitaditya I Muktapida of Kashmir. (See 731).

746 Vanaraja, Prince of Deo, laid the foundation of Anhilwara Patan of Rajasthan.

750 After a prolonged anarchy in Bengal since the death of Sasanka in 637, people of Bengal selected Gopala as their King. Gopala ruled till 770 and founded Pala dynasty in Eastern India, which lasted for about 450 years. Gopala revived Nalanda University.

760 Krishna I succeeded to the throne of Rastrakutas. His reign is famous for the rock-cut Kailasha temple of Ellora, the most extensive and sumptuous of the rock-cut shrines in India. The size is 84 mt. × 47 mt. and the height is 32.8 mt.

764 Bappa was defeated by the 21st Caliph at Mansoor. Bappa, after the defeat, departed for Persia (Iran) and perhaps never returned to India. (See 713 & 735).

770 Dharmapala succeeded Gopala in Bengal. He raised the Pala Kingdom to imperial power and virtually became the Emperor of Northern India. He founded Vikramsila university near Bhagalpur. (See 1203).

774. A Jewish colony settled down in Cochin.

779 After Lalitaditya's death in 760, four weak Kings ruled Kashmir. Then Jayapida Vinayaditya ascended the throne of Kashmir. Jayapida revived the glory of Naga (Karataka) dynasty.

Caliph Mutahid appointed Yaqub ibn Lail's Saffari as the Governor of Sind. From that date Sind became virtually independent of Khilafat. (See 712).

784 Jinasena completed 'Harivansa Purana' of the Digambar Jains.

788 Adi Sankaracharya was born at Kaladi in Kerala. He founded four 'Mathas' in four corner of India at Sringeri, Puri, Dwarka and Joshi (Badrinath), for the resurrection of Hindu religion. He attained 'Samadhi' at Badrinath in 820.

794 Govinda III, son of Dhruva, became the Rashtrakuta King and was the most remarkable ruler of his dynasty. He expanded his territory over a vast area. He shifted his capital from Nasik to Manyakheta and ruled till 814.

809 Manikya, the Indian physician, was called to the court of Karun-ur Rashid of Arabia to attend to his illness.

810 Devapala became the king of Bengal. During his region he deposed the reigning King of Kanauj and put his own nominee on Kanauj throne. Devapala had 50,000 elephants in his army. (See 816).

814 Amoghavarsha I, son of Govind III, became the Rastrakuta King. He was a devout Jain. But he did not hesitate to cut off one of his fingers and to offer it to Goddess Mahalakshmi to propitiate her to remove the epidemic which was ravaging his kingdom.

816 One Nagabhata, a descendent of Nagabhata of Gurjara-Pratihara, dynasty, captured Kanauj from the nominee of Devapala, Nagabhata's descedants ruled Kanauj till 1017 when Sultan Mahmud of Ghazni captured it.

820 Adi Sankaracharya attained Samadhi at Badrinath. (See 788).

831 The Chandellas of Bundelkhand or Jejakabhukti first came into notice, when Nanika Chandella overthrew a Parihar chief and became the lord of Bundelkhand.

840 Mihira Pratihara, commonly known as Raja Bhoj, became the King of Gurjara-Pratihara empire. He was a great patron of magic. During his rule, Gurjaras rose to a great height. His rule continued till 885. (See 1010).

855 Avantivarman of Utpala dynasty started his reign in Kashmir. He was notable for his enlightened patronage of literature, his beneficent work like drainage and irrigation schemes.

883 After Avantivarman, Sasankavarman was the next King of Kashmir. He was obsessed for his love for fiscal oppression and plunder of temple treasures.

885 Mahendrapala I, son of Raja Bhoj, succeeded to the Gurjara-Pratihara throne. During his regime, Gurjara-Pratihara empire reached its zenith. He drove the Palas of Bengal out of Magadha. (See 840).

894 The idol of Sriranganathaswamy of Srirangapatnam was installed. (See 1120).

916 Mahipala, I, the Gurjara-Pratihara King, suffered a severe set-back when Indra III, the Rastrakuta King of Decan captured Kanauj and plundered Pratihara territory upto Prayar near Allahabd.

942 Mularaja became the King of Gujarat and founded Solanki dynasty of Anhilwara. (942-997).

949 The war between Cholas and Rashtrakutas was remarkable for the death of Chola King Rajaditya I on the battlefield. Much bitterness developed between Jainism and orthodox Hinduism.

950 Kshemagupta of Pravagupta dynasty became king of Kashmir and married Didda, daughter of King Simharaja of Laharu. These two are the most notorious couple in Indian history. After Kshemagupta's death in 958, Didda virtually ruled Kashmir. She had no mercy, no scruple, indulged in sex with royal officers and murdered her two grandsons Tribhuvana and Bhimagupta to sit on Kashmir throne in 980.

955 Dhanga, the most powerful Chendella King, sat on the throne. Some of the grandest Khajuraho temples were built during his regime. He joined Jaipal to resist Subuktigin in 977.

967 Dhola Rai, the expelled son of Sova Singh of Gwalior, laid the foundation of the State of Dhandoor, later Amber and now Jaipur.

973 Nurmadi Taila II established Chalukya dynasty in Kalyani of South India. Much of his time was spent in fighting Munja, the Paramar Raja of Dhara, who claimed sixteen victories. On the seventeenth encounter in 995, Munja was caught, forced to beg from door to door and ultimately beheaded.

Al Biruni or Abu Ar Rayhan Muhammad Bin Ahmed was born in Birun of Uzbekistan. His famous history of India 'Tarikh Al Hind' gives a comprehensive survey of India of the 11th century. He also excelled in philosophy, astronomy, physics, chemistry, medicine and Sanskrit. (d. 1048).

977 Chandella King Dhanga of Khajuraho fame and King Jaipal of Lahore jointly and successfully opposed Subuktigin (See 979).

979 King Jaipal of Lahore encountered Subuktigin at Luckman. A treaty was agreed upon. (See 977).

981 The 17 mt. high world's biggest monolith statue of Gomateswara (meaning a handsome man) was erected by King Vira Pandiya on Vindhya Hill at Sravana Belgola for Bahubal, son of Vrishava, the first Tirthankar.

982 Atisa (Dipankar Srijnana), the Buddhist sage of Magadha, was born. He went to Tibet in 1038 and died near Lhasa in 1053.

997 After Taila's death the Chalukya crown was transmitted to his son Satyashraya. During his reign Chalukya kingdom suffered heavily from the invasion by the Chola king Rajaraja I.

1000 Sultan Mahmud of Ghazni, a Turk, haunted on India's border and captured some frontier posts.

1001 Sultan Mahmud of Ghazni made his first real expedition to India and began his crusade against the Hindus. He defeated King Jaipal at Peshawar on November 27. The proud king, unable to withstand the humiliation of defeat, burnt himself to death. He son Anandapal succeeded him. Mahmud's fourteenth and last expedition was in 1026. (See 1009).

1006 Mahmud had his second expedition to India against Raja Bhira Rao and captured the fortress of Bhatia in Bikaner desert.

The same year Mahmud made his third expedition against his subordinate Wali of Multan.

1007 Mahmud was on his fourth expedition to India against Sukpal, a Hindu converted to Muslim, whom he made the Governor of some of his conquered territories.

1009 Mahmud's fifth expedition was against Anandapal, son of Jaipal, and captured Nagarkote near Lahore. He carried away 7 tonnes of pure gold, 7 tonnes of jewels and 25 tonnes of gold and silver utensils from the temples in Nagarkote. (See 1001).

In Mahmud's sixth expedition he captured Narain, capital of Matsya.

1010 Mahmud's seventh expedition to India was against Abdul Fath Lodi, his own Governor of some of the conquered territories. Raja Bhoj, the renowned King of Paramar dynasty, ascended the throne of Malwa. In 1060 he was defeated by the allied armies of Gujarat and Chedi. This Raja Bhoj is different from that of Gurjara dyansty. (See 840).

Chola King Rajaraja I consecrates the magnificent Siva temple Brihadeswara at Tanjavur. He also annexed the Maldive Islands.

1012 Rajaraja I and his son Rajendra I jointly ruled the Cholas for 2 years. Rajendra I completed the conquest of Ceylon which his father began.

1013 Mahmud was on his eighth expedition for plunder of India.

1014 Mohammed's ninth expedition was aimed at Thaneswar. He sacked the town and took two lakh Hindu captives from Thaneswar to Ghazni.

1015 In his tenth expedition Mahmud tried to penetrate into Kashmir, but could advance no further than Lohkot (presently Loharin).

1017 Mahmud, in his eleventh expedition, captured Kanauj from the ruler of Gurjara-Pratihara origin, as well as he took Mathura. (See 816).

Acharya Ramanuja, the Vaishnab philosopher, was born in Sriparambudur in Chinglepet District.

1021 Mahmud advanced into India for the twelfth time to help the King of Kanauj, who was attacked by Nanda. King of Kalanjara. Trilochanapala of Lahore opposed and lost his life in the battle. Mahmud annexed Lahore to Ghazni and thus laid the foundation of future Muhammedan empire in India.

1023 Mahmud invaded India for the thirteen time. He besieged Gwalior and brought Nanda, the Chandella Raja of Kalanjara, to terms. (See 1021).

The Chola King Rajendra I of Tanjore launched a campaign in North India and attacked Mahipala I of Bengal. Rajendra I

Bibliography

Abhedananda, Swami, *Attitude of Vedanta Towards Religion. Ramakrishna* Vedanta Math, Calcutta, 1947.

Aiyangar, S.K., *Contribution of South India to Indian Culture.* Calcutta University, 1923.

Aiyangar, S.K., *Early History of Vaiṣṇavism in South India.* Oxford University Press, London, 1920.

Aiyar, G.V. Jagadisha, *South Indian Festivities.* Higginbothams Ltd., London, 1921.

Aiyar, V.V.S. (Trans.), *The Kural; or, The Maxims of Tiruvalluvar.* 3rd Edn. Dr. V.V.S. Krishnamurthy, Tiruchirapalli, 1952.

Altekar, A.S., *Education in Ancient India,* 5th Edn. Nand Kishore & Bros., Banaras, 1957.

Altekar, A.S., *Position of Women in Hindu Civilisation.* Banaras Hindu University, Banaras, 1938.

Aurobindo, Sri, *Bases of Yoga.* Arya Publishing House, Calcutta, 1949.

Aurobindo, Sri, *Essays on the Gita.* The Sri Aurobindo Library, New York, 1950.

Aurobindo, Sri, *Lights on Yoga.* Arya Publishing House, Calcutta, 1948.

Aurobindo, Sri, *Synthesis of Yoga.* The Sri Aurobindo Library, New York, 1950.

Avalon, Arthur (Sir John Woodroffe), *Kāmakalāvilāsa.* Translation. Ganesh & Co. Ltd., Madras, 1953.

Avalon, Arthur (Sir John Woodroffe), *Principles of Tantra.* Ganesh & Co. Ltd., Madras, 1952.

Avalon, Arthur (Sir John Woodroffe), *Shakti and Shakta,* Ganesh & Co. Ltd., Madras, 1951.

Avalon, Arthur (Sir John Woodroffe), *The Great Liberation (Mahānirvāṇa Tantra)*, Text and Translation. Ganesh & Co., Ltd., Madras, 1953.

Avalon, Arthur (Sir John Woodroffe), *The Serpent Power (Saṭcakra-nirūpaṇa and Pādukāpañcaka)*. Ganesh & Co. Ltd., Madras, 1953.

Avalon, Arthur, and Saubhagyvardhani, *Ānandalaharī or Wave of Bliss.* Translation. Ganesh & Co. Ltd., Madras, 1953.

Avalon, Arthur, and Avalon, Ellen, *Hymns to the Goddess.* Translation Ganesh & Co. Ltd., Madras, 1952.

Baden-Powell, B.H., *The Origin and Growth of Village Communities in India.* Swan Sonnenschein, London, 1908.

Bader, Clarisse, *Women in Ancient India, Moral and Literary Studies.* Trans. by Mary E.R. Martin. Kegan Paul, Trench, Trübner, London, 1925.

Bagchi, P.C., *Studies in the Tantras.* Calcutta university, 1939.

Bahirat, B.P., *The Philosophy of Jnanadeva.* Pandharpur Research Society.

Banerjea, J.N., *Development of Hindu Iconography.* Calcutta University, 1956.

Banerjee, G.N., *Hellenism in Ancient India.* 2nd Edn. Butterworth, Calcutta, 1920.

Banerjee, G.N., *India as Known to the Ancient World.* An Account of India's Intercoruse in Ancient Times with her Neighbours, Egypt, Western Asia, China, Further India and Indonesia. O.U.P., Calcutta, 1921.

Banerji, N.C., *Economic Life and Progress in Ancient India, being the outlines of an Economic History of Ancient India,* Calcutta University, Calcutta, 1945.

Barnett, L.D, *The Heart of India.* John Murray, London, 1913.

Barnett, L.D., *Hindu Gods and Heroes.* London, 1922.

Barnett, L.D., *Paramārthasāra of Abhinavagupta.* With Yogarāja's commentary. Translated in *Journal of the Royal Asiatic Society of Great Britain,* 1910.

Barth, A., *Religions of India.* Translated by J. Wood. Kegan Paul, Trench, Trübner & Co., London, 1921.

Barthwal, P.D., *The Nirguṇa School of Hindi Poetry.* Indian Book Shop, Banaras, 1936.

Barua, K.L., *Early History of Kamarupa.* Shillong, 1933.

Basu, Manindramohan, *Post-Caitanya Sahajiyā Cult of Bengal.* Calcutta University, 1930.

Bengeri, H.G., *Main Outlines of Haridāsa Kūṭa.* Kollegal, 1931.

Bhandarkar, R.G., *Vaiṣṇavism, Śaivism, and Minor Religious Systems.* Karl J. Trübner, Strassburg, 1923.

Bhandarkar, R.G., *Vaiṣṇavism, Śaivism, and Minor Religious Systems.* Trubner & Co., Strassburg. 1913.

Bhattacharyya, Benoytosh, *Buddhist Esoterism,* Oxford University Press, London, 1932.

Billington, Mary Frances, *Women in India.* Chapman and Hall, London, 1895.

Brahma, N. K., *The Philosophy of Hindu Sāḍhanā.* Kegan Paul, London, 1932.

Briggs, G.W., *Gorakhnāth and the Kānphaṭa Yogis.* Oxford University Press, London, 1938.

Buch, M.A., *Economic Life in Ancient India; a Systematic Survey* (2 Vols.). Author, Baroda, 1924.

Buck, C.H., *Faiths, Fairs, and Festivals of India.* Thacker Spink & Co., Calcutta, 1917.

Buhler, G., *The Laws of Manu.* Sacred Books of the East, XXV. Clarendon Press, Oxford, 1886.

Caland, W., *Vaikhānasa Śrauta-Sūtras.* Translation, Asiatic Society of Bengal, Calcutta, 1929.

Caland, W., *Vaikhānasa Smārta-Sūtras.* Translation. Asiatic Society of Bengal, Calcutta, 1927.

Carpenter, J.E., *Theism in Mediaeval India.* Constable & Co., London, 1926

Chakladar, H.C., *Social Life in Ancient India: Studies in Vātsyāyana's Kāmasūtra.* Greater India Society, Calcutta, 1929.

Chakravarti, P.C., *Doctrine of Śakti in Indian Literature.* General Printers and Publishers, Calcutta, 1940.

Chanda, R.P., *The Indo-Aryan Races.* Varendra Research Society, Rajshahi, 1916.

Chapman, J.A., *Religious Lyrics of Bengal.* Calcutta, 1926.

Chatterjee, Satish Chandra, *The Fundamentals of Hinduism: A Philosophical Study,* Das Gupta & Co., Calcutta, 1950.

Chatterji, J.C., *Kashmir Shaivaism.* The Research Department, Kashmir State, Srinagar, 1914.

Chatterji, Suniti Kumar, *The Indian Synthesis, and Racial and Cultural Intermixture in India.* Gujarat Vidya Sabha, Ahmedabad, 1953.

Chaudhuri, J.B., *the Position of Women in the Vedic Ritual.* Prachyavani Mandir, Calcutta, 1945.

Childe, V. Gordon, *The Aryans: a Study of Indo-European Origins.* Kegan Paul, Trench, Trübner, London, 1926.

Chopra, P.N., *Some Aspects of Society and Culture During the Mughal Age* (1526-1707). Shivalal Agarwala & Co., Agra, 1956.

Coomaraswamy, A.K., *Hinduism and Buddhism,* Philosophical Library, New York.

Compton, Herbert, *Indian Life in Town and Country*. George Newnes, London.

Cowell, E.B., *Śāṇḍilya Sūtras*. With Svapneśvara's commentary. Text with translation of commentary in *Bibliotheca Indica*. Calcutta, 1878.

Crooke, W., *Religion and Folk-lore of Northern India* (2 vols.). Oxford University Press, London, 1926.

Culshaw, W.J., *Tribal Heritage*. Lutterworth Press, London, 1949.

Das Gupta, Debendra Chandra, *Educational Psychology of the Ancient Hindus*. Calcutta University, Calcutta, 1949.

Das Gupta, S.B., *An Introduction to Tāntric Buddhism*. Calcutta University, 1950.

Das Gupta, S.B., *Obcure Religious Cults*. Calcutta University, 1946.

Das, Bhagavan, *Science of Social Organisation or the Laws of Manu in the Light of Ātma Vidyā* (3 vols.). Theosophical Publishing House, Adyar, Madras.

Das, Bhagavan, *The Essential Unity of All Religions*. Theosophical Publishing House, Adyar, Madras, 1940.

Das, S.K., *The Economic History of Ancient India*. Author, Howrah (Bengal), 1925.

Das, Santosh Kumar, *The Educational System of the Ancient Hindus*. Mitra Press, Calcutta, 1931.

Das, Sudhendukumar, *Śakti or Divine Power*. Calcutta University, 1934.

Dasgupta, Surendranath, *A History of Indian Philosophy* (5 vols.). Cambridge University Press.

Dasgupta, Surendranath, *Yoga as Philosophy and Religion*. Kegan Paul, London, 1924.

Dasgupta, Surendranath, *Yoga Philosophy in Relation to Other Systems of Indian Thought*. Calcutta University, 1930.

De, *S.K., Early History of the Vaiṣṇava Faith and Movement in Bengal from Sanskrit and Bengali Sources*. General Printers and Publishers, Calcutta, 1942.

Deming, W.S., *Rāmdās and the Rāmdāsīs*. Calcutta, 1928.

Desmukh, P.S., *The Origin and Development of Religion in Vedic Literature*. Oxford University Press, London, 1933.

Diksitar, Ramachandra, *Lalitā-Cult*. Madras University, 1942.

Dubois, J.A., *Hindu Manners, Cutsoms and Ceremonies*. Clarendon Press, Oxford, 1906.

Dutt, B.N., *Studies in Indian Social Polity*. Purabi Publishers, Calcutta, 1944.

Dutt, N.K., *Origin and Growth of Caste in India.* Kegan Paul, Trench, Trübner, London, 1931.

Elliot, Sir Charles, *Hinduism and Buddhism* (3 vols.). Routledge and Kegan Paul, London, 1954.

Ellis, F.W. (Comm.), *Tiru-k-Kural with Ellis' Commentary.* Ed. by R.P. Sethu Pillai. Madras University, Madras, 1955.

Farquhar, J.N., *An Outline of the Religious Literature of India.* Oxford University Press, London, 1920.

Fraser, J.N., and Edwards, J. F., *Life and Teaching of Tukārām.* Madras.

Gandhi, M.K., *Hindu Dharma.* Edited by Bharatan Kumarappa. Navajivan Publishing House, Ahmedabad, 1950.

Ghosh, Atal. Behari, *Śiva and Śakti.* Rajshahi, 1935.

Ghoshal, U.N, *Contributions to the History of the Hindu Revenue System.* Calcutta University, Calcutta, 1929.

Ghoshal, U.N., *The Agrarian System in Ancient India.* Calcutta University, Calcutta, 1930.

Ghurye, G.S. *Caste and Race in India.* Kegan Paul, Trench, Trübner, London, 1932.

Goldstucker, Theodore, *Inspired Writings of Hinduism.* Sunil Gutpa (India) Ltd., Calcutta, 1952.

Govindacharya, Alkondavilli, *The Divine Wisdom of the Drāviḍa Saints,* Madras, 1902.

Grierson, G.A., 'Notes on Tulasī Dāsa', Published in *Indian Antiquary,* 1893.

Griffith, R.T.H., *Valmiki Ramayana.* Translation. Trubner & Co., London, 1870.

Gupte, B.A., *Hindu Holidays and Ceremonials.* Thacker Spink & Co., Calcutta, 1919.

Haig, H., *Leading Ideals of Hinduism.* Susil Gupta (India) Ltd., Calcutta, 1952

Hastings, J. (Ed.), *Encyclopaedia of Religion and Ethics* (13 vols.). T. & T. Clark, Edinburgh.

Hill, W.D.P., *The Holy Lake of the Acts of Rāma.* An English Translation of Tulasīdās's *Rāmacaritamānasa.* Oxford University Press, London, 1952.

Hooper, J.S.M., *Hymns of the Āḻvārs.* Association Press, Calcutta, 1929.

Hopkins, E.W., *Epic Mythology,* Trubner & Co., Strassburg, 1915.

Hopkins, E.W., *Religions of India.* Ginn, London, 1902.

Hopkins, E.W., *The Mutual Relations of the Four Castes. According to the Mānavadharma-śāstram.* Breitkope and Hartel Leipzig, 1881.

Hume, R.E., *The Thirteen Princiapl Upanishads.* Oxford University Press, Madras, 1951.

Hutton, J.H., (Ed.), *Census Report of India for 1931.* Government of India.

Hutton, J.H., *Caste in India.* Cambridge University Press, 1952.

Hutton, J.H., *Caste in India,* 2nd Edn. O.U.P., Bombay, 1951.

Indra, *The Status of Women in Ancient India.* 2nd Edn. Motilal Banarasidas, Banaras, 1955.

Iyengar, P.T.S., *Pre-Aryan Tamil Culture,* Madras, 1930.

Iyer, C.V. Narayana, *The Origin and Early History of Śaivism in South India.* Calcutta, 1923.

Jha, Ganganath, *Manu-Smṛti.* Translation and Notes. Calcutta University, 1920-26.

Jhavery, M.B., *Comparative and Critical Study of Mantraśāstra.* Sarabhai Manilal Nawal, Ahmedabad.

Kane, P.V., *History of Dharma-śāstra* (Vols. I-IV). Bhandarkar Oriental Research Insittute, Poona.

Kapadia, K.M., *Marriage and Family in India.* 2nd Edn. O.U.P., Bombay, 1958.

Karmarkar, A.P., and Kalamdani, N.B., *Mystic Teachings of the Haridāsas of Karṇāṭaka.* Karnataka Vidyavardhaka Sangha, Dharwar, 1939.

Karmarkar, A.P., *Religions of India.* Mira Publishing House, Lonavla, 1950.

Karve, Mrs. Iravati, *Kinship Organisation in India.* Deccan College Post-Graduate and Research Institute, Poona, 1953.

Keay, F.E., *Kabir and His Followers.* Association Press, Calcutta, 1921.

Keay, Frank Ernest, *Indian Education in Ancient and Later Times: an Inquiry into its Origin, Developmental, and Ideals.* 2nd Edn. O.U.P., Calcutta, 1950.

Keith, A.B., *The Religion and Philosophy of the Veda and Upanishads* (2 vols.), Harvard Oriental Series. Cambriedge (Mass.), 1925.

Kennedy, M.T., *Chaitanya Movement: A Study of the Vaishnavism of Bengal.* Association Press, Calcutta, 1925.

Ketkar, S.V., *History of Caste in India* (2 Vols.). Taylor and Carpenter, New York, 1909-11.

Kingsbury, F., and Phillips, G. E., *Hymns of the Tamil Śaivite Saints.* Association Press, Calcutta, 1921.

Kramrisch, Stella, *The Hindu Temple,* Calcutta University, 1946.

Kumarappa, B., *The Hindu Conception of the Deity as Culminating in Rāmānuja.* Luzac & Co., London, 1934.

Kumaraswamiji, Shree, *The Vīraśaiva Philosophy and Mysticism.* V.R. Koppal, Dharwar, 1949.

Laby, R.L., *Holy Land of the Hindus.* Robert Scott. London, 1913.

Lazarus, J. (Trans.), *The Kural of Tiruvalluvar.* With the commentary of Parimelazagar and a simple and clear *padavurai.* To which is added an English trans. of the text. W. Pushparatha Chettiar, Madras, 1885.

Leidecker, K.F., *Pratyabhijnāhṛdaya* (*The Secret of Recognition*). Translation with notes. The Adyar Library, Madras, 1938.

Macdonell, *A. A., Vedic Mythology.* Trubner & Co., Strassburg, 1897.

Macdonell, A.A., *Hymns from the Rigveda.* Association Press, Calcutta, 1923.

Macnicol, N., *Indian Theism.* Oxford University Press, London, 1915.

Macnicol., N., *Psalms of Marāṭhā Saints.* Association Press, Calcutta, 1919.

Madhavananda, Swami, *Bṛhadāraṇyaka Upaniṣad.* Text with translation of Śaṅkara's commentary. Advaita Ashrama, Calcutta, 1950.

Madhavananda, Swami, and Majumdar, R.C., *Great Women of India.* Advaita Ashram, Almora, 1953.

Majumdar, D.N., *Races and Cultures of India.* 2nd Edn. Universal Publishers, Lucknow, 1950.

Majumdar, R.C., *Ancient Indian Colonies in the Far East* (3 Vols.). Punjab Sanskrit Book Depot, Lahore, 1927-44.

Marshall, J., *Mohenjo-daro and the Indus Civilisation.* Arthur Probsthain, London, 1931.

Max Muller, F., *Vedic Hymns.* Sacred Books of the East, XXXII. Clarendon Press, Oxford, 1891.

Mitra, D.N., *The Position of Women in Hindu Law.* Calcutta University, Calcutta, 1913.

Monier-Williams, M., *Hinduism.* Susil Gupta (India) Ltd., Calcutta, 1951.

Monier-Williams, M., *Religious Thought and Life in India.* London, 1891.

Morgan, K.W., (Ed.), *The Religion of the Hindus.* Roland Press, New York, 1953.

Mukerji, Abhay Charan, *Hindu Fasts and Feasts.* The Indian Press, Allabahad, 1918.

Mukharji, D.P., *Diversities; Essays in Economics, Sociology and Other Social Problems.* People's Publishing House, New Delhi, 1958.

Mukherjee, Radha Kamal, *The Foundations of Indian Economics.* Longmans and Green, London, 1911.

Mukherji, Radha Kumud, *Ancient Indian Education.* 2nd Edn. Macmillan, London, 1951.

Nandimath, S.C., *Handbook of Virashaivism.* Edited by Literary Committee. L.E. Association, Dharwar, 1942.

Nath, R.M., *The Background of Assamese Culture.* A.K. Nath, Shillong, 1948.

Nath, Radha Govinda, *The Yogis of Bengal.* Mani Bhusan Nath, Calcutta, 1909.

Nikhilananda, Swami, *Essence of Hinduism.* Ramakrishna-Vivekananda Center, New York, 1946.

Nikhilananda, Swami, *The Bhagavad-Gītā.* Translated with notes, comments, and introduction. Ramakrishna-Vivekananda Center, New York, 1944.

Nikhilananda, Swami, *The Upanishads* (2 vols.). Harper & Brothers, New York.

Nirvedananda, Swami, *Hinduism at a Glance,* Vidyamandira, Dhakuria, 1946.

Nivedita, Sister, *Religion and Dharma,* Advaita Ashrama, Calcutta, 1952.

Noble, Margaret Elizabeth (Sister Nivedita), *The Web of Indian Life.* Longmans Green & Co., Bombay, 1918.

O'Malley, L.S.S., *Indian Caste Customs.* Cambridge University Press, Cambridge, 1932.

Oman, J.C., *Indian Life: Religious and Scoial.* Fisher Unwin, London, 1879.

Oman, J.C., *Mystics, Ascetics, and Saints of India.* London, 1903.

Pal, D.N., *Śiva and Śakti: An Elaborate Discoruse on Hindu Religion and Mythology* (2 vols.). Calcutta, 1910.

Pandey, Kantichandra, *Abhinavagupta: An Historical and Philosophical Study,* Chowkhamba Sanskrit Series office, Banaras, 1936.

Pawate, S.D., *Virashaiva Philosophy of the Shaivagamas.* W.B. Bile Angadi, Hubli, 1927.

Pillai, J.M. Nallaswami, *Śivajnāna-bodham.* Translated with notes and introduction. Dharmapuram Adhinam, 1945.

Pillai, J.M. Nallaswami, *Śivajñāna-siddhiyār* (*Supakkam*) of Aruṇandi Śivam. Translated with notes. Dharmapuram Adhinam, 1948.

Pillai, J.M. Nallaswami, *Studies in Śaiva Siddhānta.* Meykandan Press, Madras, 1911.

Pillai, Tiru G.S., *Introduction and History of Śaiva Siddhānta.* Annamalai University, 1948.

Pinkham, M.W., *Women in the Sacred Scriptures of Hinduism.* Columbia University, New York, 1941.

Pope, G.U., and Others (Trans.), *Tiru-k-Kural.* With trans. in English by G.U. Pope, W.H. Drew, John Lazarus, and F.W. Ellis. South India Saiva Siddhanta Works Publishing Society, Madras, 1958.

Popley, H.A. (Trans.), *The Sacred Kural: or The Tamil Veda of Tiruvalluvar.* Selected and trans. with introduction and notes. 2nd Rev. Edn. with fresh trans. Y.M.C.A., Calcutta, 1958.

Prabhu, Pandharinath, *Hindu Social Organisation: A Study in Social, Psychological, and Ideological Foundations.* New Rev. Edn. Popular Book Depot, Bombay, 1954.

Radhakrishnan, S., (Ed.), *History of Philosophy: Eastern and Western,* Sponsored by the Ministry of Education, Government of India. George Allen & Unwin, London, 1952.

Radhakrishnan, S., *Bhagavad-Gītā.* Translation. George Allen & Unwin, London, 1948.

Radhakrishnan, S., *East and West in Religion,* George Allen & Unwin, London, 1933.

Radhakrishnan, S., *Indian Philosophy* (2 vols.)., George Allen & Unwin, London, 1948.

Radhakrishnan, S., *Principal Upaniṣads,* Edited with introduction, text, translation, and notes, George Allen & Unwin, London, 1953.

Radhakrishnan, S., *Religion and Society.* George Allen & Unwin. London, 1947.

Radhakrishnan, S., *The Hindu View of Life.* George Allen & Unwin, London, 1925.

Raja, C.K., *Some Aspects of Education in Ancient India.* Adyar, 1950.

Rajagopalachariar, T., *The Vaishnavite Reformers of India.* G.A. Natesan & Co., Madras, 1909.

Ranade, R.D., *Mysticism in Maharashtra.* Poona.

Rao, C. Hayavadana, *Indian Caste System: a Study.* Bangalore Press, Bangalore, 1931.

Rao, Shakuntala Sastri, *Women in the Scred Laws.* Bhavan's Book. Bombay, 1953.

Rao, Shakuntala Sastri,, *Women in the Vedic Age.* Bharatiya Vidyabhavan, Bombay, 1954.

Rao, T.A. Gopinath, *Elements of Hindu Iconography.* Madras, 1916.

Rao, T.A. Gopinath, *History of Śrī Vaiṣṇavas.* Madras University, 1923.

Rau, S. Subra, *Śrīmad Bhāgavata Purāṇam.* Translation. Tirupati, 1928.

Rawlison, H.G., *Intercourse between India and the Western World, from the Earliest Times to the Fall of Rome.* Cambridge University, Cambridge, 1916.

Ray, J.C., *Ancient Indian Life.* P.R. Sen, Calcutta, 1948.

Raychaudhuri, G.K., *Hindu Customs and Manners.* M.M. Mazumdar, Calcutta, 1888.

Raychaudhuri, H.C., *Materials for the Study of the Early History of the Vaiṣṇava Sect.* Calcutta University, 1936.

Renou, Louis, *Religions of Ancient India.* Translated by Sheila M. Fynn. London University, The Athlone Press, London, 1953.

Roy, P.C., *The Mahabharata* (11 vols.), Translation, Oriental Publishing Co., Calcutta.

Roy, R.L., *Bases of Peace in Hindu Political Economy.* Bhagalpur, 1943.

Sakhare, M.R., *History and Philosophy of Liṅgāyata Religion.* Belgaum, 1942.

Saltore, B.A., *Social and Political Life in the Vijayanagar Empire.* Madras, 1934.

Sankalia, Hasmukh D., *The University of Nalanda,* B.G. Paul, Madras, 1934.

Sanyal, J.M., *Śrīmad Bhāgavatam* (5 vols.), Translation. Oriental Publishing Co., Calcutta.

Sarkar, Jadunath, *Chaitanya's Life and Teachings.* Translation of Kṛṣṇadāsa Kavirāja's *Caitanya Bhāgavata.* M.C. Sarkar & Sons. Calcutta, 1932.

Sarkar, S.C. *Some Aspects of the Earliest Social History of India, Pre-Buddhistic Ages.* O.U.P., London, 1920.

Sastri, H. Krishna, *South Indian Images of Gods and Goddesses.* Government Press, Madras, 1916.

Sastri, Nilakantha K.A., *South Indian Influence in the Far East.* Hind Kitabs, Bombay, 1949.

Sastri, R. Anantakrishna, *Śakti-Sūtra.* With notes. The Adyar Library, Madras, 1896.

Sastri, R. Anantakrishna, *Lalitā Sahasranāma Stotra.* Translation, The Adyar Library, Madras, 1925.

Sastri, S.S. Suryanarayana, *Śivādvaitanirṇaya* of Appaya Dīkṣita. With introduction, translation, and notes. Madras.

Schrader, F.O., *Introduction to the Pāñcarātra and the Ahirbudhnya Saṁhitā.* The Adyar Library, Madras, 1916.

Sakhare, M.R., *History and Philosophy of Liṅgāyata Religion.* Belgaum, 1942 introduction, translation, and notes. Madras.

Sen, D.C., *Chaitanya and His Age.* Calcutta University, 1922.

Sen, D.C., *The Vaiṣṇava Literature of Mediaeval Bengal.* Calcutta University, 1917.

Sen, K.M., *Mediaeval Mysticism of India.* Luzac, London, 1936.

Sen, Kshitimohan, *Mediaeval Mysticism of India.* Translated by Manomohan Ghosh. Luzac & Co., London, 1929.

Sen, M.L., *The Ramayana* (3 vols.). Translation, Oriental Publishing Co., Calcutta.

Senart, Emile, *Caste in India, the Facts and the System.* Tans. by Sir E. Denison Ross. Methuen, London, 1930.

Shah, K.T., *Ancient Foundations of Economics in India.* Vora & Co., Bombay, 1954.

Sharvananda, Swami, *Iśa, Kena, Kaṭha, Praśna, Muṇḍaka, Māṇḍūkya, Taittirīya,* and *Aitareya Upaniṣads.* Text and translation with notes. Sri Ramakrishna Math, Madras.

Singh, Mohan, *Gorakhnāth and Mediaeval Hindu Mysticism.* Lahore, 1937.

Singh, Mohan, *Kabīr and Bhakt Movement.* Atma Ram & Sons. Lahore, 1934.

Singh, Pritam, *Saints and Sages of India.* Oriental Publishing Co., Calcutta.

Sivapādasundaram, S., *The Śaiva School of Hinduism.* George Allen & Unwin, London, 1934.

Subramanian, K.R., *Origin of Śaivism and Its History in the Tamil Land.* Madras University, 1927.

Swarupananda, Swami, *Śrīmad Bhagavad-Gītā.* Advaita Ashrama, Calcutta, 1948.

Tagore, Rabindranath, *One Hundred Poems of Kabir.* Macmillan & Co., Calcutta, 1943.

Tarn, W.W., *The Greeks in Bactria and India.* Cambridge University Press, Cambridge, 1938.

Thompson, E. J., and Spencer, A.M., *Bengali Religious Lyrics: Śākta.* Association Press, Calcutta, 1923.

Tilak, B.G., *Śrīmad Bhagavadgītā Rahasya or Karma-yoga-śāstra* (2 vols.). Translated by B.S. Sukhthankar. Tilak Brothers, Poona, 1935-36.

Tirtha, Bhakti Pradip, *Chaitanya Mahaprabhu.* Gaudiya Mission, Calcutta, 1947.

Tyagisananda, Swami, *Śvetāśvatara Upaniṣad.* Text and translation with notes. Sri Ramakrishna Math, Madras.

Tyagisananda, Swami, *Nārada Bhakti-Sūtras.* Tedt and translation with notes. Sri Ramakrishna Math, Madras, 1952.

Upadhyaya, B.S. Women in the Rigveda. 2nd Rev. and Enl. Edn. Nand Kishore & Bros., Banaras, 1941.

Varadachariar, S., *The Hindu Social System.* 1946.

Vasu, Nagendra Nath, *The Social History of Kāmarūpa.* Calcutta, 1926.

Vasu, Srischandra, *Haṭhayoga-pradīpikā.* Text and translation. Panini Office, Allahabad.

Venkataramanayya, N., *Rudra-Śiva.* Madras University, 1941.

Venkateswara, S.V., *Indian Culture Through the Ages* (2 Vols.). Longmans Gree & Co., London, 1928-32.

Vireswarananda, Swami, *Śrīmad Bhagavad-Gītā.* Text with translation of Śrīdhara's gloss. Sri Ramakrishna Math, Madras, 1948.

Viswanatha, S.V., *Racial Synthesis in Hindu Culture.* Kegan Paul, Trench, Trübner, London, 1928.

Vivekananda, Swami, *Our Women.* 2nd Edn. Advaita Ashram, Mayavati, 1946.

Waddell, L.A., *The Buddhism of Tibet of Lamaism.* W.H. Allen & Co., London, 1895.

Westcott, G.H., *Kabir and the Kabir Panth.* Susil Gutpa (India) Ltd., Calcutta, 1953.

Wilkins, W.J., *Modern Hinduism.* Thacker Spink & Co., Calcutta, 1900.

Wilson, H.H., *Essays and Lectures on the Religions of the Hindus* (2 vols.), Edited by R. Rost. Trubner & Co., London, 1861.

Wilson, H.H., *The Viṣṇu Purāṇa.* Tanslation. Edited by F. Hall. Trubner & Co., London, 1864-77.

Wright, Caleb, *Oriental Customs, or Life in India.* Author, Boston, 1860.